HAMMOND

The New Comparative World Atlas

Mapmakers for the 21st Century

New Comparative World Atlas

ENTIRE CONTENTS
© COPYRIGHT 2000 BY
HAMMOND WORLD ATLAS CORPORATION
All rights reserved. No part of this book may
be reproduced or utilized in any form or by any
means, electronic or mechanical, including
photocopying, recording or by any information
storage and retrieval system, without permission
in writing from the Publisher.
Printed in The United States of America

LIBRARY OF CONGRESS
CATALOGING-IN-PUBLICATION DATA

Hammond World Atlas Corporation.
    Hammond new comparative world atlas.
        p. cm.
    Includes index.
    ISBN 0-8437-1379-8 (hc)
    ISBN 0-8437-1380-1 (sc)
    1. Atlases.
        I. Title. New comparative world atlas
    II. Title.
    G1021. H2738   2000
    912--DC21
                                00-039570
                                        CIP
                                        MAPS

Contents

INTERPRETING MAPS

Designed to enhance your knowledge and enjoyment of maps, these pages explain map scales and projections, describe how to locate information quickly and show you how to weave together the sections of this atlas to gain a more dynamic world view.

QUICK REFERENCE GUIDE

The world at your fingertips: a concise, current alphabetical listing of the world's continents, countries, states, provinces and territories, with the size, population and capital of each. Page numbers and reference keys for each entry are visible at a glance.

GLOBAL RELATIONSHIPS

Beginning with general world physical and political maps, subsequent chapters highlight a variety of the earth's natural features, dealing first with its structure and then with its air, water and land components. Next, maps, charts and graphs unveil the complex relationships between people and their environments. Coverage includes: demographic trends, population distribution and growth, and global energy production; assessing the consequences of pollution: acid rain, deforestation, ozone depletion and global warming; also revealing comparisons of GNP per capita and literacy and life expectancy around the globe.

MAPS OF THE WORLD

This new collection of regional maps artfully balances political and physical detail while proprietary map projections present the most distortion-free views of the continents yet seen. Special thematic maps are included in each continental section. Numbers following each entry indicate map scale (M = million).

Europe and Northern Asia

Asia

Australia and Pacific

Africa, Polar Regions

North America

South America

POPULATIONS AND INDEX

City population figures are given for all major cities, including capitals. A Master Index lists places and features appearing in this atlas, complete with page numbers, latitude and longitude.

Using This Atlas

Albania
Alberta, Canada
Algeria
American Samoa
Andorra
Angola
Anguilla

Quick Reference Guide

This concise guide lists continents, countries, states, provinces and territories in alphabetical order, complete with the size, population and capital of each. Page numbers and alpha-numeric reference keys are visible at a glance.

A

Aberdeen, Scot. ....
Abidjan, Côte d'Ivoire ....
Abilene, Texas ....
Abu Dhabi,* Un. Arab Emirates
Abuja,* Nigeria ....
Acapulco, Mex. ....
Accra,* Ghana ....
Aconcagua (mt.) ....
Adana, Turkey ....
Dahna' (desert)

Master Index

When you're looking for a specific place or physical feature, your quickest route is the Master Index. This 2,000-entry alphabetical index lists both the page number and latitude-longitude coordinates for major places and features found on the Regional Maps.

This New Comparative World Atlas has been thoughtfully designed to be easy and enjoyable to use, both as a general reference and as a valuable addition to the classroom. A short time spent familiarizing yourself with its organization will help you to benefit fully from its use.

MAP PROJECTIONS

This chapter explores some of the most widely used examples of how map-makers project the curved earth's surface onto a flat plane. Included is Hammond's new Optimal Conformal Projection which keeps scale distortion over selected areas to the minimum degree possible.

GLOBAL RELATIONSHIPS

Double spread World Physical and World Political maps are accompanied by Land Elevation/Ocean Depth Profiles and Comparative Land Areas and Population graphics. World thematic maps, charts and diagrams highlight important social, cultural, economic and geographic factors affecting today's world. Here, readers can explore complex relationships among such topics as population growth, environmental problems, climate and agriculture or compare worldwide standards of living, resources and manufacturing.

CONTINENT COMPARISONS

Eight thematic maps are shown for each continent (except Antarctica) enabling the map reader to visualize a variety of topics for the same region or to compare similar topics for different regions.

REGIONAL MAPS

This atlas section is grouped by continent starting with facing-page physical and political maps. Following two pages of thematic topics, in-depth regional maps offer abundant detail

WORLD THEMATIC TOPIC

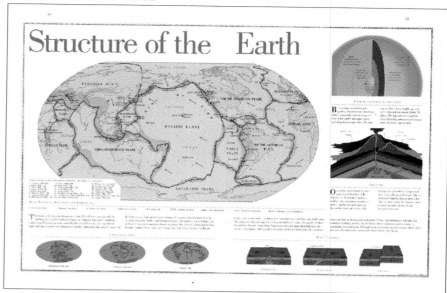

CONTINENT PHYSICAL AND POLITICAL MAPS

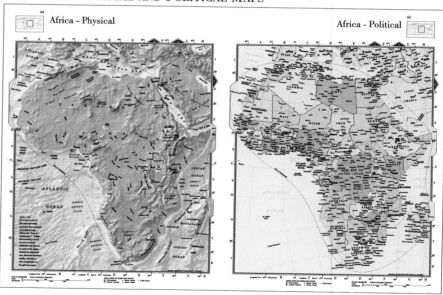

CONTINENT THEMATIC MAPS

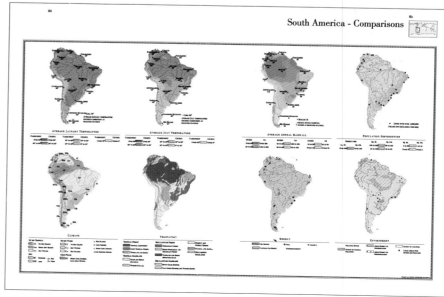

REGIONAL MAP

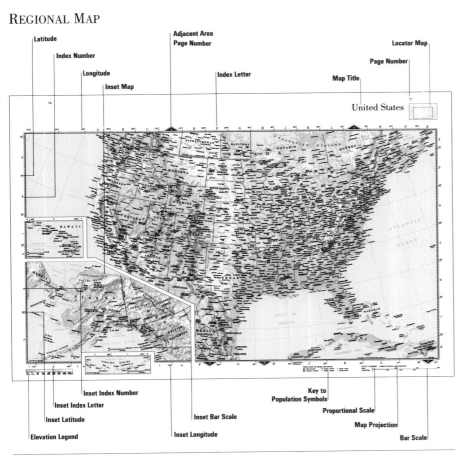

Latitude
Index Number
Longitude
Inset Map
Adjacent Area
Page Number
Index Letter
Map Title
Locator Map
Page Number

United States

Inset Index Number
Inset Index Letter
Inset Latitude
Elevation Legend
Inset Bar Scale
Inset Longitude
Key to
Population Symbols
Proportional Scale
Map Projection
Bar Scale

SYMBOLS USED ON REGIONAL MAPS

First Order (National) Boundary	Intermittent Lake	⩾ Pass
First Order Water Boundary	Dry Lake	⚓ Ruins
First Order Disputed Boundary	Salt Pan	● Falls
Second Order (Internal) Boundary	Desert/Sand Area	✳ Rapids
Third Order (Internal) Boundary	Swamp	● Dam
Undefined Boundary	Lava Flow	▲ Point Elevation
International Date Line	Glacier	🌲 Park
Shoreline, River	Stockholm First Order (National) Capital	■ Point of Interest
Intermittent River	Lausanne Second Order (Internal) Capital	⌣ Well
Canal/Aqueduct		
Highways/Roads		
Railroads		
Lake, Reservoir		

Below Sea Lev.	Sea Level	200 700	500 1,600	1,000 3,300	1,500 5,000	2,000 6,500	4,000 13,000	6,000 m. 19,700 ft.

The colors in this bar represent elevation ranges of land areas above or below sea level. Boundaries between colors are labeled both in feet and meters. Selective shading highlights those regions with significant relief variations.

PRINCIPAL MAP ABBREVIATIONS

ARCH.	ARCHIPELAGO	HAR.	HARBOR	PK.	PEAK
AUT.	AUTONOMOUS	I., IS.	ISLAND(S)	PLAT.	PLATEAU
B.	BAY	INT'L	INTERNATIONAL	PN	PARK NATIONAL
C.	CAPE	L.	LAKE	PRSV.	PRESERVE
CAN.	CANAL	LAG.	LAGOON	PT.	POINT
CAP.	CAPITAL	MT.	MOUNT	R.	RIVER
CHAN.	CHANNEL	MTN.	MOUNTAIN	RA.	RANGE
CR.	CREEK	MTS.	MOUNTAINS	REP.	REPUBLIC
DES.	DESERT	NAT'L	NATIONAL	RES.	RESERVOIR, RESERVATION
FD.	FIORD, FJORD	No.	NORTHERN		
FED.	FEDERAL	NP	NATIONAL PARK	SA.	SIERRA
FK.	FORK	OBL.	OBLAST	SD.	SOUND
FT.	FORT	OCC.	OCCUPIED	So.	SOUTHERN
G.	GULF	OKR.	OKRUG	STR.	STRAIT
GD.	GRAND	PASSG.	PASSAGE	TERR.	TERRITORY
GT.	GREAT	PEN.	PENINSULA	VOL.	VOLCANO

including boundaries, cities, transportation networks, rivers and major mountain peaks. Map backgrounds are shown in a pleasing combination of elevation coloration and relief shading, with boundary bands defining the extent of each nation's internal and external limits.

CITY POPULATIONS
In addition to population symbols locating cities and towns on the regional maps, an alphabetical listing by country provides at a glance the population of all major cities plus the country's capital.

WORLD STATISTICS
These tables list the dimensions of the earth's principal mountains, islands, rivers and lakes, along with other useful geographic information.

MASTER INDEX
This is an A to Z listing of names found on the world, continent and regional maps. Each entry is accompanied by a page location, as well as latitude and longitude coordinates.

MAP SCALES
A map's scale is the relationship of any length on that map to an identical length on the earth's surface. A scale of 1:7,000,000 means that one inch on the map represents 7,000,000 inches (110 miles, 178 kilometers) on the earth's surface. Thus, a 1:7,000,000 scale is larger than a 1:14,000,000 scale just as 1/7 is larger than 1/14.

Along with these proportional scales, each map is accompanied by a linear (bar) scale, useful in making accurate measurements between places on the maps.

In this atlas, the most densely populated regions are shown at a scale of 1:10,500,000. Other major regions are presented at 1:14,000,000 and smaller scales, allowing you to accurately compare areas and distances of similar regions.

Boundary Policies
This atlas observes the boundary policies of the U.S. Department of State. Boundary disputes are customarily handled with a special symbol treatment, but de facto boundaries are favored if they seem to have any degree of permanence, in the belief that boundaries should reflect current geographic and political realities. The portrayal of independent nations in the atlas follows their recognition by the United Nations and/or the United States government.

Hammond also uses
accepted conventional names for certain major foreign places. Usually, space permits the inclusion of the local form in parentheses. To make the maps more readily understandable to English-speaking readers, many foreign physical features are translated into more recognizable English forms.

A Word About Names
Our source for all foreign names and physical names in the United States is the decision lists of the U.S. Board of Geographic Names, which contain hundreds of thousands of place names. If a place is not listed, the Atlas follows the name form appearing on official foreign maps or in official gazetteers of the country concerned. For rendering domestic city, town and village names, this atlas follows the forms and spelling of the U.S. Postal Service.

Map Projections

There is only one way to represent a sphere with absolute precision: on a globe. All attempts to project our planet's surface onto a plane unevenly stretch or tear the sphere as it flattens, inevitably distorting shapes, areas, distances and/or directions.

Map makers show features on the curved surface of the earth by utilizing an evenly-spaced, imaginary grid pattern on the globe. Points and lines on this pattern are then transferred, or projected, to a corresponding flat surface pattern which has been previously selected and constructed from one of a wide variety of mathematical formulas.

In order to understand some of the most widely used map projections, a brief explanation of the earth's grid pattern is necessary.

The earth rotates around its *axis* once a day. The two end points of this axis are the North and South *poles*; the line circling the earth midway between the poles is the *equator*. The arc from the equator to either pole is divided into 90 degrees. The distance, expressed in degrees, from the equator (0 degrees) north or south to any point is its *latitude*, and circles of equal latitude are called *parallels*. On maps, it is customary to show parallels of evenly-spaced degrees such as every fifth or every tenth degree.

The equator is divided into 360 degrees. Lines circling the globe from pole to pole through the degree points on the equator are called *meridians*. All meridians are equal in length, but by international agreement the meridian passing through the Greenwich Observatory near London has been chosen as the *prime meridian*.

The distance, expressed in degrees, from the prime meridian (0 degrees) east or west to any point is its *longitude*. While meridians are all equal in length, parallels become shorter as they approach the poles. Whereas one degree of latitude represents approximately 69 miles (112 kilometers) anywhere on the globe, a degree of longitude varies from 69 miles (112 kilometers) at the equator to zero at the poles. Each degree of latitude and longitude is divided into 60 minutes and each minute into 60 seconds. One minute of latitude equals one nautical mile (1.15 land miles or 1.85 kilometers).

On a flat surface, any regular set of parallels and meridians upon which a map can be drawn makes a *map projection*. Since representing a sphere on a flat plane always creates distortion, only the parallels or the meridians or some other set of lines can be *true* (the same length as on a globe at corresponding scale).

The larger the area covered by the map the larger the amount of distortion; thus, distortion is greatest on world maps. Many maps seek to preserve either true area relationships (equal-area projections) or true angles and shapes (conformal projections). Other maps are more concerned with achieving true distance and directional accuracy. Some maps reflect an overall balance by compromise instead of trying to preserve any single true relationship.

WORLD MAP PROJECTIONS

A globe's surface can be transformed to fit within any outline on a flat surface. In fact, such shapes as diamonds, hearts, stars and even stylistic butterflies have enclosed a map of the earth. However, three traditional shapes - rectangles, circles and ovals - are used to portray most maps of the world.

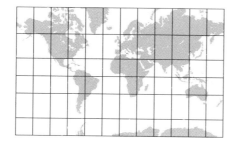

Mercator Projection
A rectangular- shaped map with vertical meridians and horizontal parallels, it is the only map on which a straight line, drawn anywhere on the map, indicates true direction along its entire length. The map has reasonably true shapes and distances within 15 degrees of the equator, but distortion increases dramatically into the higher latitudes.

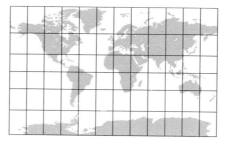

Miller Cylindrical Projection
Similar in appearance to the Mercator Projection, the Miller Cylindrical lessens distortions in the higher latitudes by closing up the spacing between parallels. Although this destroys the unique navigational property or the Mercator, it does present a more realistic view of land areas in the northern parts of Europe, Asia and North America.

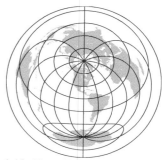

Azimuthal Equidistant Projection
A circular-shaped projection whose oblique view is the only projection in which directions and distances are depicted accurately from the projection's center point to any other place on the globe. Any straight line passing through the center is a great circle route. Distortion of areas and shapes increases away from the center.

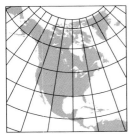

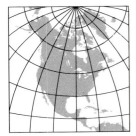

Polyconic Projection

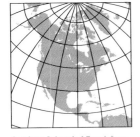

Lambert Azimuthal Equal-Area
Projection

OTHER MAP PROJECTIONS

Since continents and smaller regions occupy only a part of the entire earth's surface, other projections can be employed to minimize distortion and, where possible, preserve true shapes, areas, distances or directions. But, although smaller in size, the areas being mapped are still parts of a sphere and the flattening process will still result in distortions in the maps.

Conic Projections

These maps are created by mathematically projecting points and lines from a globe onto a cone which caps the globe. The cone can be placed either tangent to the globe at a preselected parallel or it can intersect the globe at two preselected parallels. The use of two standard parallels, one near the top of the map, the other near the bottom of the map, reduces the scale error. In one type of conic projection, Albers, the parallels are spaced evenly to make the projection equal-area. In the Lambert Conformal Conic Projection the parallels are spaced so that any small quadrangle of the grid will have the same shape as on the globe.

Polyconic Projection

Best suited for maps with a long north-south orientation, this projection is mathematically based upon an infinite number of cones tangent to an infinite number of points (parallels) on the globe. All meridians are curved lines except for the central meridian, which shows true distance and direction.

Gnomonic Projection

Viewing the surface of the globe from its center point creates this projection with very bad distortions away from the map's center. However, this projection has a unique quality - all great circles (shortest lines between points on a sphere) are shown as straight lines. Therefore, the path of the shortest distance between any two points on the map is a straight line.

Lambert Azimuthal Equal-Area Projection

Mathematically projected on a plane surface tangent to any point on a globe, this is the most common projection (also known as Zenithal Equal-Area) used for maps of the Eastern and Western hemispheres. It is also a good projection for continents, as it shows correct areas with little distortion of shape.

Hammond's Optimal Conformal Projection

As its name implies, this new conformal projection presents the optimal view of an area by reducing shifts in scale over an entire region to the minimum degree possible. While conformal maps generally preserve all small shapes, large shapes can become very distorted because of varying scales, causing considerable inaccuracy in distance measurements. Consequently, unlike other projections, the Optimal Comformal does not use one standard formula to construct a map. Each map is a unique projection - the optimal projection for that particular area. The result is the most distortion-free conformal map possible.

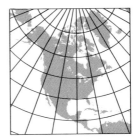

Lambert Conformal Conic
Projection

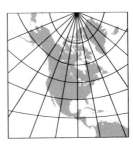

Gnomonic Projection

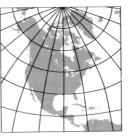

Optimal Conformal Projection

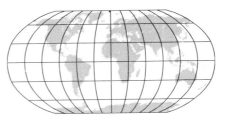

Orthographic Projection

This projection looks like a picture of a globe. It is neither conformal nor equal-area. Although the distortion on the peripheries is extreme, we see it correctly, because the eye perceives it not as a map but as a picture of a three-dimensional globe. Obviously, only a hemisphere (half globe) can be shown.

Mollweide Projection

An early example of an oval-shaped (also called pseudocylindrical) projection is this equal-area map of the earth within an ellipse. Shapes are elongated in the lower latitudes. Since its presentation in 1805 it has been an inspiration for similar oval-shaped maps and has even been "interrupted" to minimize distortion of continental or ocean areas.

Robinson Projection

This modern, oval-shaped projection uses tabular coordinates rather than mathematical formulas to make the world "look right." Although not true with respect to shapes, sizes, distances or directions, its compromising features show a better balance of size and shape in high latitude lands and very low distortion near the equator.

Quick Reference Guide

This concise alphabetical reference lists continents, countries, states, territories, possessions and other major geographical areas, complete with the size, population and capital or chief town of each. Page numbers and alpha-numeric reference keys (which refer to the grid squares of latitude and longitude on each map) are visible at a glance. The population figures are the latest and most reliable figures obtainable.

Place	Square Miles	Square Kilometers	Population	Capital or Chief Town	Page/ Index Ref.
A Afghanistan*	250,000	647,500	26,668,251	Kabul	49/F 6
Africa	11,701,147	30,306,000	705,924,000	....	65
Alabama, U.S.	52,237	135,293	4,273,084	Montgomery	78/C 4
Alaska, U.S.	615,230	1,593,444	607,007	Juneau	76
Albania*	11,100	28,749	3,401,126	Tiranë	44/C 3
Alberta, Canada	255,285	661,185	2,964,700	Edmonton	79/F 4
Algeria*	919,591	2,381,740	31,787,647	Algiers	68/F 2
Andorra*	174	450	67,673	Andorra la Vella	42/E 5
Angola*	481,351	1,246,700	11,486,729	Luanda	70/C 3
Antarctica	5,500,000	14,245,000	....	....	71
Antigua and Barbuda*	170	440	64,461	St. John's	81/J 4
Argentina*	1,068,296	2,766,890	37,214,757	Buenos Aires	88/D 4
Arizona, U.S.	114,006	295,276	4,428,068	Phoenix	76/D 5
Arkansas, U.S.	53,182	137,742	2,509,793	Little Rock	77/H 4
Armenia*	11,506	29,800	3,396,184	Yerevan	45/C 4
Asia	17,159,867	44,444,100	3,407,967,000	....	49
Australia*	2,967,893	7,686,850	18,950,108	Canberra	59
Austria*	32,375	83,851	8,148,007	Vienna	42/G 4
Azerbaijan*	33,436	86,600	7,955,772	Baku	45/D 4
B Bahamas, The*	5,382	13,939	287,548	Nassau	81/F 2
Bahrain*	240	622	641,539	Manama	52/F 3
Bangladesh*	55,598	144,000	129,146,695	Dhaka	53/E 4
Barbados*	166	430	259,248	Bridgetown	81/J 5
Belarus*	80,154	207,600	10,390,697	Minsk	43/G 5
Belgium*	11,780	30,513	10,185,894	Brussels	42/E 3
Belize*	8,865	22,960	241,546	Belmopan	80/D 4
Benin*	43,483	112,620	6,516,630	Porto-Novo	68/F 5
Bhutan*	18,147	47,000	1,996,221	Thimphu	53/E 3
Bolivia*	424,163	1,098,582	8,139,180	La Paz; Sucre	86/F 7
Bosnia & Herzegovina*	19,781	51,233	3,591,618	Sarajevo	44/C 3
Botswana*	231,803	600,370	1,479,039	Gaborone	70/D 5
Brazil*	3,286,470	8,511,965	173,790,810	Brasília	83/D 3
British Columbia, Canada	365,946	947,800	4,023,100	Victoria	79/F 4
Brunei*	2,228	5,770	330,689	Bandar Seri Begawan	56/E 4
Bulgaria*	42,823	110,912	8,155,828	Sofia	44/D 3
Burkina Faso*	105,869	274,200	11,892,029	Ouagadougou	68/E 5
Burundi*	10,745	27,830	5,930,805	Bujumbura	70/E 1
C California, U.S.	158,869	411,470	31,878,234	Sacramento	76/C 4
Cambodia*	69,900	181,040	11,918,865	Phnom Penh	56/C 3
Cameroon*	183,568	475,441	15,891,531	Yaoundé	68/H 7
Canada*	3,851,787	9,976,139	31,330,255	Ottawa	79
Cape Verde*	1,556	4,030	411,487	Praia	12/H 5
Central African Republic*	240,533	622,980	3,515,657	Bangui	69/J 6
Chad*	495,752	1,283,998	7,760,252	N'Djamena	69/J 4
Chile*	292,258	756,950	15,155,495	Santiago	88/B 3
China, People's Rep. of*	3,705,386	9,596,960	1,256,167,701	Beijing	54/G 4
China, Republic of (Taiwan)	13,892	35,980	22,319,222	Taipei	55/M 7
Colombia*	439,733	1,138,910	40,036,927	Bogotá	86/D 3
Colorado, U.S.	104,100	269,618	3,822,676	Denver	76/E 4
Comoros*	838	2,170	580,509	Moroni	65/G 6
Congo, Dem. Rep. of the	905,563	2,345,410	51,987,773	Kinshasa	65/E 5
Congo, Rep. of the*	132,046	342,000	2,775,659	Brazzaville	65/D 4
Connecticut, U.S.	5,544	14,358	3,274,238	Hartford	78/F 2
Costa Rica*	19,730	51,100	3,743,677	San José	80/E 5
Côte d'Ivoire*	124,502	322,460	16,190,105	Yamoussoukro	68/D 5
Croatia*	22,050	56,538	4,681,015	Zagreb	44/C 2
Cuba*	42,803	110,860	11,139,412	Havana	81/F 3
Cyprus*	3,571	9,250	759,048	Nicosia	52/B 1
Czech Republic*	30,387	78,703	10,283,762	Prague	44/B 2
D Delaware, U.S.	2,396	6,206	724,842	Dover	78/E 3
Denmark*	16,629	43,069	5,374,554	Copenhagen	43/C 4
District of Columbia, U.S.	68	177	543,213	Washington	78/E 3
Djibouti*	8,494	22,000	454,294	Djibouti	69/P 5
Dominica*	290	751	63,944	Roseau	81/J 4
Dominican Republic*	18,815	48,730	8,261,536	Santo Domingo	81/H 4
E Ecuador*	109,483	283,561	12,782,161	Quito	86/C 4
Egypt*	386,659	1,001,447	68,494,584	Cairo	69/L 2
El Salvador*	8,124	21,040	5,925,374	San Salvador	80/C 5

Place	Square Miles	Square Kilometers	Population	Capital or Chief Town	Page/ Index Ref.
England, U.K.	50,356	130,423	49,089,100	London	42/D 3
Equatorial Guinea*	10,831	28,052	477,763	Malabo	68/G 7
Eritrea*	46,842	121,320	4,142,481	Asmara	69/N 5
Estonia*	17,413	45,100	1,398,140	Tallinn	43/G 3
Ethiopia*	435,184	1,127,127	60,967,436	Addis Ababa	69/N 5
Europe	4,066,019	10,531,000	732,653,000	....	39
F Fiji*	7,055	18,272	823,376	Suva	62/G 6
Finland*	130,128	337,032	5,164,825	Helsinki	43/G 3
Florida, U.S.	59,928	155,214	14,399,985	Tallahassee	78/D 5
France*	211,208	547,030	59,128,187	Paris	42/E 4
French Guiana	35,135	91,000	173,246	Cayenne	87/H 3
French Polynesia	1,522	3,941	246,171	Papeete	63/L 6
G Gabon*	103,347	267,670	1,244,192	Libreville	68/H 7
Gambia, The*	4,363	11,300	1,381,496	Banjul	68/B 5
Gaza Strip	139	360	1,162,777	Gaza	52/B 2
Georgia*	26,911	69,700	5,034,051	T'bilisi	45/C 4
Georgia, U.S.	58,977	152,750	7,353,225	Atlanta	78/D 4
Germany*	137,803	356,910	82,081,365	Berlin	42/F 3
Ghana*	92,100	238,540	19,271,744	Accra	68/E 6
Greece*	50,942	131,940	10,750,705	Athens	44/D 4
Greenland, Denmark	840,000	2,175,600	60,324	Nuuk (Godthåb)	72/N 2
Grenada*	131	340	97,913	St. George's	81/J 5
Guadeloupe	687	1,779	425,317	Basse-Terre	81/J 4
Guam	209	541	154,623	Hagåtña	62/D 3
Guatemala*	42,042	108,889	12,669,576	Guatemala	80/C 4
Guinea*	94,927	245,860	7,610,869	Conakry	68/C 5
Guinea-Bissau*	13,946	36,120	1,263,341	Bissau	68/B 5
Guyana*	83,000	214,970	703,399	Georgetown	86/G 3
H Haiti*	10,714	27,750	6,991,589	Port-au-Prince	81/G 4
Hawaii, U.S.	6,459	16,729	1,183,723	Honolulu	76
Honduras*	43,277	112,087	6,130,135	Tegucigalpa	80/D 4
Hong Kong, China	402	1,040	6,966,929	Victoria	55/K 7
Hungary*	35,919	93,030	10,167,182	Budapest	44/C 2
I Iceland*	39,768	103,000	274,141	Reykjavík	39/B 2
Idaho, U.S.	83,574	216,456	1,189,251	Boise	76/C 3
Illinois, U.S.	57,918	150,007	11,846,544	Springfield	78/B 2
India*	1,269,339	3,287,588	1,017,645,163	New Delhi	53/C 4
Indiana, U.S.	36,420	94,328	5,840,528	Indianapolis	78/C 2
Indonesia*	741,096	1,919,440	219,266,557	Jakarta	56/E 6
Iowa, U.S.	56,275	145,752	2,851,792	Des Moines	77/H 3
Iran*	636,293	1,648,000	65,865,302	Tehran	52/F 2
Iraq*	168,753	437,072	23,150,926	Baghdad	52/D 2
Ireland*	27,136	70,282	3,647,348	Dublin	42/C 3
Ireland, Northern, U.K.	5,459	14,138	1,663,300	Belfast	42/C 3
Israel*	8,019	20,770	5,851,913	Jerusalem	52/B 2
Italy*	116,305	301,230	56,686,568	Rome	39/F 4
J Jamaica*	4,243	10,990	2,668,740	Kingston	81/F 4
Japan*	145,882	377,835	126,434,470	Tokyo	55/Q 4
Jordan*	34,445	89,213	4,700,843	Amman	52/C 2
K Kansas, U.S.	82,282	213,110	2,572,150	Topeka	77/G 4
Kazakhstan*	1,049,150	2,717,300	16,816,150	Astana	46/G 5
Kentucky, U.S.	40,411	104,665	3,883,723	Frankfort	77/J 4
Kenya*	224,960	582,646	29,250,541	Nairobi	65/F 4
Kiribati*	277	717	87,025	Tarawa	62/H 5
Korea, North*	46,540	120,539	21,687,550	P'yŏngyang	55/N 3
Korea, South*	38,023	98,480	47,350,529	Seoul	55/N 4
Kuwait*	6,880	17,820	2,067,728	Kuwait	52/E 3
Kyrgyzstan*	76,641	198,500	4,584,341	Bishkek	46/H 5
L Laos*	91,428	236,800	5,556,821	Vientiane	49/K 8
Latvia*	24,749	64,100	2,326,689	Riga	43/G 4
Lebanon*	4,015	10,399	3,619,971	Beirut	52/B 2
Lesotho*	11,718	30,350	2,166,520	Maseru	70/E 6
Liberia*	43,000	111,370	3,089,980	Monrovia	68/D 6
Libya*	679,358	1,759,537	5,114,032	Tripoli	69/J 2
Liechtenstein*	62	160	32,410	Vaduz	42/F 4
Lithuania*	25,174	65,200	3,571,552	Vilnius	43/F 4
Louisiana, U.S.	49,651	128,595	4,350,579	Baton Rouge	77/H 5
Luxembourg*	999	2,587	432,577	Luxembourg	42/F 4

* United Nations member (Yugoslavia suspended)

Place	Square Miles	Square Kilometers	Population	Capital or Chief Town	Page/Index Ref.
M					
Macedonia, Former Yugoslav					
Republic of *￼	9,781	25,333	2,035,044	Skopje	44/D 3
Madagascar*	226,657	587,041	15,294,535	Antananarivo	70/K10
Maine, U.S.	33,741	87,388	1,243,316	Augusta	78/G 1
Malawi*	45,745	118,480	10,154,299	Lilongwe	70/F 3
Malaysia*	127,316	329,750	21,820,143	Kuala Lumpur	56/D 4
Maldives*	116	300	310,425	Male	49/G 9
Mali*	478,764	1,240,000	10,750,686	Bamako	68/E 4
Malta*	124	320	383,285	Valletta	44/B 4
Manitoba, Canada	250,946	649,951	1,143,500	Winnipeg	79/H 4
Marshall Islands*	70	181	68,088	Majuro	62/G 3
Maryland, U.S.	12,297	31,849	5,071,604	Annapolis	78/E 3
Massachusetts, U.S.	9,241	23,934	6,092,352	Boston	78/F 2
Mauritania*	397,953	1,030,700	2,660,155	Nouakchott	68/C 4
Mauritius *	718	1,860	1,196,172	Port Louis	13/M 7
Mexico *	761,601	1,972,546	102,026,691	Mexico	80/A 3
Michigan, U.S.	96,705	250,465	9,594,350	Lansing	78/C 1
Micronesia, Federated					
States of*	271	702	133,144	Palikir	62/D 4
Minnesota, U.S.	86,943	225,182	4,657,758	St. Paul	77/G 2
Mississippi, U.S.	48,286	125,060	2,716,115	Jackson	78/B 4
Missouri, U.S.	69,709	180,546	5,358,692	Jefferson City	77/H 4
Moldova*	13,012	33,700	4,466,758	Chişinău	44/E 2
Monaco*	0.7	1.9	32,231	....	42/F 5
Mongolia*	606,163	1,569,962	2,654,572	Ulaanbaatar	54/G 2
Montana, U.S.	147,046	380,849	879,372	Helena	76/D 2
Morocco *	172,414	446,550	30,205,387	Rabat	68/C 1
Mozambique *	309,494	801,590	19,614,345	Maputo	70/G 4
Myanmar (Burma)*	261,969	678,500	48,852,098	Yangon	49/J 7
N					
Namibia*	318,694	825,418	1,674,116	Windhoek	70/C 5
Nauru	8	21	10,704	Yaren (district)	62/F 5
Nebraska, U.S.	77,358	200,358	1,652,093	Lincoln	76/F 3
Nepal*	54,363	140,800	24,920,211	Kathmandu	53/D 3
Netherlands*	14,413	37,330	15,878,304	The Hague; Amsterdam	42/F 3
Nevada, U.S.	110,567	286,367	1,603,163	Carson City	76/C 4
New Brunswick, Canada	28,355	73,440	755,000	Fredericton	79/L 5
Newfoundland, Canada	156,649	405,721	541,000	St. John's	79/L 4
New Hampshire, U.S.	9,283	24,044	1,162,481	Concord	78/F 2
New Jersey, U.S.	8,215	21,277	7,987,933	Trenton	78/F 2
New Mexico, U.S.	121,598	314,939	1,713,407	Santa Fe	76/E 5
New York, U.S.	53,989	139,833	18,184,774	Albany	78/E 2
New Zealand*	103,736	268,676	3,697,850	Wellington	59/H 6
Nicaragua*	49,998	129,494	4,850,976	Managua	80/D 5
Niger*	489,189	1,267,000	10,260,316	Niamey	68/G 4
Nigeria*	356,668	923,770	117,170,948	Abuja	68/G 6
North America	9,355,975	24,232,000	443,438,000	....	73
North Carolina, U.S.	52,672	136,421	7,322,870	Raleigh	78/D 3
North Dakota, U.S.	70,704	183,123	643,539	Bismarck	76/F 2
Northern Ireland, U.K.	5,459	14,138	1,663,300	Belfast	42/C 3
Northwest Territories, Canada	1,322,905	3,426,328	41,600	Yellowknife	79/F 3
Norway*	125,181	324,220	4,455,707	Oslo	43/C 3
Nova Scotia, Canada	21,425	55,491	939,800	Halifax	79/L 5
Nunavut, Canada	733,590	1,900,000	27,000	Iqaluit	79/G 3
O					
Ohio, U.S.	44,828	116,103	11,172,782	Columbus	78/D 2
Oklahoma, U.S.	69,903	181,048	3,300,902	Oklahoma City	77/G 4
Oman*	82,031	212,460	2,532,556	Muscat	52/G 4
Ontario, Canada	412,580	1,068,582	11,513,800	Toronto	79/H 4
Oregon, U.S.	97,132	251,571	3,203,735	Salem	76/B 3
P					
Pakistan*	310,403	803,944	141,145,344	Islamabad	49/F 7
Palau*	177	458	18,827	Koror	62/C 4
Panama*	30,193	78,200	2,821,085	Panamá	80/E 6
Papua New Guinea*	178,259	461,690	4,811,939	Port Moresby	62/D 5
Paraguay*	157,047	406,752	5,579,503	Asunción	83/C 5
Pennsylvania, U.S.	46,058	119,291	12,056,112	Harrisburg	78/E 2
Peru*	496,223	1,285,220	27,135,689	Lima	86/C 5
Philippines*	115,830	300,000	80,961,430	Manila	57/H 3
Poland*	120,725	312,678	38,644,184	Warsaw	39/F 3
Portugal*	35,552	92,080	9,902,147	Lisbon	42/C 6
Prince Edward Island, Canada	2,184	5,657	138,000	Charlottetown	79/L 5
Puerto Rico, U.S.	3,508	9,085	3,817,833	San Juan	81/H 4
Q					
Qatar*	4,247	11,000	749,542	Doha	52/F 3
Québec, Canada	594,857	1,540,680	7,345,400	Québec	79/K 4
R					
Réunion, France	969	2,510	730,201	St-Denis	13/M 7
Rhode Island, U.S.	1,231	3,189	990,225	Providence	78/F 2
Romania*	91,699	237,500	22,291,200	Bucharest	44/D 2

Place	Square Miles	Square Kilometers	Population	Capital or Chief Town	Page/Index Ref.
Russia*	6,592,735	17,075,200	145,904,542	Moscow	46/H 3
Rwanda*	10,169	26,337	8,336,995	Kigali	70/E 1
S					
Saint Kitts and Nevis*	104	269	43,441	Basseterre	81/J 4
Saint Lucia*	239	620	155,678	Castries	81/J 5
Saint Vincent & the Grenadines*	131	340	121,188	Kingstown	81/J 5
Samoa*	1,104	2,860	235,302	Apia	63/H 6
San Marino*	23.4	60.6	25,215	San Marino	42/G 5
São Tomé and Príncipe*	371	960	159,832	São Tomé	68/F 7
Saskatchewan, Canada	251,865	652,330	1,027,800	Regina	79/G 4
Saudi Arabia*	756,981	1,960,582	22,245,751	Riyadh	52/D 4
Scotland, U.K.	30,414	78,772	5,128,000	Edinburgh	42/C 2
Senegal*	75,749	196,190	10,390,296	Dakar	68/B 5
Seychelles*	176	455	79,672	Victoria	13/M 6
Sierra Leone*	27,699	71,740	5,509,263	Freetown	68/C 6
Singapore*	244	632.6	3,571,710	Singapore	56/C 5
Slovakia*	18,859	48,845	5,401,134	Bratislava	44/C 2
Slovenia*	7,836	20,296	1,970,056	Ljubljana	44/B 2
Solomon Islands*	10,985	28,450	470,000	Honiara	62/E 6
Somalia*	246,200	637,658	7,433,922	Mogadishu	69/Q 6
South Africa*	471,008	1,219,912	43,981,758	Cape Town; Pretoria	70/D 6
South America	6,879,916	17,819,000	314,335,000	....	83
South Carolina, U.S.	31,189	80,779	3,698,746	Columbia	78/D 4
South Dakota, U.S.	77,121	199,744	732,405	Pierre	76/F 3
Spain*	194,884	504,750	39,208,236	Madrid	42/D 5
Sri Lanka*	25,332	65,610	19,355,053	Colombo	53/D 7
Sudan*	967,494	2,505,809	35,530,371	Khartoum	69/L 5
Suriname*	63,039	163,270	434,093	Paramaribo	87/G 3
Swaziland*	6,703	17,360	1,004,072	Mbabane	70/F 6
Sweden*	173,731	449,964	8,938,559	Stockholm	43/D 3
Switzerland	15,943	41,292	7,288,715	Bern	42/F 4
Syria*	71,498	185,180	17,758,925	Damascus	52/C 1
T					
Taiwan	13,892	35,980	22,319,222	T'aipei	55/M 7
Tajikistan*	55,251	143,100	6,194,373	Dushanbe	46/H 6
Tanzania*	364,699	945,090	31,962,769	Dar es Salaam	70/F 2
Tennessee, U.S.	42,146	109,158	5,319,654	Nashville	78/C 3
Texas, U.S.	267,277	692,248	19,128,261	Austin	76/F 5
Thailand*	198,455	513,998	61,163,833	Bangkok	56/C 2
Togo*	21,927	56,790	5,262,611	Lomé	68/F 6
Tonga	289	748	109,959	Nuku'alofa	63/H 7
Trinidad and Tobago*	1,980	5,128	1,086,908	Port-of-Spain	81/J 5
Tunisia*	63,170	163,610	9,645,499	Tunis	68/G 1
Turkey*	301,382	780,580	66,620,120	Ankara	44/F 4
Turkmenistan*	188,455	488,100	4,435,507	Ashkhabad	46/F 6
Tuvalu	10	26	10,730	Funafuti	62/G 5
U					
Uganda*	91,135	236,040	22,804,973	Kampala	69/M 7
Ukraine*	233,089	603,700	49,506,779	Kiev	44/E 2
United Arab Emirates*	29,182	75,581	2,386,472	Abu Dhabi	52/F 4
United Kingdom*	94,525	244,820	59,113,439	London	42/D 2
United States*	3,618,765	9,372,610	274,943,496	Washington, D.C.	76
Uruguay*	68,039	176,220	3,332,782	Montevideo	88/E 3
Utah, U.S.	84,904	219,902	2,000,494	Salt Lake City	76/D 4
Uzbekistan*	172,741	447,400	24,422,518	Tashkent	46/G 5
V					
Vanuatu*	5,699	14,760	192,848	Port-Vila	62/F 6
Vatican City	0.17	0.44	870	....	42/G 5
Venezuela*	352,143	912,050	23,595,822	Caracas	82/E 2
Vermont, U.S.	9,614	24,900	588,654	Montpelier	78/F 2
Vietnam*	127,243	329,560	78,349,503	Hanoi	49/K 8
Virginia, U.S.	42,326	109,625	6,675,451	Richmond	78/E 3
Virgin Islands, British	59	153	13,368	Road Town	81/J 4
Virgin Islands, U.S.	136	352	97,240	Charlotte Amalie	81/H 4
W					
Wales, U.K.	8,017	20,764	2,921,100	Cardiff	42/D 3
Washington, U.S.	70,637	182,949	5,532,939	Olympia	76/B 2
West Bank	2,263	5,860	1,661,749	....	52/C 2
Western Sahara	102,703	266,000	244,943	....	68/B 3
West Virginia, U.S.	24,231	62,758	1,825,754	Charleston	78/D 3
Wisconsin, U.S.	65,499	169,643	5,159,795	Madison	78/B 1
World	(land) 57,505,734	148,940,000	6,041,580,566	....	12
Wyoming, U.S.	97,818	253,349	481,400	Cheyenne	76/E 3
Y					
Yemen*	203,849	527,970	17,521,085	Sanaa	52/E 6
Yugoslavia*	39,517	102,350	11,210,243	Belgrade	44/D 3
Yukon Territory, Canada	186,660	483,450	30,600	Whitehorse	79/D 3
Z					
Zambia*	290,583	752,610	9,872,007	Lusaka	70/E 3
Zimbabwe*	150,803	390,580	11,272,013	Harare	70/E 4

World - Physical

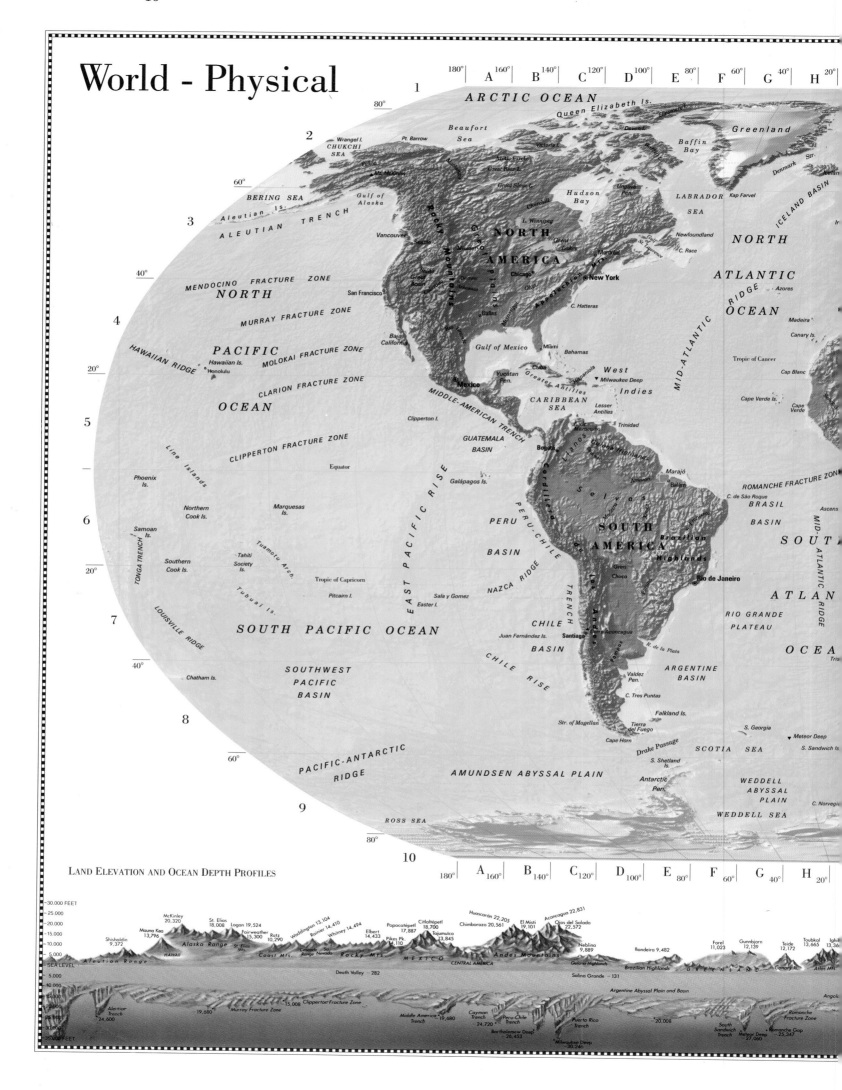

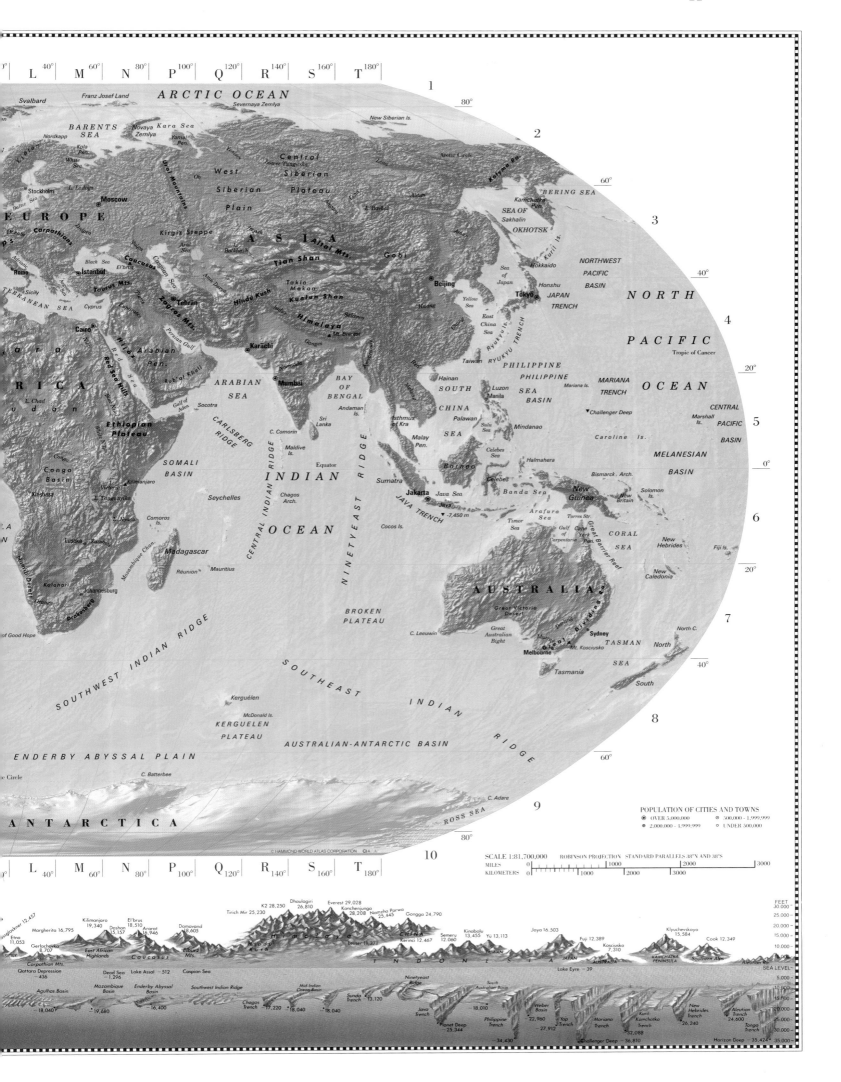

World - Political

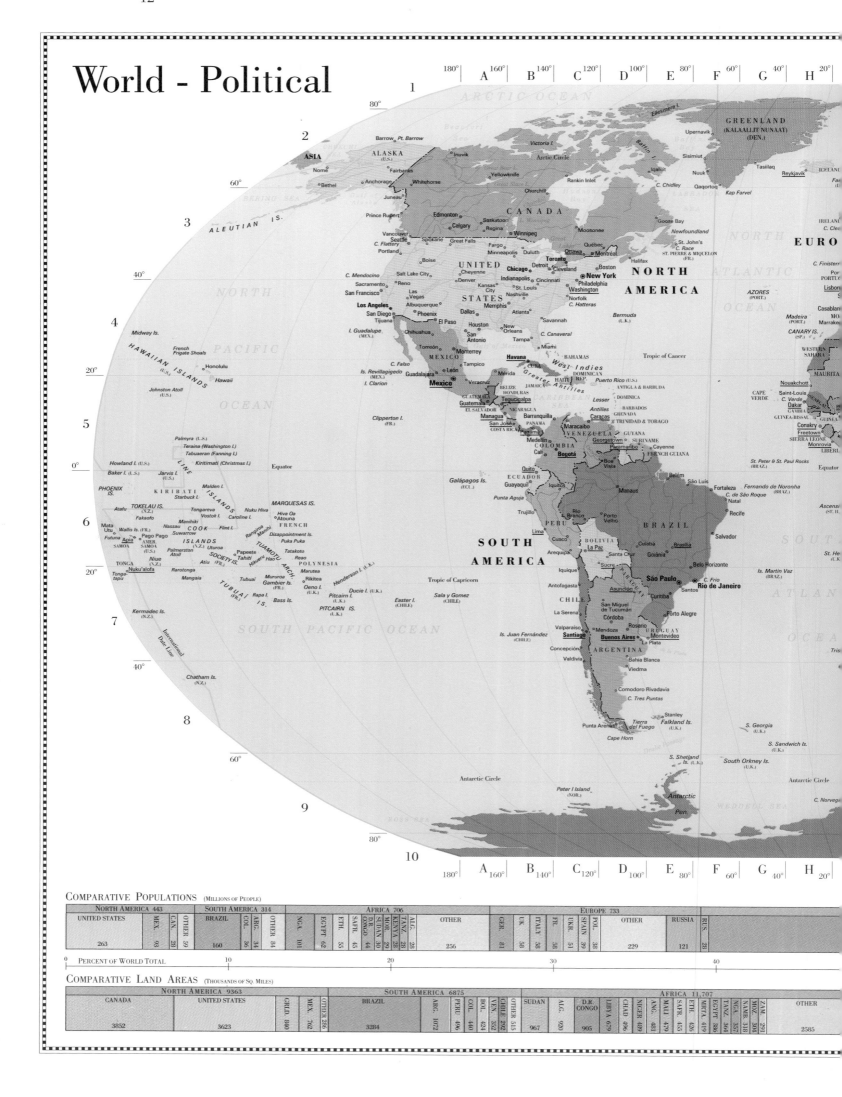

COMPARATIVE POPULATIONS (MILLIONS OF PEOPLE)

NORTH AMERICA 443				SOUTH AMERICA 314				AFRICA 706										EUROPE 733								RUSSIA	
UNITED STATES	MEX.	CAN.	OTHER	BRAZIL	COL.	ARG.	OTHER	NGA.	EGYPT	ETH.	SAFR.	D.R. CONGO	SUDAN	KENYA	TANZ.	ALG.	OTHER	GER.	UK	ITALY	FR.	UKR.	SPAIN	POL.	OTHER	RUSSIA	RUS.
263	93	29	59	160	36	34	84	101	62	55	45	44	30	28	28	28	256	81	58	58	58	51	39	38	229	121	28

0	10	20	30	40

PERCENT OF WORLD TOTAL

COMPARATIVE LAND AREAS (THOUSANDS OF SQ. MILES)

NORTH AMERICA 9363					SOUTH AMERICA 6875							AFRICA 11,707													
CANADA	UNITED STATES	GRLD.	MEX.	OTHER	BRAZIL	ARG.	PERU	COL.	BOL.	VEN.	CHILE	SUDAN	ALG.	D.R. CONGO	LIBYA	CHAD	NIGER	ANG.	MALI	SAFR.	ETH.	MRTA.	EGYPT	TANZ.	NGA.	NAMB.	MOZ.	ZAM.	OTHER
3852	3623	840	762	286	3284	1072	496	440	424	352	292	967	920	905	679	496	489	481	479	471	455	426	419	386	364	357	318	303	291	2585

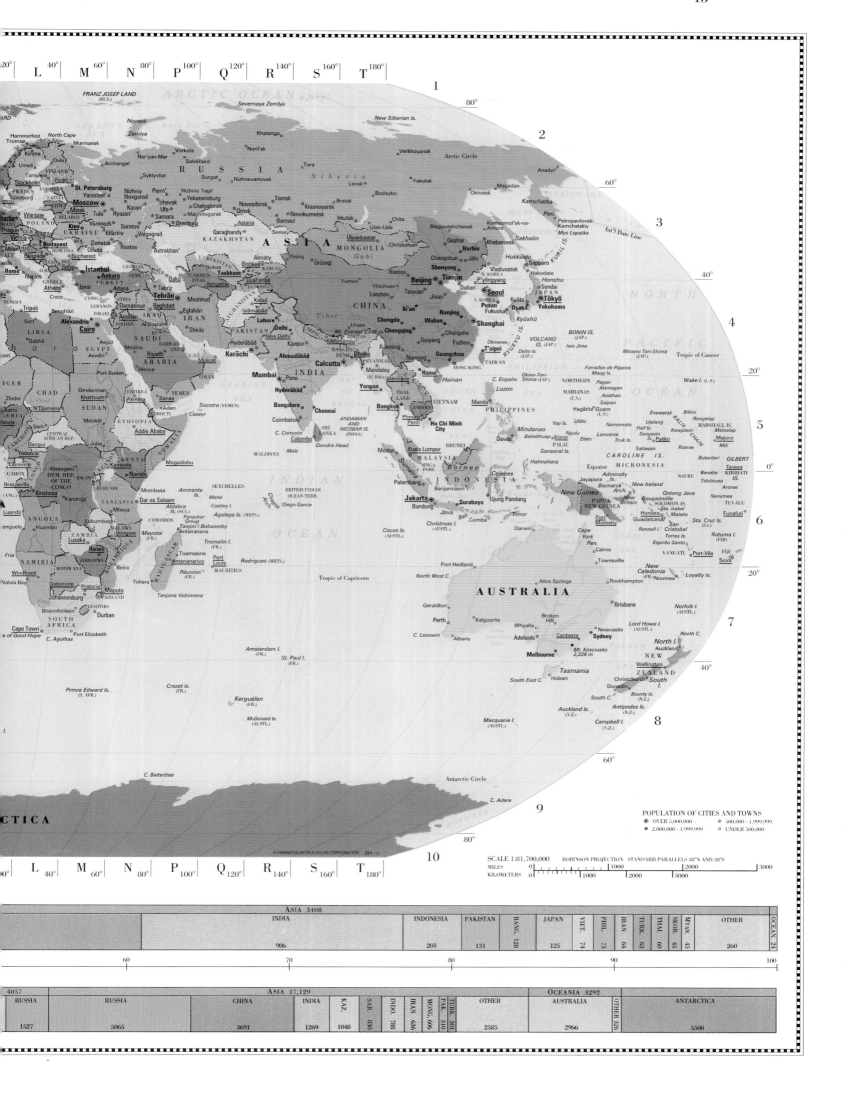

Structure of the

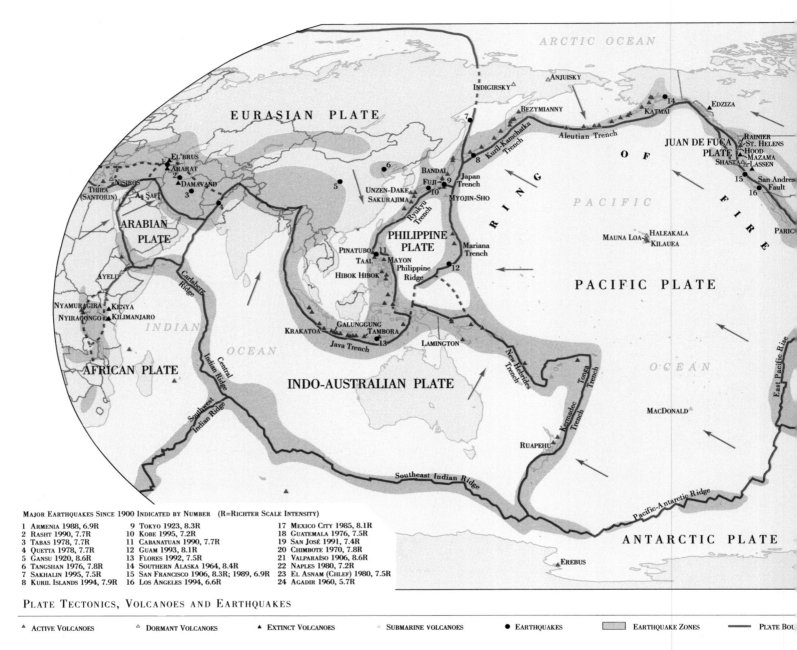

MAJOR EARTHQUAKES SINCE 1900 INDICATED BY NUMBER   (R=RICHTER SCALE INTENSITY)

1 ARMENIA 1988, 6.9R	9 TOKYO 1923, 8.3R	17 MEXICO CITY 1985, 8.1R
2 RASHT 1990, 7.7R	10 KOBE 1995, 7.2R	18 GUATEMALA 1976, 7.5R
3 TABAS 1978, 7.7R	11 CABANATUAN 1990, 7.7R	19 SAN JOSÉ 1991, 7.4R
4 QUETTA 1978, 7.7R	12 GUAM 1993, 8.1R	20 CHIMBOTE 1970, 7.8R
5 GANSU 1920, 8.6R	13 FLORES 1992, 7.5R	21 VALPARAÍSO 1906, 8.6R
6 TANGSHAN 1976, 7.8R	14 SOUTHERN ALASKA 1964, 8.4R	22 NAPLES 1980, 7.2R
7 SAKHALIN 1995, 7.5R	15 SAN FRANCISCO 1906, 8.3R; 1989, 6.9R	23 EL ASNAM (CHLEF) 1980, 7.5R
8 KURIL ISLANDS 1994, 7.9R	16 LOS ANGELES 1994, 6.6R	24 AGADIR 1960, 5.7R

PLATE TECTONICS, VOLCANOES AND EARTHQUAKES

▲ ACTIVE VOLCANOES   △ DORMANT VOLCANOES   ▲ EXTINCT VOLCANOES   ᐃ SUBMARINE VOLCANOES   ● EARTHQUAKES   ▨ EARTHQUAKE ZONES   ━━ PLATE BOU

T he making of continents began more than 200 million years ago with the splitting of a gigantic landmass known as Pangaea. Two super continents, Laurasia and Gondwana, were formed by the initial division. Over a period of many millions of years these landmasses further subdivided into smaller parts and drifted across a single great ocean, forming the oceans and continents of today. In terms of current theory, called plate tectonics, the earth's crust is divided into at least 15 rigid rock segments, known as plates, that float on a semi-molten layer of upper mantle. Seven plates are of major size and, except for the vast Pacific

CONTINENTAL DRIFT

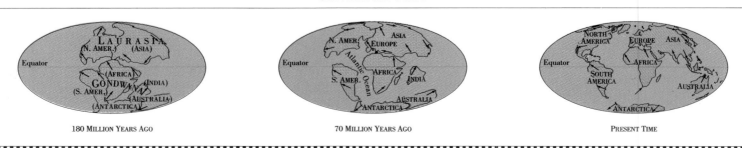

180 MILLION YEARS AGO   70 MILLION YEARS AGO   PRESENT TIME

Earth

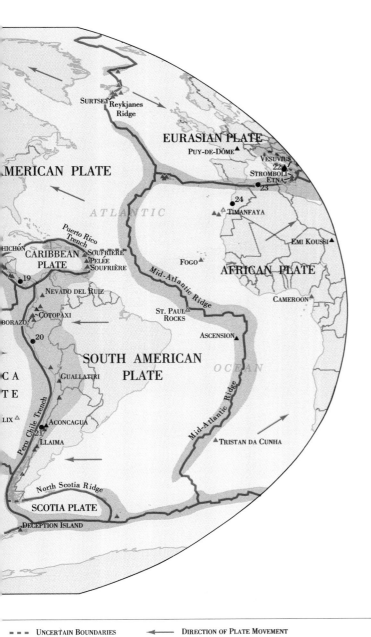

UNCERTAIN BOUNDARIES ⟵ DIRECTION OF PLATE MOVEMENT

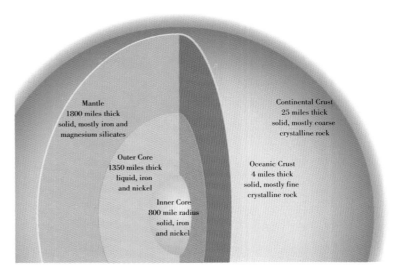

INTERIOR AND CRUST OF THE EARTH

B y studying records of earthquakes, scientists have developed
a fairly reasonable picture (cross section) of the earth's principal layers,
including their composition. The inner
core is a very dense, highly-pressur-
ized, extremely hot (about 9,000° F.)
sphere. Moving outward toward the
crust, densities, pressures and temperatures decrease significantly.

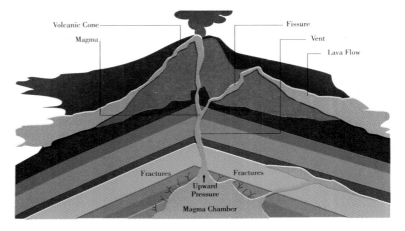

VOLCANOES

O ne of the earth's most dynamic
and colorful builders is the
volcano. In the mantle, magma—
molten rock containing compressed
gases—probes for weak spots in
the earth's crust and bursts forth
through the ground in an eruption of
fiery lava, ash, gas and steam. After a
period of eruption, lasting from a few
days to many years, the magma ceases
to push upward and the volcano
becomes dormant.

Plate, carry a continental landmass with surrounding ocean floor and island areas.
The plates are slow-moving, driven by powerful forces within the mantle. At their
boundaries they are either slowly separating with new material added from the
mantle, converging, with one plate being forced down (subducted) and consumed
under another, or sliding past each other. Almost all earthquake, volcanic and
mountain-building activity closely follows these boundaries and is related to
movements between them. Although these movements may be no more than inches
per year, the destructive power unleashed can be cataclysmic.

PLATE TECTONICS

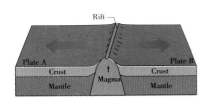

SEPARATING PLATES

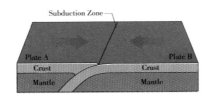

CONVERGING PLATES

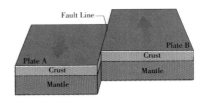

SLIDING PLATES

Atmosphere &

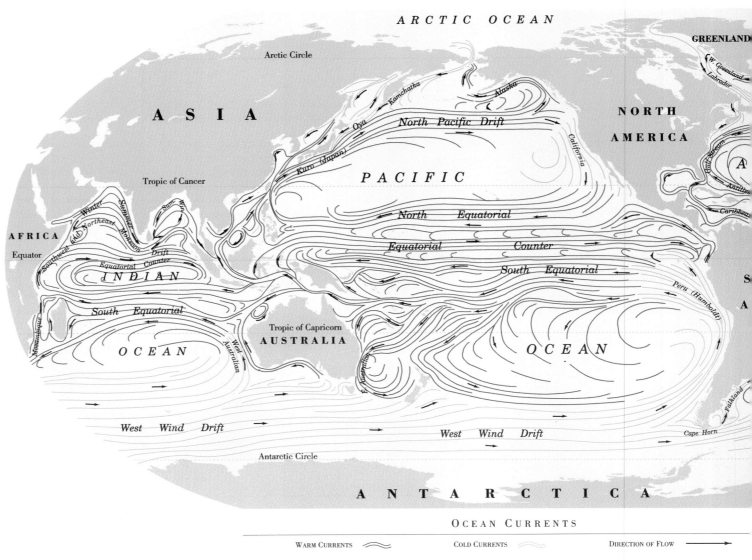

ARCTIC OCEAN

Arctic Circle

ASIA

GREENLAND

NORTH

AMERICA

North Pacific Drift

Komchatka

Alaska

Oya

Kuro (Japan)

California

Tropic of Cancer

PACIFIC

North   Equatorial

AFRICA

Winter

Northeast

Summer

Monsoon

S.W.

Wint.

Equator

Southwest (S.W.)

Drift

Equatorial   Counter

Equatorial   Counter

Counter

INDIAN

Antilles

Caribbean

South   Equatorial

South   Equatorial

Peru (Humboldt)

Mozambique

Tropic of Capricorn

Peru (Humboldt)

OCEAN

West
Australian

AUSTRALIA

OCEAN

E. Australian

Falkland

West   Wind   Drift

West   Wind   Drift

Cape Horn

Antarctic Circle

ANTARCTICA

Ocean Currents

WARM CURRENTS ≈   COLD CURRENTS ≈   DIRECTION OF FLOW ⟶

Hurricane

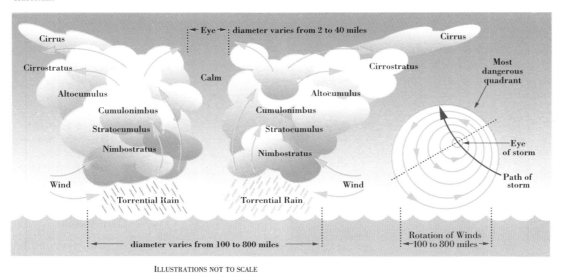

Cirrus   Eye → diameter varies from 2 to 40 miles   Cirrus

Cirrostratus   Cirrostratus   Most
dangerous
quadrant

Calm

Altocumulus   Altocumulus

Cumulonimbus   Cumulonimbus

Stratocumulus   Stratocumulus

Nimbostratus   Nimbostratus   Eye
of storm

Wind   Wind   Path of
storm

Torrential Rain   Torrential Rain

← diameter varies from 100 to 800 miles →   Rotation of Winds
← 100 to 800 miles →

ILLUSTRATIONS NOT TO SCALE

Hurricanes are great whirling storms accompanied by violent destructive winds, torrential rains and high waves and tides. They originate over the oceans, and usually move from lower to higher latitudes with increasing speed, size and intensity. Movement over land quickly reduces their force. Hurricane winds cause severe property damage, but drowning is the greatest cause of hurricane deaths. Floods can be the hurricane's most serious threat.

Oceans

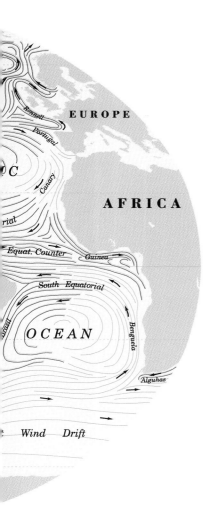

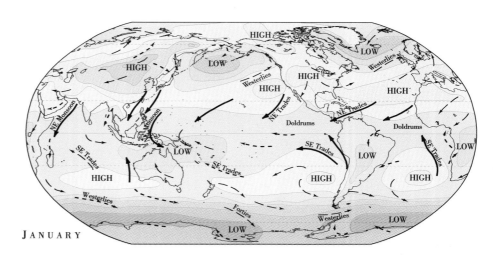

JANUARY

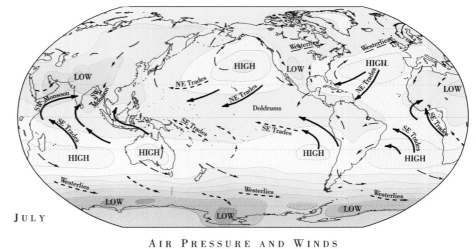

JULY

AIR PRESSURE AND WINDS

PRESSURE IN MILLIBARS				WINDS	
OVER 1038	1020 TO 1026	1002 TO 1008	984 TO 990	LESS OFTEN	→
1032 TO 1038	1014 TO 1020	996 TO 1002	UNDER 984	MORE OFTEN	--→
1026 TO 1032	1008 TO 1014	990 TO 996		CONSTANT	→

Warm Front

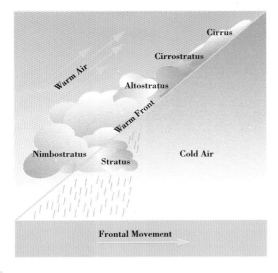

Cold Front

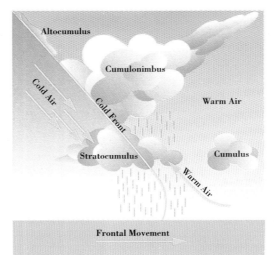

A front is the boundary surface between two air masses which have different characteristics, primarily different temperatures. Depending upon the amount of moisture in the warm air, warm fronts usually produce steady, moderate precipitation over a broad area ahead of the front on the ground. Cold fronts tend to move faster than warm fronts. They are generally confined to a narrower frontal zone but may contain dense thunderheads and severe storms.

Climate

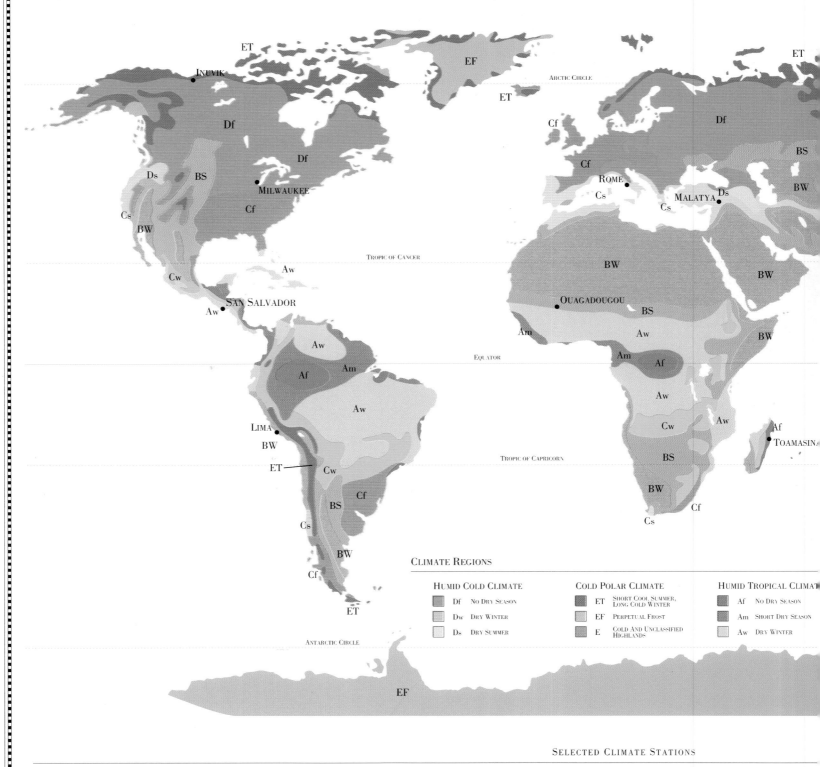

ET

INUVIK

EF

ARCTIC CIRCLE

ET

Df

Cf

Df

BS

Df

BW

Ds

BS

Cf

ROME

Cs

MALATYA

Ds

Cs

Cf

MILWAUKEE

Cs

BW

Cf

TROPIC OF CANCER

BW

BW

Cw

Aw

BW

Aw

OUAGADOUGOU

SAN SALVADOR

BS

Am

Aw

Aw

Am

EQUATOR

Af

Aw

Am

Af

Aw

Aw

Af

Cw

TOAMASINA

LIMA

Aw

BW

Cf

BS

ET

Cw

TROPIC OF CAPRICORN

Cf

BS

Cs

BW

Cf

BW

Cs

Cf

BW

Cs

ET

ANTARCTIC CIRCLE

CLIMATE REGIONS

HUMID COLD CLIMATE

Df	NO DRY SEASON
Dw	DRY WINTER
Ds	DRY SUMMER

COLD POLAR CLIMATE

ET	SHORT COOL SUMMER, LONG COLD WINTER
EF	PERPETUAL FROST
E	COLD AND UNCLASSIFIED HIGHLANDS

HUMID TROPICAL CLIMATE

Af	NO DRY SEASON
Am	SHORT DRY SEASON
Aw	DRY WINTER

EF

SELECTED CLIMATE STATIONS

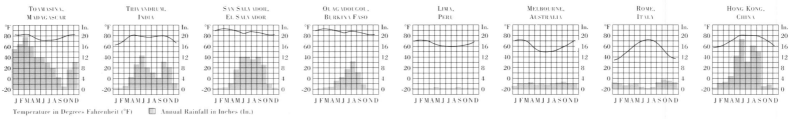

TOAMASINA, MADAGASCAR | TRIVANDRUM, INDIA | SAN SALVADOR, EL SALVADOR | OUAGADOUGOU, BURKINA FASO | LIMA, PERU | MELBOURNE, AUSTRALIA | ROME, ITALY | HONG KONG, CHINA

Temperature in Degrees Fahrenheit (°F)   Annual Rainfall in Inches (In.)

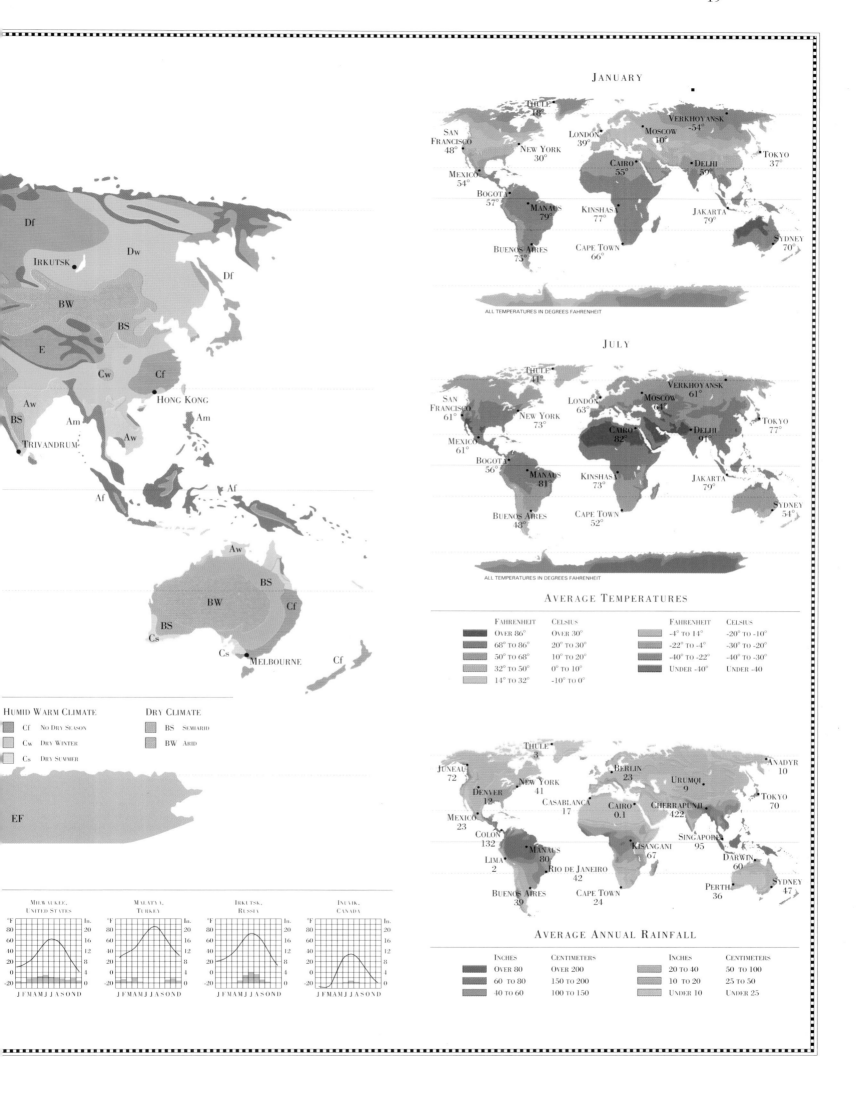

JANUARY

THULE 18°
SAN FRANCISCO 48°
LONDON 39°
VERKHOYANSK -54°
MOSCOW 10°
NEW YORK 30°
CAIRO 55°
DELHI 59°
TOKYO 37°
MEXICO 54°
BOGOTA 57°
MANAUS 79°
KINSHASA 77°
JAKARTA 79°
BUENOS AIRES 73°
CAPE TOWN 66°
SYDNEY 70°

ALL TEMPERATURES IN DEGREES FAHRENHEIT

JULY

THULE 41°
SAN FRANCISCO 61°
LONDON 63°
VERKHOYANSK 61°
MOSCOW 64°
NEW YORK 73°
CAIRO 82°
DELHI 91°
TOKYO 77°
MEXICO 61°
BOGOTA 56°
MANAUS 81°
KINSHASA 73°
JAKARTA 79°
BUENOS AIRES 48°
CAPE TOWN 52°
SYDNEY 54°

ALL TEMPERATURES IN DEGREES FAHRENHEIT

AVERAGE TEMPERATURES

FAHRENHEIT	CELSIUS	FAHRENHEIT	CELSIUS
OVER 86°	OVER 30°	-4° TO 14°	-20° TO -10°
68° TO 86°	20° TO 30°	-22° TO -4°	-30° TO -20°
50° TO 68°	10° TO 20°	-40° TO -22°	-40° TO -30°
32° TO 50°	0° TO 10°	UNDER -40°	UNDER -40
14° TO 32°	-10° TO 0°		

HUMID WARM CLIMATE
Cf No Dry Season
Cw Dry Winter
Cs Dry Summer

DRY CLIMATE
BS Semiarid
BW Arid

Df
Dw
Df
IRKUTSK
BW
BS
E
Cw
Cf
HONG KONG
Aw
Am
BS
Am
TRIVANDRUM
Aw
Af
Af
Aw
BS
BW
BS
Cf
Cs
Cs
MELBOURNE
Cf
EF

THULE 3
JUNEAU 72
BERLIN 23
ANADYR 10
NEW YORK 41
URUMQI 9
DENVER 12
CASABLANCA 17
CAIRO 0.1
CHERRAPUNJI 422
TOKYO 70
MEXICO 23
COLON 132
SINGAPORE 95
LIMA 2
MANAUS 80
KISANGANI 67
DARWIN 60
RIO DE JANEIRO 42
PERTH 36
SYDNEY 47
BUENOS AIRES 39
CAPE TOWN 24

AVERAGE ANNUAL RAINFALL

INCHES	CENTIMETERS	INCHES	CENTIMETERS
OVER 80	OVER 200	20 TO 40	50 TO 100
60 TO 80	150 TO 200	10 TO 20	25 TO 50
40 TO 60	100 TO 150	UNDER 10	UNDER 25

MILWAUKEE, UNITED STATES
MALATYA, TURKEY
IRKUTSK, RUSSIA
INUVIK, CANADA

J F M A M J J A S O N D

Vegetation & Soils

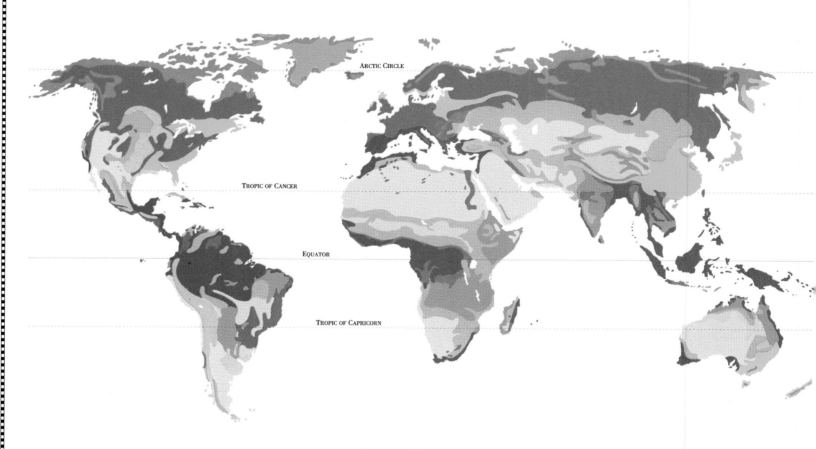

ARCTIC CIRCLE

TROPIC OF CANCER

EQUATOR

TROPIC OF CAPRICORN

NATURAL VEGETATION

NEEDLELEAF FOREST
Found in higher latitudes with shorter growing seasons, and dominated by pure stands of soft-wood, evergreen conifers (cone-bearing trees) such as pine, fir and spruce. The light under-growth consists of small shrubs, mosses, lichens and pine needles.

BROADLEAF FOREST
Found in the middle latitudes, this forest of deciduous (seasonal leaf-shedding) trees includes the hardwoods maple, hickory and oak. The forest floor is relatively barren, except for thick leaf cover during colder months.

MIXED NEEDLELEAF AND BROADLEAF FOREST
A transitional zone between northern soft-woods and temperate hardwoods.

WOODLAND AND SHRUB (MEDITERRANEAN)
A mid-latitude area of broadleaf evergreens, dense growths of woody shrubs and open grassy woodland, characterized by pronounced dry summers and wet winters.

SHORT GRASS (STEPPE)
A mid-latitude, semi-arid area usually found on the fringe of desert regions, with continu-ous short-grass cover up to 8" (20cm.) tall, used chiefly to graze livestock.

TALL GRASS (PRAIRIE)
Mid-latitude, semi-moist areas with continu-ous tall-grass cover up to 24" (61cm.) in height, used for agricultural purposes. Rain-fall is insufficient to support larger plants.

TROPICAL RAIN FOREST (SELVA)
A dense, evergreen forest of tall, varied hard-wood trees with a thick broadleaf canopy and a dark, moist interior with minimal under-growth.

LIGHT TROPICAL FOREST (TROPICAL SEMIDECIDUOUS OR MONSOON FOREST)
As above, with more widely spaced trees, heavier undergrowth, larger concentrations of single species. Dry season prevents most trees from remaining evergreen. Found in monsoon areas.

TROPICAL WOODLAND AND SHRUB (THORN FOREST)
Longer dry season results in low trees with thick bark and smaller leaves. Dense under-growth of thorny plants, brambles and grasses. Transition belt between denser forests and grasslands.

TROPICAL GRASSLAND AND SHRUB (SAVANNA)
Stiff, sharp-edged grasses, from 2' to 12' (0.6m. to 3.7m.) high, with large areas of bare ground. Scattered shrubs and low trees in some areas.

WOODED SAVANNA
A transitional area where savanna joins a trop-ical or shrub forest, with low trees and shrubs dotting the grasslands.

DESERT AND DESERT SHRUB
Barren stretches of soft brown, yellow or red sand and rock wastes with isolated patches of short grass and stunted bushes, turning bright green when fed by infrequent precipitation.

RIVER VALLEY AND OASIS
River valleys are lush, fertile lands, with var-ied vegetation. An oasis is a fertile or verdant spot found in a desert near a natural spring or pool.

HEATH AND MOOR
A heath is open, uncultivated land covered with low, flowering evergreen shrubs such as heather. Moors are often high and poorly drained lands, with patches of heath and peat bogs.

TUNDRA AND ALPINE
An area of scarce moisture and short, cool summers where trees cannot survive. A per-manently frozen subsoil supports low-growing lichens, mosses and stunted shrubs.

UNCLASSIFIED HIGHLANDS
Sequential bands or vertical zones of all vege-tation types, which generally follow the warm-to-cold upward patterns found in correspond-ing areas of vegetation. (Map scale does not permit delineation of these areas.)

PERMANENT ICE COVER
Permanently ice and snow-covered terrain found in polar regions and atop high moun-tains.

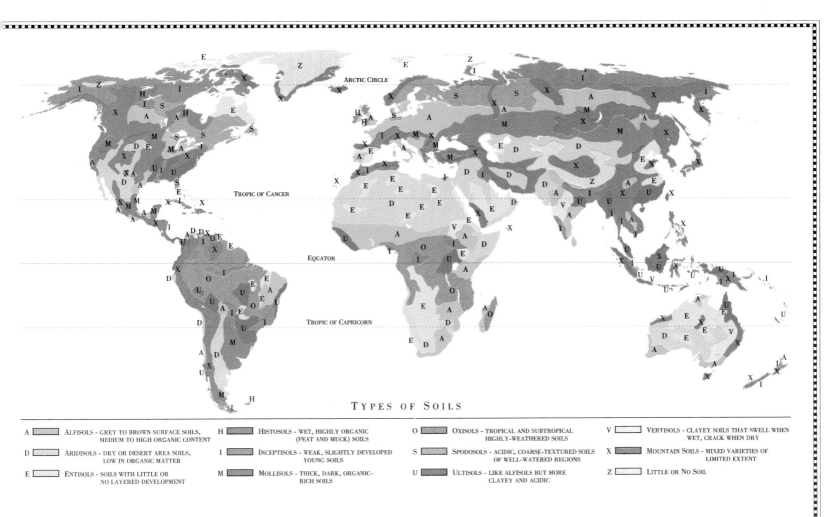

TYPES OF SOILS

A ALFISOLS - GREY TO BROWN SURFACE SOILS, MEDIUM TO HIGH ORGANIC CONTENT	**H** HISTOSOLS - WET, HIGHLY ORGANIC (PEAT AND MUCK) SOILS	**O** OXISOLS - TROPICAL AND SUBTROPICAL HIGHLY-WEATHERED SOILS	**V** VERTISOLS - CLAYEY SOILS THAT SWELL WHEN WET, CRACK WHEN DRY
D ARIDISOLS - DRY OR DESERT AREA SOILS, LOW IN ORGANIC MATTER	**I** INCEPTISOLS - WEAK, SLIGHTLY DEVELOPED YOUNG SOILS	**S** SPODOSOLS - ACIDIC, COARSE-TEXTURED SOILS OF WELL-WATERED REGIONS	**X** MOUNTAIN SOILS - MIXED VARIETIES OF LIMITED EXTENT
E ENTISOLS - SOILS WITH LITTLE OR NO LAYERED DEVELOPMENT	**M** MOLLISOLS - THICK, DARK, ORGANIC-RICH SOILS	**U** ULTISOLS - LIKE ALFISOLS BUT MORE CLAYEY AND ACIDIC	**Z** LITTLE OR NO SOIL

TYPES OF VEGETATION

Needleleaf Forest

These typically coniferous soft-wood forests of Europe, Asia and North America cover about 9 percent of the earth's land.

Broadleaf Forest

Located in the most pleasant hab-itable climatic regions, temperate broadleaf forests have suffered the greatest destruction by people.

Mixed Forest

These hardwood and softwood forests, when added to the broadleaf forest area, are home to over half the world's population.

Prairie

Unique to the Americas, tall grass prairie lands have been success-fully cultivated to become great grain fields of the world

Steppe

Slightly more moist than desert, steppe areas are sometimes cul-tivated but more often used for livestock ranching and herding.

Tropical Rain Forest

Teak, mahogany, balsawood, quinine, cocoa and rubber are some of the major products found in the world's tropical rain forest regions.

Savanna

A place of winter droughts and summer rainfall, these tropical grass and shrub areas are home to a wide variety of big-game animals.

Mediterranean

In addition to southern Europe and northern Africa, this vege-tation also can be found in California, Chile, South Africa and Western Australia.

Desert Shrub

One-fifth of the world's land is desert and desert shrub, too dry for farming and ranching and populated largely by nomads and oases-dwellers.

Tundra

Found along the Arctic fringe of North America and Eurasia, tundra is of little economic sig-nificance except for mineral exploitation.

Environmental Concerns

DESERTIFICATION AND ACID RAIN DAMAGE

AREAS OF PRODUCTIVE DRYLANDS DESERTIFIED BY EARLY 1980'S

AREAS OF DAMAGE FROM ACID RAIN AND OTHER AIRBORNE POLLUTANTS

Sun

reflected back to space

solar radiation

Greenhouse gases in atmosphere: carbon dioxide, methane, nitrous oxide, water vapor, industrial gases, ozone

A t m o s p h e r e

absorbed by clouds and atmosphere

absorbed by clouds and greenhouse gases

heat radiates back into atmophere

reradiated back to earth

about 50% of sun's radiation reaches ground and is converted to infrared (heat) radiation

Earth

GREENHOUSE EFFECT

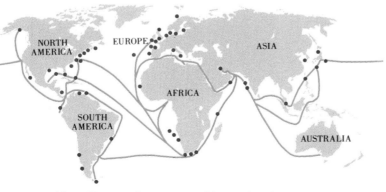

MAIN TANKER ROUTES AND MAJOR OIL SPILLS

ROUTES OF VERY LARGE CRUDE OIL CARRIERS   ● MAJOR OIL SPILLS

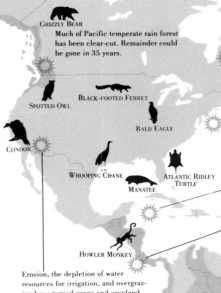

GRIZZLY BEAR
Much of Pacific temperate rain forest has been clear-cut. Remainder could be gone in 35 years.

WOODLAND CARIBOU

HUMPBACK
Hydroelectric power pro and development in Que are disrupting wildlife habitats.

Commercial fishing hary in the northwest Atlanti declined over 30 percen since 1970.

SPOTTED OWL   BLACK-FOOTED FERRET

BALD EAGLE

CONDOR

Fragile barrier beaches of the Atla coast have been damaged by agricu tural runoff sewage and overdevel ment.

WHOOPING CRANE

MANATEE

ATLANTIC RIDLEY TURTLE

Ecological balance in coral reefs of Gulf and Caribbean area is being upset by a booming tourist industry

At the present rate of clearing, ha Central America's rain forest will appear by the year 2000.

One-third of Guinea's tropical fo expected to disappear in the next decade

HOWLER MONKEY

Erosion, the depletion of water resources for irrigation, and overgraz ing have turned range and cropland into desert.

GALÁPAGOS TORTOISE

BLACK CAIMAN

JAGUAR

VICUNA

Every year over 5000 square miles (13,000 sq km) of rain forest is destroyed in Brazil's Amazon Basin.

CHINCHILLA

GOLDEN LION TAMARIN

GIANT ARMADILLO

The Atlantic waters off Patagonia have suffere over-fishing and oil sp

Southern Chile's rain forest is threat ened by development.

BLUE WHALE

Acid Rain

Acid rain of nitric and sulfuric acids has killed all life in thousands of lakes, and over 15 million acres (6 million hectares) of virgin forest in Europe and North America are dead or dying.

Deforestation

Each year, 50 million acres (20 million hectares) of tropical rainforests are be ing felled by loggers. Trees remove carbon dioxide from the atmosphere and are vital to the prevention of soil erosion.

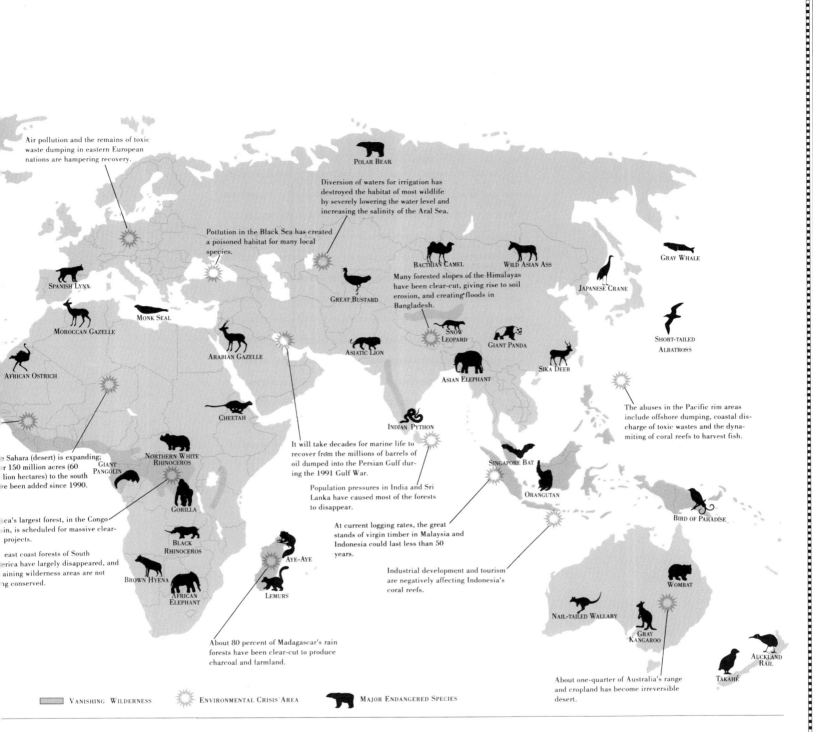

Air pollution and the remains of toxic waste dumping in eastern European nations are hampering recovery.

POLAR BEAR

Diversion of waters for irrigation has destroyed the habitat of most wildlife by severely lowering the water level and increasing the salinity of the Aral Sea.

Pollution in the Black Sea has created a poisoned habitat for many local species.

GRAY WHALE

BACTRIAN CAMEL   **WILD ASIAN ASS**

Many forested slopes of the Himalayas have been clear-cut, giving rise to soil erosion, and creating floods in Bangladesh.

GREAT BUSTARD

JAPANESE CRANE

SPANISH LYNX

MONK SEAL

MOROCCAN GAZELLE

SNOW LEOPARD

GIANT PANDA

SHORT-TAILED ALBATROSS

ARABIAN GAZELLE

ASIATIC LION

SIKA DEER

AFRICAN OSTRICH

CHEETAH

ASIAN ELEPHANT

INDIAN PYTHON

The abuses in the Pacific rim areas include offshore dumping, coastal discharge of toxic wastes and the dynamiting of coral reefs to harvest fish.

e Sahara (desert) is expanding; r 150 million acres (60 lion hectares) to the south ve been added since 1990.

GIANT PANGOLIN

NORTHERN WHITE RHINOCEROS

It will take decades for marine life to recover from the millions of barrels of oil dumped into the Persian Gulf during the 1991 Gulf War.

SINGAPORE BAT

ca's largest forest, in the Congo in, is scheduled for massive clear-projects.

GORILLA

Population pressures in India and Sri Lanka have caused most of the forests to disappear.

ORANGUTAN

BIRD OF PARADISE

east coast forests of South erica have largely disappeared, and aining wilderness areas are not g conserved.

BLACK RHINOCEROS

AYE-AYE

At current logging rates, the great stands of virgin timber in Malaysia and Indonesia could last less than 50 years.

BROWN HYENA

AFRICAN ELEPHANT

LEMURS

Industrial development and tourism are negatively affecting Indonesia's coral reefs.

WOMBAT

NAIL-TAILED WALLABY

GRAY KANGAROO

AUCKLAND RAIL

About 80 percent of Madagascar's rain forests have been clear-cut to produce charcoal and farmland.

TAKAHÉ

About one-quarter of Australia's range and cropland has become irreversible desert.

▬ VANISHING WILDERNESS   ✦ ENVIRONMENTAL CRISIS AREA   🐻 MAJOR ENDANGERED SPECIES

Extinction

Biologists estimate that over 50,000 plant and animal species inhabiting the world's rain forests are disappearing each year due to pollution, unchecked hunting and the destruction of natural habitats.

Air Pollution

Billions of tons of industrial emissions and toxic pollutants are released into the air each year, depleting our ozone layer, killing our forests and lakes with acid rain and threatening our health.

Water Pollution

Only 3 percent of the earth's water is fresh. Pollution from cities, farms and factories has made much of it unfit to drink. In the developing world, most sewage flows untreated into lakes and rivers.

Ozone Depletion

The layer of ozone in the stratosphere shields earth from harmful ultraviolet radiation. But man-made gases are destroying this vital barrier, increasing the risk of skin cancer and eye disease.

Population

World's Largest Urban Areas

Millions of Inhabitants

TOKYO, Japan 26.5

NEW YORK, U.S. 18.0

SÃO PAULO, Brazil 16.9

OSAKA, Japan 16.9

SEOUL, Korea, 15.8

MEXICO, Mexico 15.5

SHANGHAI, China 14.7

MUMBAI, India 14.5

LOS ANGELES, U.S. 14.5

MOSCOW, Russia 13.1

BEIJING, China 12.0

CALCUTTA, India 11.4

LONDON, U.K. 11.1

RIO DE JANEIRO, Brazil 11.0

JAKARTA, Indonesia 11.0

Urban & Rural Population Components

Selected Countries

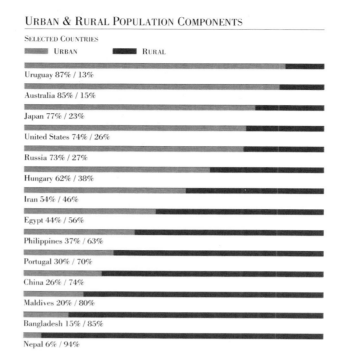

■ URBAN ■ RURAL

Uruguay 87% / 13%

Australia 85% / 15%

Japan 77% / 23%

United States 74% / 26%

Russia 73% / 27%

Hungary 62% / 38%

Iran 54% / 46%

Egypt 44% / 56%

Philippines 37% / 63%

Portugal 30% / 70%

China 26% / 74%

Maldives 20% / 80%

Bangladesh 15% / 85%

Nepal 6% / 94%

Age Distribution

United States

Switzerland

Angola

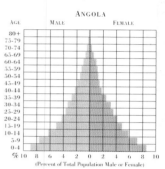

Source: U.S. Bureau of the Census, International Database

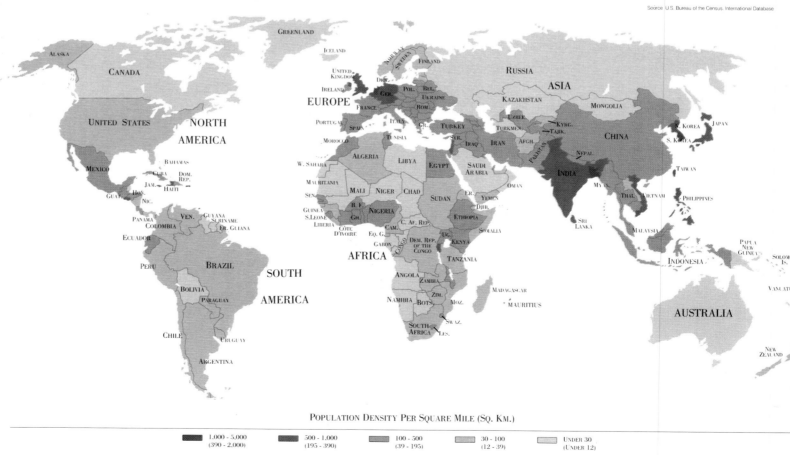

POPULATION DENSITY PER SQUARE MILE (SQ. KM.)

1,000 - 5,000 (390 - 2,000)	500 - 1,000 (195 - 390)	100 - 500 (39 - 195)	30 - 100 (12 - 39)	UNDER 30 (UNDER 12)

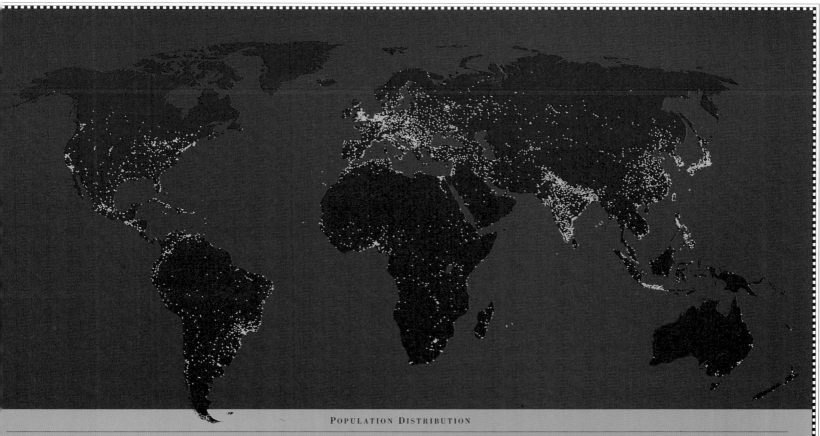

POPULATION DISTRIBUTION

This map provides a dramatic perspective by illuminating populated areas with one point of light for each city over 50,000 residents. Over 675 million people live in cities with populations in excess of 500,000. According to the latest census data, there are 10,000 people per square mile (3,860 per sq km) in London. In New York, there are 11,000 (4,250). Hong Kong has over 16,000 people per square mile (6,200 per sq km), and the Tokyo-Yokohama agglomeration includes over 25,000 (9,650). During the last decade, the movement to the cities has accelerated dramatically, particulary in developing nations. In Lagos, Nigeria, where there are over 24,000 people per square mile (9,290 per sq km), most live in shantytowns. In São Paulo, Brazil, 2,000 buses arrive each day, bringing field hands, farm workers and their families in search of a better life. Tokyo, Mexico and Mumbai are the world's largest urban agglomerations. According to the United Nations, 15 of the 20 largest urban agglomerations are located in less-industrialized nations.

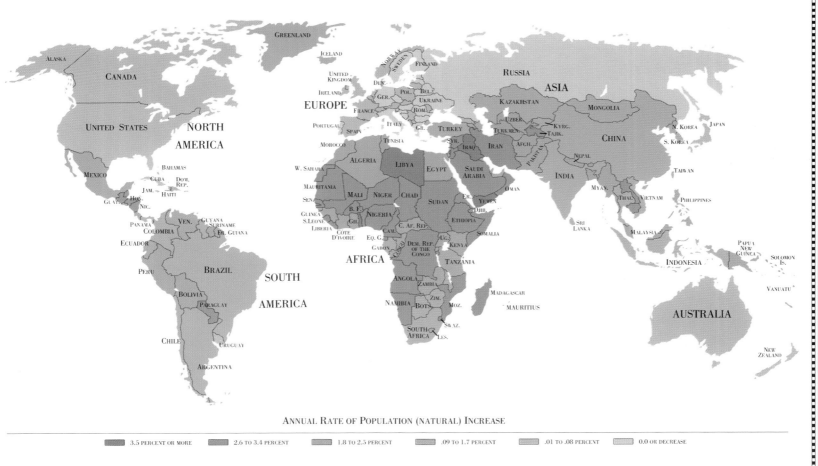

ANNUAL RATE OF POPULATION (NATURAL) INCREASE

3.5 PERCENT OR MORE	2.6 TO 3.4 PERCENT	1.8 TO 2.5 PERCENT	.09 TO 1.7 PERCENT	.01 TO .08 PERCENT	0.0 OR DECREASE

Source: U.S. Bureau of the Census, International Database

© HAMMOND WORLD ATLAS CORPORATION   CJ-#-A-A

Languages & Religions

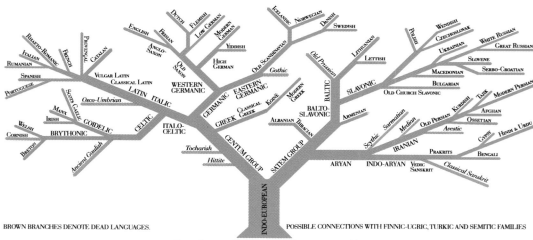

BROWN BRANCHES DENOTE DEAD LANGUAGES.

POSSIBLE CONNECTIONS WITH FINNIC-UGRIC, TURKIC AND SEMITIC FAMILIES

THE INDO-EUROPEAN LANGUAGE TREE

The most well-established family tree is Indo-European. Spoken by more than 2.5 billion people, it contains dozens of languages. Some linguists theorize that all people - and all languages - are descended from a tiny population that lived in Africa some 200,000 years ago.

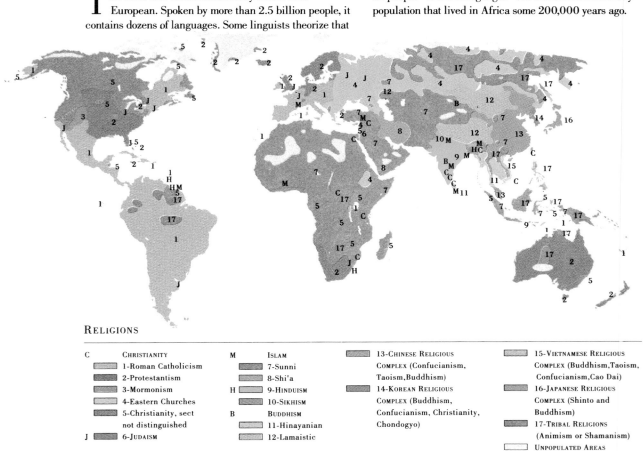

RELIGIONS

C	CHRISTIANITY	
	1-Roman Catholicism	
	2-Protestantism	
	3-Mormonism	
	4-Eastern Churches	
	5-Christianity, sect not distinguished	
J	6-JUDAISM	

M	ISLAM	
	7-Sunni	
	8-Shi'a	
H	9-HINDUISM	
	10-SIKHISM	
B	BUDDHISM	
	11-Hinayanian	
	12-Lamaistic	

13-CHINESE RELIGIOUS COMPLEX (Confucianism, Taoism, Buddhism)

14-KOREAN RELIGIOUS COMPLEX (Buddhism, Confucianism, Christianity, Chondogyo)

15-VIETNAMESE RELIGIOUS COMPLEX (Buddhism, Taoism, Confucianism, Cao Dai)

16-JAPANESE RELIGIOUS COMPLEX (Shinto and Buddhism)

17-TRIBAL RELIGIONS (Animism or Shamanism)

UNPOPULATED AREAS

Important Local Minorities are Indicated by Letter

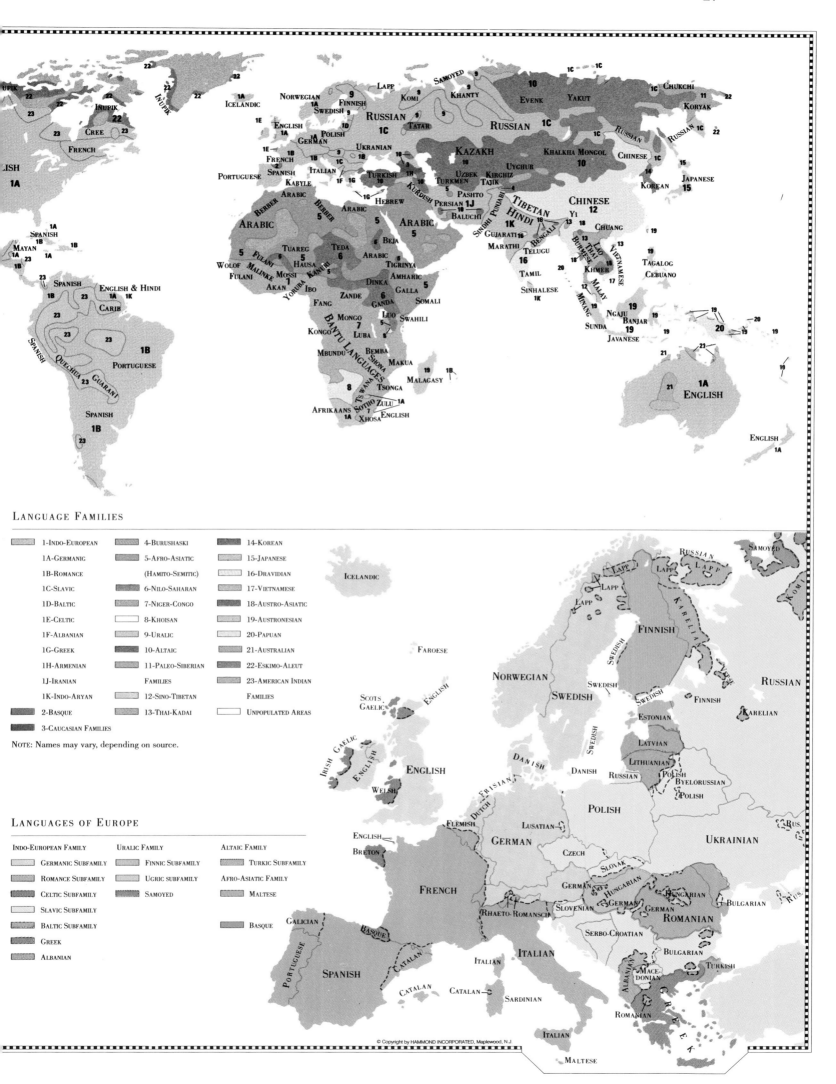

Standards of Living

ALASKA

CANADA

GREENL

UNITED STATES

UNITED STATES
The economic and political influence of women has risen substantially. In a number of fields, women's salaries are now nearly equal to men's.

MEXICO

BAHAMAS

CUBA

JAM. DOM. REP.

HAITI

BEL. HON.

GUAT.

EL. SAL. NIC.

C. R.

SOUTH AMERICA
Political unrest, rising inflation and slow economic growth continue to thwart efforts to bring unity and prosperity to the nations of South America.

LATIN AMERICA
The gulf between rich and poor continues to widen, despite efforts to reform oppressive governments, increase literacy and relieve overburdened cities.

PANAMA VENEZUELA GUYANA

SURINAME

COLOMBIA FR. GUIANA

ECUADOR

PERU BRAZIL

BOLIVIA

PARAGUAY

CHILE

URUGUAY

ARGENTINA

EUROPE

NORTH AMERICA

ASIA

AFRICA

SOUTH AMERICA

AUSTRALIA

LITERATE PERCENT OF POPULATION

80 AND ABOVE	40-59	0-19
60-79	20-39	

EUROPE

NORTH AMERICA

ASIA

AFRICA

SOUTH AMERICA

AUSTRALIA

YEARS OF LIFE EXPECTANCY (MEN AND WOMEN)

70 AND ABOVE	50-59	0-39
60-69	40-49	

EUROPE

NORTH AMERICA

ASIA

AFRICA

SOUTH AMERICA

AUSTRALIA

INFANT DEATHS PER 1,000 LIVE BIRTHS

150 AND MORE	50-99	0-24
100-149	25-49	

GROSS NATIONAL PRODUCT GROWTH RATES

BEST PERCENTAGE		WORST PERCENTAGE	
THAILAND	8.2	GEORGIA	-18.6
SOUTH KOREA	7.8	ARMENIA	-12.9
SINGAPORE	6.9	AZERBAIJAN	-12.2
CHINA	6.9	TAJIKISTAN	-11.7
BOTSWANA	6.6	LITHUANIA	-7.8
MALDIVES	6.5	CAMEROON	-6.6
CHILE	6.2	KAZAKHSTAN	-6.5
INDONESIA	6.0	ESTONIA	-6.4
MALAYSIA	5.7	NICARAGUA	-6.4
MAURITIUS	5.6	JORDAN	-6.3
BELIZE	5.3	ROMANIA	-6.2
MALTA	5.3	LATVIA	-6.2
CYPRUS	5.2	ALBANIA	-6.0
IRELAND	5.2	KYRGYZSTAN	-5.4
ST. KITTS & NEVIS	4.7	CÔTE D'IVOIRE	-5.2
SEYCHELLES	4.5	UKRAINE	-5.1
ST. VINCENT & GRENADINES	4.4	HAITI	-5.0
DOMINICA	4.2	RUSSIA	-4.4
PORTUGAL	4.0	MONGOLIA	-3.3
ST. LUCIA	4.0	SLOVAKIA	-3.3

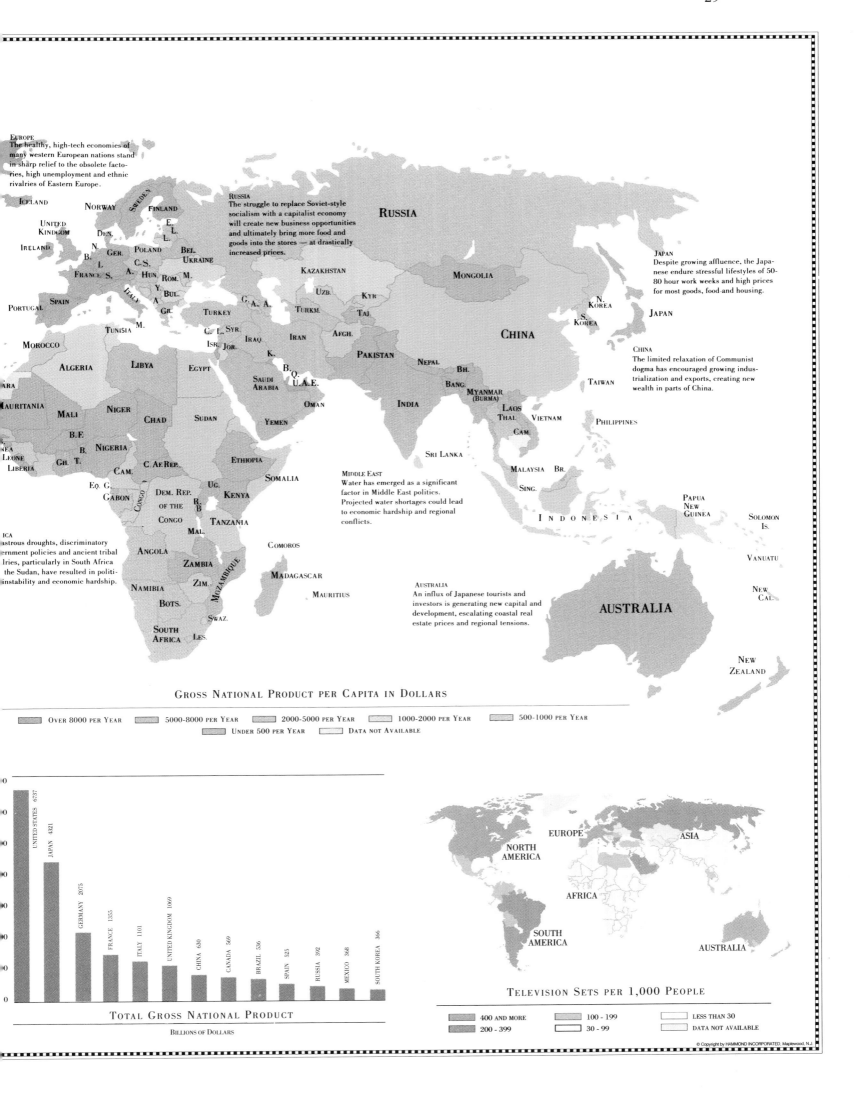

EUROPE
The healthy, high-tech economies of many western European nations stand in sharp relief to the obsolete factories, high unemployment and ethnic rivalries of Eastern Europe.

RUSSIA
The struggle to replace Soviet-style socialism with a capitalist economy will create new business opportunities and ultimately bring more food and goods into the stores — at drastically increased prices.

JAPAN
Despite growing affluence, the Japanese endure stressful lifestyles of 50-80 hour work weeks and high prices for most goods, food and housing.

CHINA
The limited relaxation of Communist dogma has encouraged growing industrialization and exports, creating new wealth in parts of China.

MIDDLE EAST
Water has emerged as a significant factor in Middle East politics. Projected water shortages could lead to economic hardship and regional conflicts.

AUSTRALIA
An influx of Japanese tourists and investors is generating new capital and development, escalating coastal real estate prices and regional tensions.

...astrous droughts, discriminatory ...ernment policies and ancient tribal ...lries, particularly in South Africa ...the Sudan, have resulted in politi-...instability and economic hardship.

GROSS NATIONAL PRODUCT PER CAPITA IN DOLLARS

OVER 8000 PER YEAR   5000-8000 PER YEAR   2000-5000 PER YEAR   1000-2000 PER YEAR   500-1000 PER YEAR   UNDER 500 PER YEAR   DATA NOT AVAILABLE

TOTAL GROSS NATIONAL PRODUCT
BILLIONS OF DOLLARS

UNITED STATES 6737
JAPAN 4321
GERMANY 2075
FRANCE 1355
ITALY 1101
UNITED KINGDOM 1069
CHINA 630
CANADA 569
BRAZIL 536
SPAIN 525
RUSSIA 392
MEXICO 368
SOUTH KOREA 366

TELEVISION SETS PER 1,000 PEOPLE

400 AND MORE   200 - 399   100 - 199   30 - 99   LESS THAN 30   DATA NOT AVAILABLE

Agriculture & Manufacturing

TOP FIVE WORLD PRODUCERS OF SELECTED AGRICULTURAL COMMODITIES

	1	2	3	4	5
WHEAT	CHINA	UNITED STATES	INDIA	RUSSIA	FRANCE
RICE	CHINA	INDIA	INDONESIA	BANGLADESH	MYANMAR (BURMA)
OATS	RUSSIA	CANADA	UNITED STATES	GERMANY	UKRAINE
CORN (MAIZE)	UNITED STATES	CHINA	BRAZIL	MEXICO	FRANCE
SOYBEANS	UNITED STATES	BRAZIL	CHINA	ARGENTINA	INDIA
POTATOES	CHINA	RUSSIA	POLAND	UNITED STATES	UKRAINE
COFFEE	BRAZIL	COLOMBIA	INDONESIA	MEXICO	ETHIOPIA
TEA	INDIA	CHINA	SRI LANKA	KENYA	TURKEY
TOBACCO	CHINA	UNITED STATES	BRAZIL	INDIA	TURKEY
COTTON	CHINA	UNITED STATES	INDIA	PAKISTAN	UZBEKISTAN
CATTLE (STOCK)	BRAZIL	UNITED STATES	CHINA	ARGENTINA	RUSSIA
SHEEP (STOCK)	AUSTRALIA	CHINA	NEW ZEALAND	RUSSIA	INDIA
HOGS (STOCK)	CHINA	UNITED STATES	BRAZIL	RUSSIA	GERMANY
COW'S MILK	UNITED STATES	RUSSIA	INDIA	GERMANY	FRANCE
HEN'S EGGS	CHINA	UNITED STATES	JAPAN	RUSSIA	INDIA
WOOL	AUSTRALIA	NEW ZEALAND	CHINA	RUSSIA	KAZAKHSTAN
ROUNDWOOD	UNITED STATES	RUSSIA	CHINA	INDIA	BRAZIL
NATURAL RUBBER	THAILAND	INDONESIA	MALAYSIA	INDIA	CHINA
FISH CATCHES	CHINA	JAPAN	PERU	CHILE	RUSSIA

Names in Black Indicate More Than 10% of Total World Production

HERDING
SHIFTING CROPS
LIVESTOCK RANCHIN[G]

PERCENT OF TOTAL EMPLOYMENT IN AGRICULTURE, MANUFACTURING AND OTHER INDUSTRIES

AGRICULTURE (INCLUDES FORESTRY AND FISHING)
MANUFACTURING
CONSTRUCTION
TRADE AND COMMERCE
FINANCE, INSURANCE, REAL ESTATE
SERVICES
OTHER (INCLUDES MINING, UTILITIES, TRANSPORTATION)

0   20   40   60   80   100

India
China
Indonesia
Pakistan
Mexico
Brazil
Spain
Argentina
Italy
Japan
France
Canada
Australia
Germany
United States
United Kingdom

Finance, Insurance, Real Estate Data Included With "Other" for India, China, Indonesia and Pakistan

SEATTLE - TACOMA
SAN FRANCISCO - SAN JOSE
SOUTHERN CALIFORNIA
CHICAGO
ST. L[OUIS]
DE[TROIT]
HO[USTON]
MEXICO - PUEBLA
SANTIAGO - VALPA[RAISO]

▲ AIRCRAFT
△ MOTOR VEHICLES
▽ SHIPBUILDING

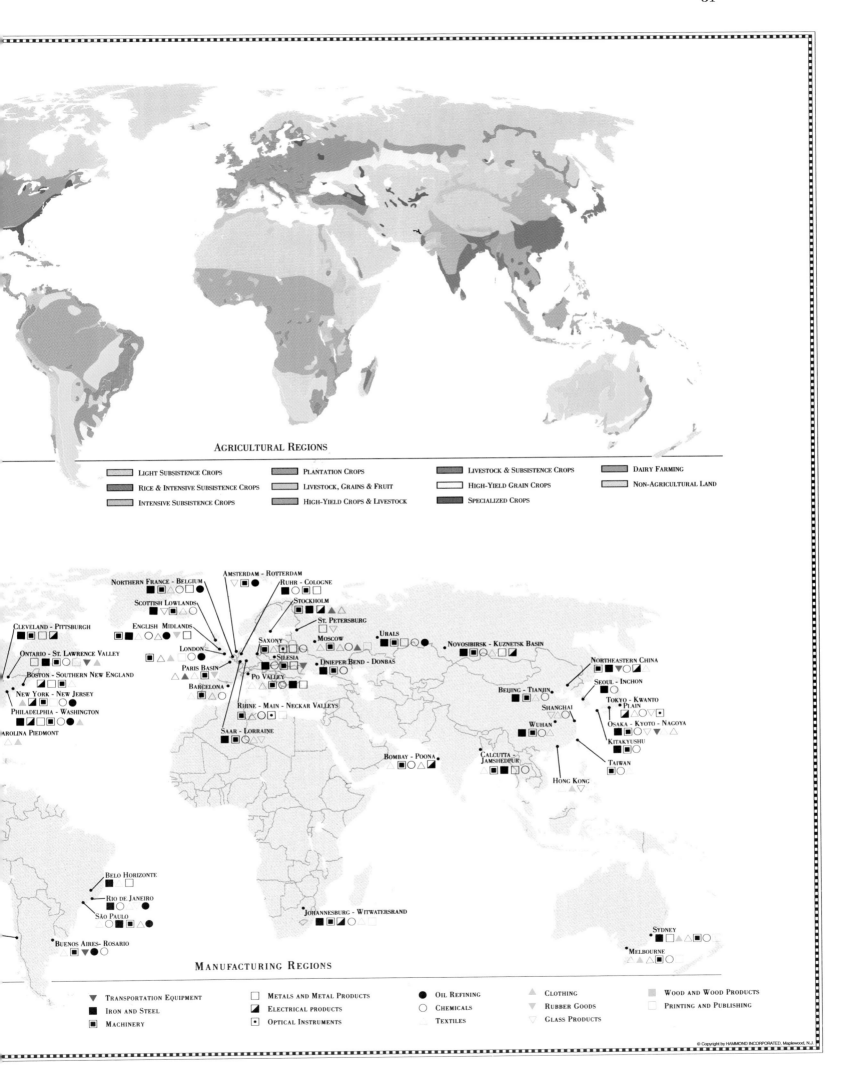

AGRICULTURAL REGIONS

MANUFACTURING REGIONS

Energy & Resources

ALASKA

UNITEI

MEXI

TOP FIVE WORLD PRODUCERS OF SELECTED MINERAL COMMODITIES

MINERAL FUELS	1	2	3	4	5
CRUDE OIL	SAUDI ARABIA	RUSSIA	UNITED STATES	IRAN	CHINA
GASOLINE	UNITED STATES	RUSSIA	JAPAN	CHINA	UNITED KINGDOM
NATURAL GAS	RUSSIA	UNITED STATES	CANADA	NETHERLANDS	TURKMENISTAN
COAL (AND LIGNITE)	CHINA	UNITED STATES	RUSSIA	GERMANY	INDIA
URANIUM-BEARING ORES	CANADA	NIGER	KAZAKHSTAN	RUSSIA	UZBEKISTAN

METALS					
CHROMITE	KAZAKHSTAN	SOUTH AFRICA	INDIA	FINLAND	TURKEY
IRON ORE	BRAZIL	AUSTRALIA	CHINA	RUSSIA	UKRAINE
MANGANESE ORE	UKRAINE	CHINA	SOUTH AFRICA	AUSTRALIA	BRAZIL
MINE NICKEL	RUSSIA	CANADA	NEW CALEDONIA	INDONESIA	AUSTRALIA
MINE SILVER	MEXICO	UNITED STATES	PERU	AUSTRALIA	CANADA
BAUXITE	AUSTRALIA	GUINEA	JAMAICA	BRAZIL	RUSSIA
ALUMINUM	UNITED STATES	RUSSIA	CANADA	AUSTRALIA	CHINA
MINE GOLD	SOUTH AFRICA	UNITED STATES	AUSTRALIA	CHINA	CANADA
MINE COPPER	CHILE	UNITED STATES	CANADA	RUSSIA	PERU
MINE LEAD	AUSTRALIA	CHINA	UNITED STATES	PERU	CANADA
MINE TIN	CHINA	INDONESIA	BRAZIL	BOLIVIA	PERU
MINE ZINC	CANADA	AUSTRALIA	CHINA	PERU	UNITED STATES

NONMETALS					
NATURAL DIAMOND	AUSTRALIA	BOTSWANA	RUSSIA	DEM. REP. CONGO	SOUTH AFRICA
POTASH	CANADA	GERMANY	RUSSIA	BELARUS	UNITED STATES
PHOSPHATE ROCK	UNITED STATES	CHINA	MOROCCO	RUSSIA	KAZAKHSTAN
SULFUR (ALL FORMS)	UNITED STATES	CANADA	CHINA	JAPAN	POLAND

Names in Black Indicate More Than 10% of Total World Production

COMMERCIAL ENERGY PRODUCTION/CONSUMPTION

PERCENTAGE OF WORLD TOTAL
▢ PRODUCTION   ▢ CONSUMPTION

United States 20% / 25%

Russia 12% / 17.2%

China 9% / 8.9%

Saudi Arabia 5.8% / 0.9%

Canada 3.6% / 2.7%

United Kingdom 2.7% / 2.9%

Iran 2.5% / 0.9%

Mexico 2.4% / 1.5%

India 2.3% / 2.8%

Indonesia 2.0% / 0.7%

Germany 2.0% / 4.3%

Australia 2% / 1.2%

Venezuela 1.9% / 0.6%

Norway 1.8% / 0.3%

NATIONS WITH HIGHEST PERCENTAGE OF NUCLEAR POWER PRODUCTION

▢ NUCLEAR   ▢ THERMAL   ▢ HYDROELECTRIC

Belgium 98% / 1% / 1%

France 75% / 11% / 14%

South Korea 71% / 21% / 8%

Japan 65% / 9% / 26%

Finland 58% / 42%

Sweden 43% / 57%

Spain 41% / 40% / 19%

Switzerland 39% / 61%

Germany 26% / 71% / 3%

Hungary 22% / 78%

Ukraine 21% / 77% / 2%

Bulgaria 17% / 80% / 3%

United Kingdom 11% / 88% / 1%

United States 10% / 86% / 4%

OIL FIELDS

NATURAL GAS FIELDS

● MAJOR COAL DEPOSITS

▲ OIL SANDS

◆ OIL SHALE

✶ MAJOR URANIUM DEPOSITS

■ IMPORTANT PEAT DEPOSITS

IRON AND FERROALLOY METALS

1 COBALT	5 MOLYBDENUM
2 CHROMIUM	6 NICKEL
3 IRON ORE	7 VANADIUM
4 MANGANESE	8 TUNGSTEN

OTHER METALS

1 SILVER	7 PLATINUM
2 BAUXITE	8 ANTIMONY
3 GOLD	9 TIN
4 COPPER	10 TITANIUM
5 MERCURY	11 ZINC
6 LEAD	

NONMETALS

1 ASBESTOS	10 MICA
2 BORAX	11 NITRATES
3 DIAMONDS	12 OPALS
4 EMERALDS	13 PHOSPHATES
5 FLUORSPAR	14 PEARLS
6 GRAPHITE	15 RUBIES
7 IODINE	16 SULFUR
8 JADE	17 SAPPHIRES
9 POTASH	

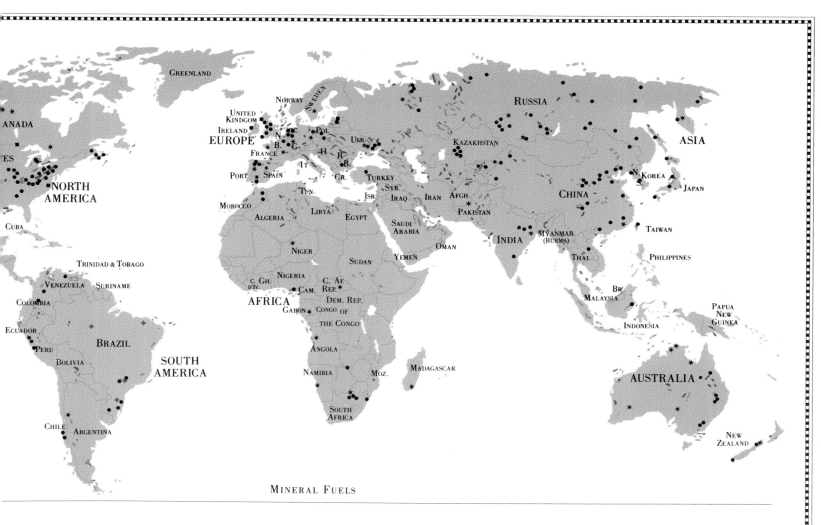

MINERAL FUELS

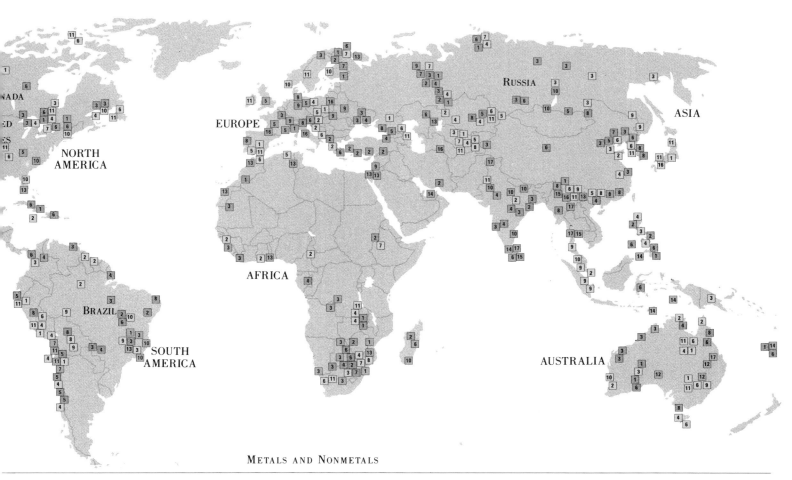

METALS AND NONMETALS

Transportation & Trade

WORLD EXPORTS BY REGIONS

PERCENT (BY VALUE) OF TOTAL EXPORTS

- TO EUROPEAN COMMUNITY
- TO UNITED STATES
- TO ASIA (EXCLUDING JAPAN)
- TO JAPAN
- TO EUROPEAN FREE TRADE ASSN.
- TO CANADA
- TO LATIN AMERICA
- TO AFRICA
- TO OTHERS

EUROPEAN COMMUNITY
25 / 20 / 17 / 8 / 5 / 5 / 20

UNITED STATES
24 / 20 / 20 / 15 / 12 / 9

ASIA (EXCLUDING JAPAN)
33 / 25 / 22 / 20

JAPAN
37 / 29 / 19 / 4 / 11

EUROPEAN FREE TRADE ASSN.
68 / 9 / 7 / 16

CANADA
76 / 8 / 6 / 5 / 5

LATIN AMERICA
43 / 30 / 8 / 7 / 12

AFRICA
62 / 20 / 6 / 12

AUSTRALIA AND NEW ZEALAND
35 / 28 / 13 / 11 / 13

TRADE BALANCES OF LEADING EXPORT NATIONS

VALUE IN BILLIONS OF DOLLARS

- ANNUAL EXPORTS
- ANNUAL IMPORTS   (DATA BASED ON AVERAGE, 1992-1994)

| 0 | 50 | 100 | 150 | | 150 | 200 | 300 | 400 | 500 | 600 |

United States 468 / 596

Germany 402 / 363

Japan 365 / 249

France 244 / 240

United Kingdom 192 / 215

Italy 179 / 175

Canada 140 / 131

Belgium 117 / 120

China 99 / 100

Taiwan 87 / 78

South Korea 85 / 88

Spain 69 / 95

Sweden 55 / 48

| 0 | 50 | 100 |

Mexico 46 / 64

Australia 45 / 44

Russia 43 / 33

Saudi Arabia 43 / 27

Brazil 39 / 26

Indonesia 36 / 28

Thailand 35 / 44

South Africa 24 / 19

India 22 / 24

Iran 16 / 21

Turkey 15 / 24

Venezuela 15 / 10

Argentina 14 / 17

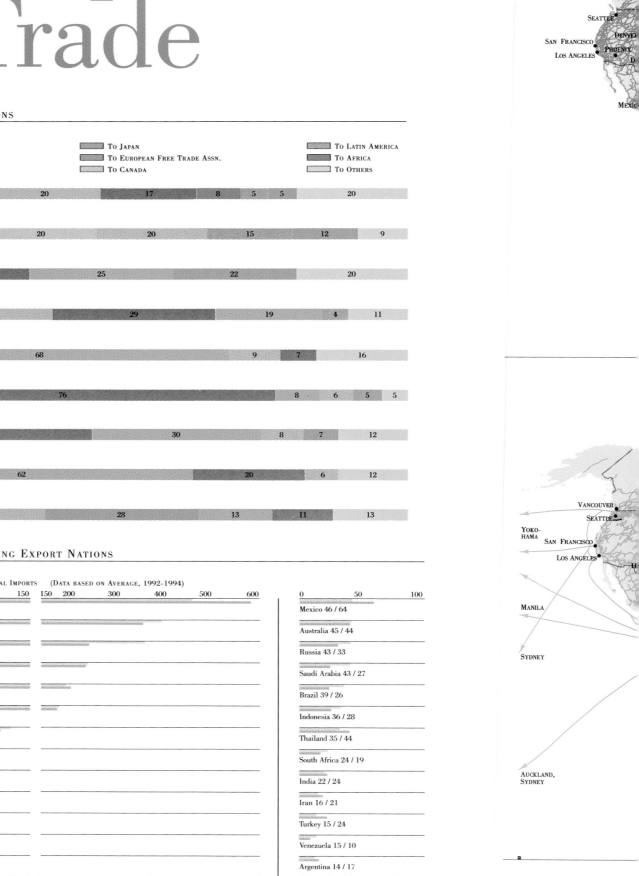

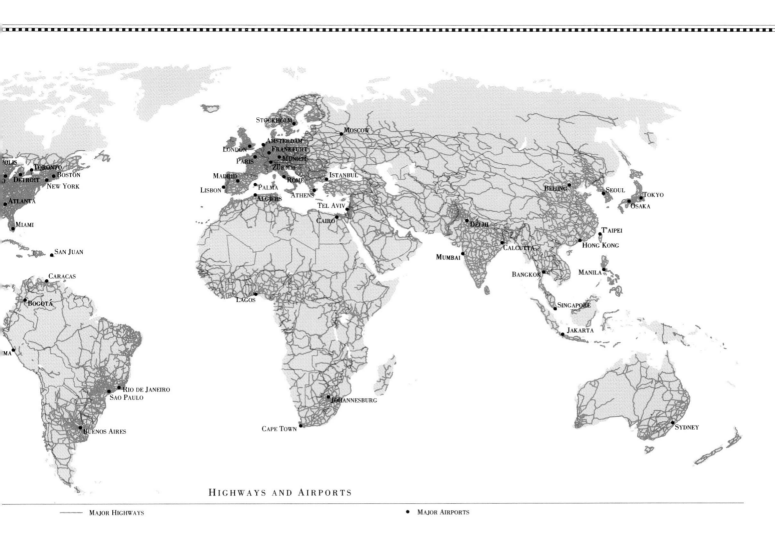

HIGHWAYS AND AIRPORTS

——— MAJOR HIGHWAYS   • MAJOR AIRPORTS

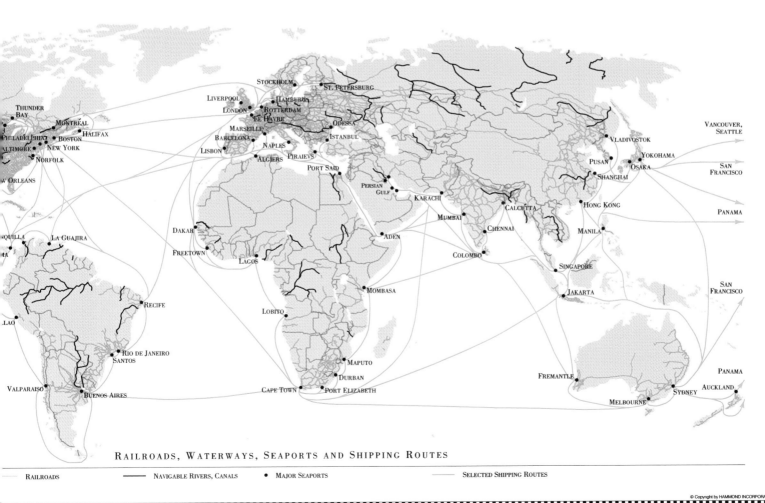

RAILROADS, WATERWAYS, SEAPORTS AND SHIPPING ROUTES

RAILROADS   ——— NAVIGABLE RIVERS, CANALS   • MAJOR SEAPORTS   ——— SELECTED SHIPPING ROUTES

Global Politics

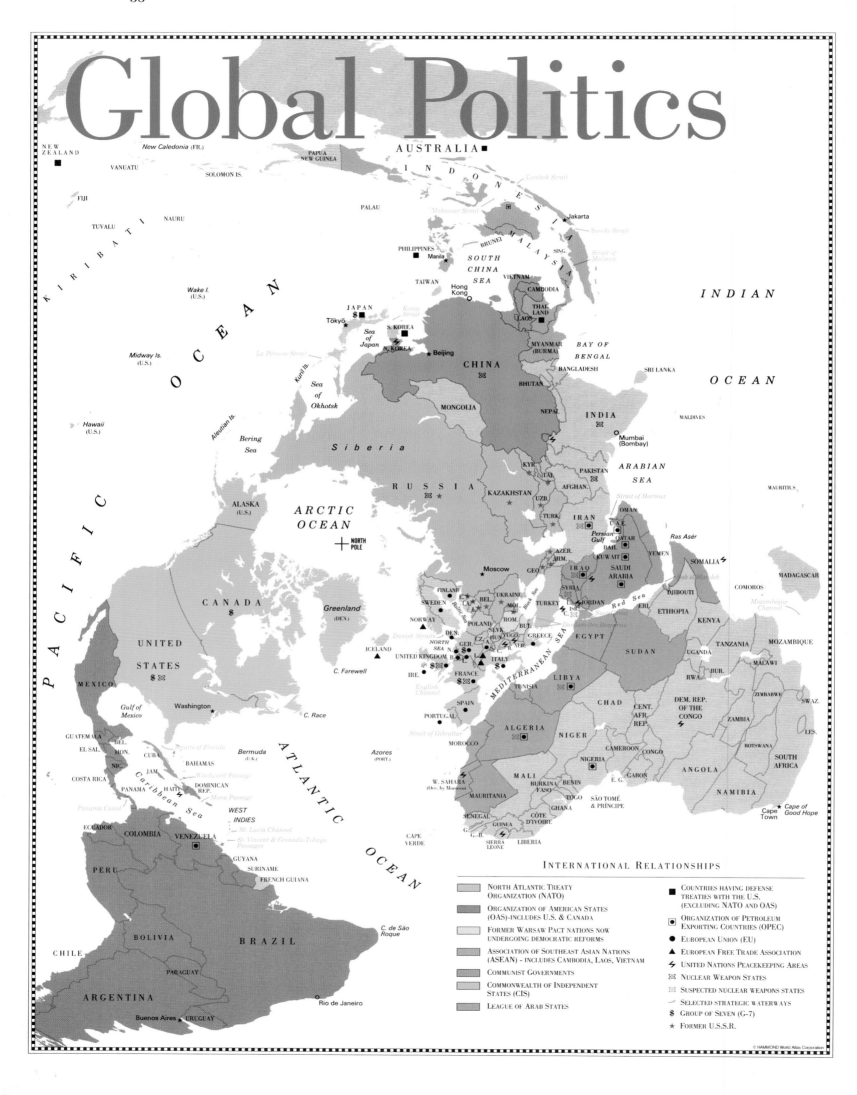

NEW
ZEALAND
New Caledonia (FR.)
AUSTRALIA
VANUATU
PAPUA
NEW GUINEA
SOLOMON IS.
INDONESIA
FIJI
PALAU
Jakarta
TUVALU
NAURU
Makassar Strait
Sunda Strait
Lombok Strait
PHILIPPINES
BRUNEI
MALAYSIA
SING.
KIRIBATI
Manila
SOUTH
CHINA
SEA
Strait of
Malacca
Wake I.
(U.S.)
TAIWAN
VIETNAM
CAMBODIA
THAI
LAND
INDIAN
JAPAN
Hong
Kong
LAOS
Tōkyō
Korea
Strait
S. KOREA
MYANMAR
(BURMA)
BAY OF
BENGAL
OCEAN
Midway Is.
(U.S.)
Sea
of
Japan
N. KOREA
Beijing
CHINA
BANGLADESH
SRI LANKA
OCEAN
La Perouse Strait
Sea
of
Okhotsk
MONGOLIA
NEPAL
BHUTAN
INDIA
MALDIVES
Kuril Is.
Hawaii
(U.S.)
Siberia
KYR.
Mumbai
(Bombay)
ARABIAN
SEA
Aleutian Is.
Bering
Sea
RUSSIA
KAZAKHSTAN
TAJ.
AFGHAN.
PAKISTAN
MAURITIUS
ALASKA
(U.S.)
UZB.
TURK.
IRAN
OMAN
Strait of Hormuz
ARCTIC
OCEAN
NORTH
POLE
Moscow
GEO.
AZER.
ARM.
U.A.E.
Persian
Gulf
QATAR
BAH.
KUWAIT
YEMEN
Ras Asér
SOMALIA
MADAGASCAR
CANADA
Greenland
(DEN.)
FINLAND
SWEDEN
UKRAINE
MOL.
IRAQ
SAUDI
ARABIA
SYRIA
JORDAN
Red Sea
Bab el Mandeb
DJIBOUTI
ERI.
COMOROS
Mozambique
Channel
UNITED
STATES
NORWAY
DEN.
BEL.
POLAND
ROM.
TURKEY
ISR.
Dardanelles/Bosporus
ETHIOPIA
KENYA
TANZANIA
MOZAMBIQUE
C. Farewell
ICELAND
UNITED KINGDOM
GER.
CZ.
SVK.
HUN.
YUGO.
BUL.
GREECE
EGYPT
SUDAN
UGANDA
MALAWI
IRE.
FRANCE
ITALY
LIBYA
CHAD
CENT.
AFR.
REP.
DEM. REP.
OF THE
CONGO
ZAMBIA
ZIMBABWE
SWAZ.
Washington
C. Race
SPAIN
TUNISIA
ALGERIA
NIGER
CAMEROON
CONGO
GABON
ANGOLA
BOTSWANA
SOUTH
AFRICA
NAMIBIA
LES.
Gulf of
Mexico
PORTUGAL
Strait of Gibraltar
MOROCCO
MALI
NIGERIA
E. G.
Cape of
Good Hope
MEXICO
Azores
(PORT.)
W. SAHARA
(Occ. by Morocco)
BURKINA
FASO
BENIN
TOGO
SÃO TOMÉ
& PRÍNCIPE
Cape
Town
GUATEMALA
EL SAL.
BEL.
HON.
NIC.
CUBA
BAHAMAS
Bermuda
(U.K.)
MAURITANIA
SENEGAL
GHANA
CÔTE
D'IVOIRE
COSTA RICA
JAM.
HAITI
DOMINICAN
REP.
G.-B.
GUINEA
LIBERIA
PANAMA
Panama Canal
Caribbean Sea
Windward Passage
Mona Passage
WEST
INDIES
ATLANTIC
G.
G.-B.
SIERRA
LEONE
ECUADOR
COLOMBIA
VENEZUELA
St. Lucia Channel
St. Vincent & Grenada-Tobago
Passages
CAPE
VERDE
PERU
GUYANA
SURINAME
FRENCH GUIANA
OCEAN
Rio de Janeiro
C. de São
Roque
BOLIVIA
BRAZIL
CHILE
PARAGUAY
ARGENTINA
URUGUAY
Buenos Aires

INTERNATIONAL RELATIONSHIPS

NORTH ATLANTIC TREATY
ORGANIZATION (NATO)

ORGANIZATION OF AMERICAN STATES
(OAS)-INCLUDES U.S. & CANADA

FORMER WARSAW PACT NATIONS NOW
UNDERGOING DEMOCRATIC REFORMS

ASSOCIATION OF SOUTHEAST ASIAN NATIONS
(ASEAN) - INCLUDES CAMBODIA, LAOS, VIETNAM

COMMUNIST GOVERNMENTS

COMMONWEALTH OF INDEPENDENT
STATES (CIS)

LEAGUE OF ARAB STATES

■ COUNTRIES HAVING DEFENSE
TREATIES WITH THE U.S.
(EXCLUDING NATO AND OAS)

⊡ ORGANIZATION OF PETROLEUM
EXPORTING COUNTRIES (OPEC)

● EUROPEAN UNION (EU)

▲ EUROPEAN FREE TRADE ASSOCIATION

⚡ UNITED NATIONS PEACEKEEPING AREAS

⊠ NUCLEAR WEAPON STATES

⊠ SUSPECTED NUCLEAR WEAPONS STATES

SELECTED STRATEGIC WATERWAYS

$ GROUP OF SEVEN (G-7)

★ FORMER U.S.S.R.

© HAMMOND World Atlas Corporation

Europe - Physical

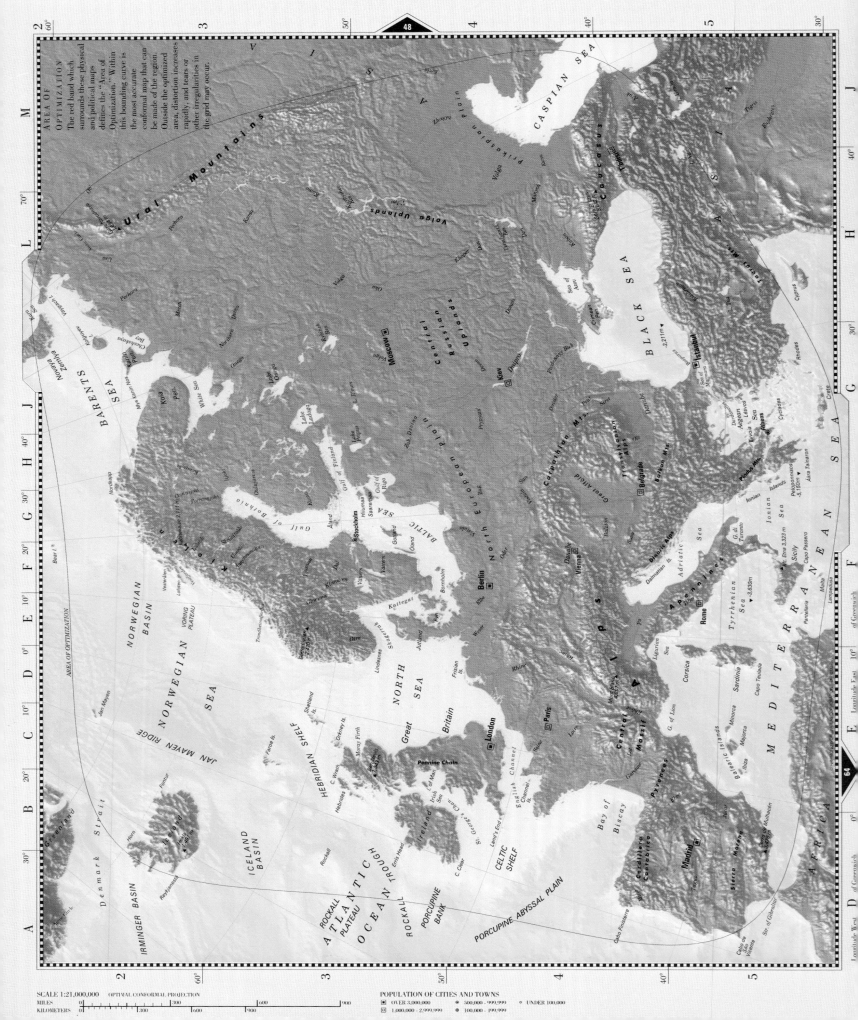

AREA OF OPTIMIZATION
The red band which surrounds these physical and political maps defines the "Area of Optimization." Within this bounding curve is the most accurate conformal map that can be made of the region. Outside the optimized area, distortion increases rapidly, and tears or other irregularities in the grid may occur.

SCALE 1:21,000,000   OPTIMAL CONFORMAL PROJECTION

MILES

KILOMETERS

POPULATION OF CITIES AND TOWNS

□ OVER 3,000,000   ● 500,000 - 999,999   ○ UNDER 100,000

▣ 1,000,000 - 2,999,999   ◉ 100,000 - 199,999

Europe - Political

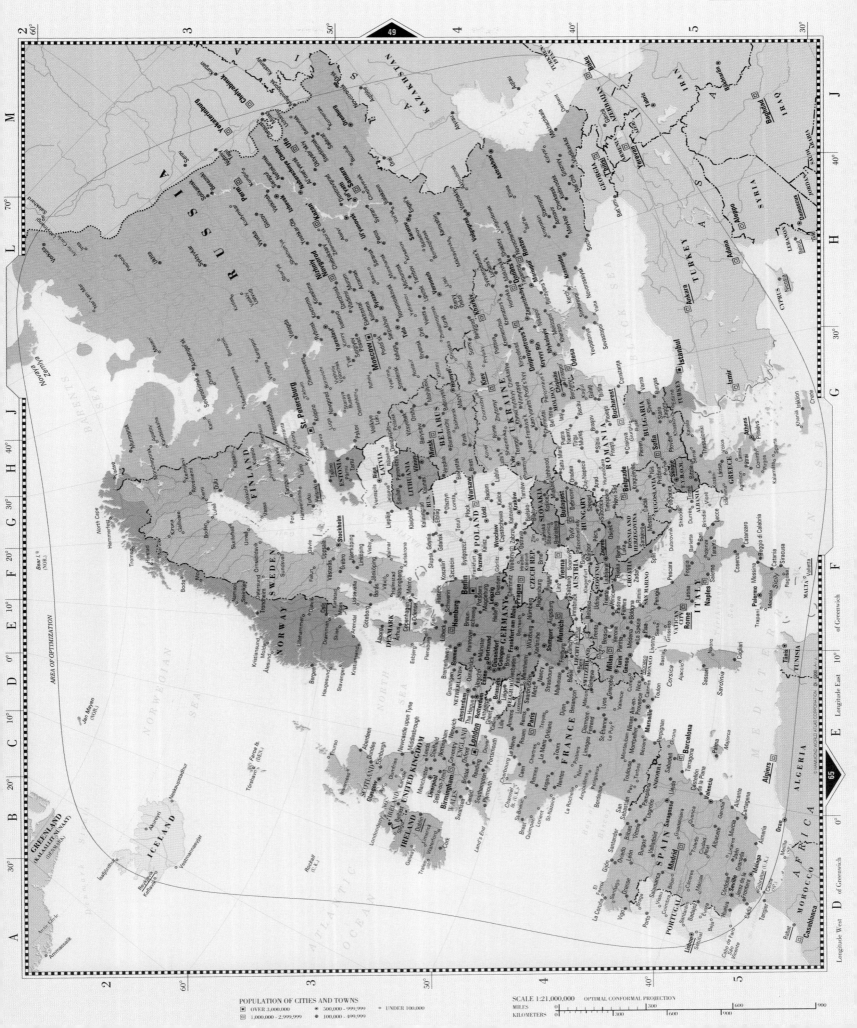

POPULATION OF CITIES AND TOWNS

▣ OVER 3,000,000   ● 500,000 - 999,999   ○ UNDER 100,000
▢ 1,000,000 - 2,999,999   ● 100,000 - 499,999

SCALE 1:21,000,000   OPTIMAL CONFORMAL PROJECTION

MILES   0   300   600   900

KILOMETERS   0   300   600   900

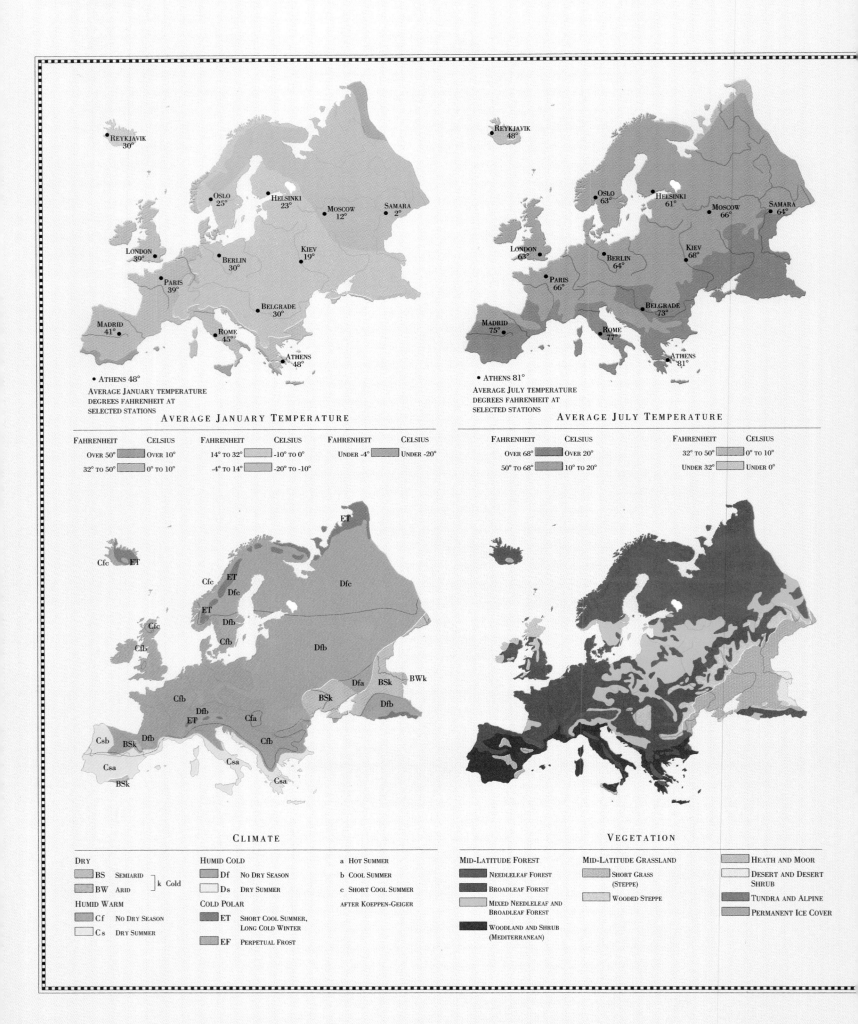

REYKJAVIK 30°
OSLO 25°
HELSINKI 23°
MOSCOW 12°
SAMARA 2°
LONDON 39°
BERLIN 30°
KIEV 19°
PARIS 39°
BELGRADE 30°
MADRID 41°
ROME 45°
ATHENS 48°

• ATHENS 48°
AVERAGE JANUARY TEMPERATURE
DEGREES FAHRENHEIT AT
SELECTED STATIONS

AVERAGE JANUARY TEMPERATURE

FAHRENHEIT	CELSIUS	FAHRENHEIT	CELSIUS	FAHRENHEIT	CELSIUS
OVER 50°	OVER 10°	14° TO 32°	-10° TO 0°	UNDER -4°	UNDER -20°
32° TO 50°	0° TO 10°	-4° TO 14°	-20° TO -10°		

REYKJAVIK 48°
OSLO 63°
HELSINKI 61°
MOSCOW 66°
SAMARA 64°
LONDON 63°
BERLIN 64°
KIEV 68°
PARIS 66°
BELGRADE 73°
MADRID 75°
ROME 77°
ATHENS 81°

• ATHENS 81°
AVERAGE JULY TEMPERATURE
DEGREES FAHRENHEIT AT
SELECTED STATIONS

AVERAGE JULY TEMPERATURE

FAHRENHEIT	CELSIUS	FAHRENHEIT	CELSIUS
OVER 68°	OVER 20°	32° TO 50°	0° TO 10°
50° TO 68°	10° TO 20°	UNDER 32°	UNDER 0°

ET
Cfc   ET
Cfc   ET
Dfc
ET
Dfb
Cfc
Cfb
Dfb
Dfc
Dfb
Dfa   BSk   BWk
BSk
Cfb
Dfb
Dfb   Dfb
ET
Cfa
Csb   BSk   Dfb
Csa
Csa
Csa
BSk

CLIMATE

DRY
BS SEMIARID
BW ARID } k Cold
HUMID WARM
Cf NO DRY SEASON
Cs DRY SUMMER

HUMID COLD
Df NO DRY SEASON
Ds DRY SUMMER
COLD POLAR
ET SHORT COOL SUMMER, LONG COLD WINTER
EF PERPETUAL FROST

a HOT SUMMER
b COOL SUMMER
c SHORT COOL SUMMER
AFTER KOEPPEN-GEIGER

VEGETATION

MID-LATITUDE FOREST
NEEDLELEAF FOREST
BROADLEAF FOREST
MIXED NEEDLELEAF AND BROADLEAF FOREST
WOODLAND AND SHRUB (MEDITERRANEAN)

MID-LATITUDE GRASSLAND
SHORT GRASS (STEPPE)
WOODED STEPPE

HEATH AND MOOR
DESERT AND DESERT SHRUB
TUNDRA AND ALPINE
PERMANENT ICE COVER

Europe - Comparisons

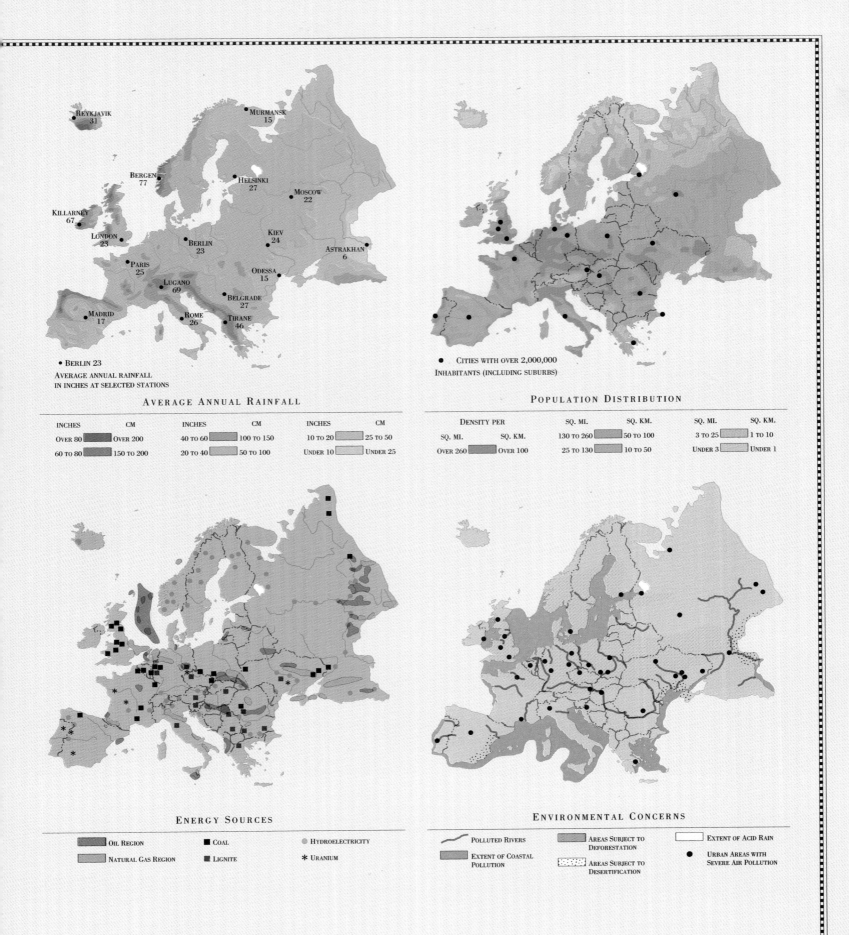

Average Annual Rainfall

• BERLIN 23
AVERAGE ANNUAL RAINFALL
IN INCHES AT SELECTED STATIONS

REYKJAVIK 31 · MURMANSK 15 · BERGEN 77 · HELSINKI 27 · MOSCOW 22 · KILLARNEY 67 · LONDON 23 · BERLIN 23 · KIEV 24 · ASTRAKHAN 6 · PARIS 25 · ODESSA 15 · LUGANO 69 · BELGRADE 27 · MADRID 17 · ROME 26 · TIRANE 46

INCHES	CM	INCHES	CM	INCHES	CM
OVER 80	OVER 200	40 TO 60	100 TO 150	10 TO 20	25 TO 50
60 TO 80	150 TO 200	20 TO 40	50 TO 100	UNDER 10	UNDER 25

Population Distribution

• CITIES WITH OVER 2,000,000
INHABITANTS (INCLUDING SUBURBS)

DENSITY PER		SQ. MI.	SQ. KM.	SQ. MI.	SQ. KM.
SQ. MI.	SQ. KM.	130 TO 260	50 TO 100	3 TO 25	1 TO 10
OVER 260	OVER 100	25 TO 130	10 TO 50	UNDER 3	UNDER 1

Energy Sources

OIL REGION	COAL	HYDROELECTRICITY
NATURAL GAS REGION	LIGNITE	URANIUM

Environmental Concerns

POLLUTED RIVERS	AREAS SUBJECT TO DEFORESTATION	EXTENT OF ACID RAIN
EXTENT OF COASTAL POLLUTION	AREAS SUBJECT TO DESERTIFICATION	URBAN AREAS WITH SEVERE AIR POLLUTION

© Copyright by HAMMOND INCORPORATED, Maplewood, N.J.

Western Europe

MILES

KILOMETERS

POPULATION OF CITIES AND TOWNS

| ■ | OVER 2,000,000 | ● | 500,000 - 999,999 | ● | 100,000 - 249,999 | ⊙ | 10,000 - 29,999 |
| □ | 1,000,000 - 1,999,999 | ◉ | 250,000 - 499,999 | ● | 30,000 - 99,999 | ○ | UNDER 10,000 |

| | Below Sea Level | Sea Level | 200 700 | 500 1,600 | 1,000 3,300 | 1,500 5,000 | 2,000 6,500 | 4,000 13,000 | 6,000 m. 19,700 ft. |

Northern Europe

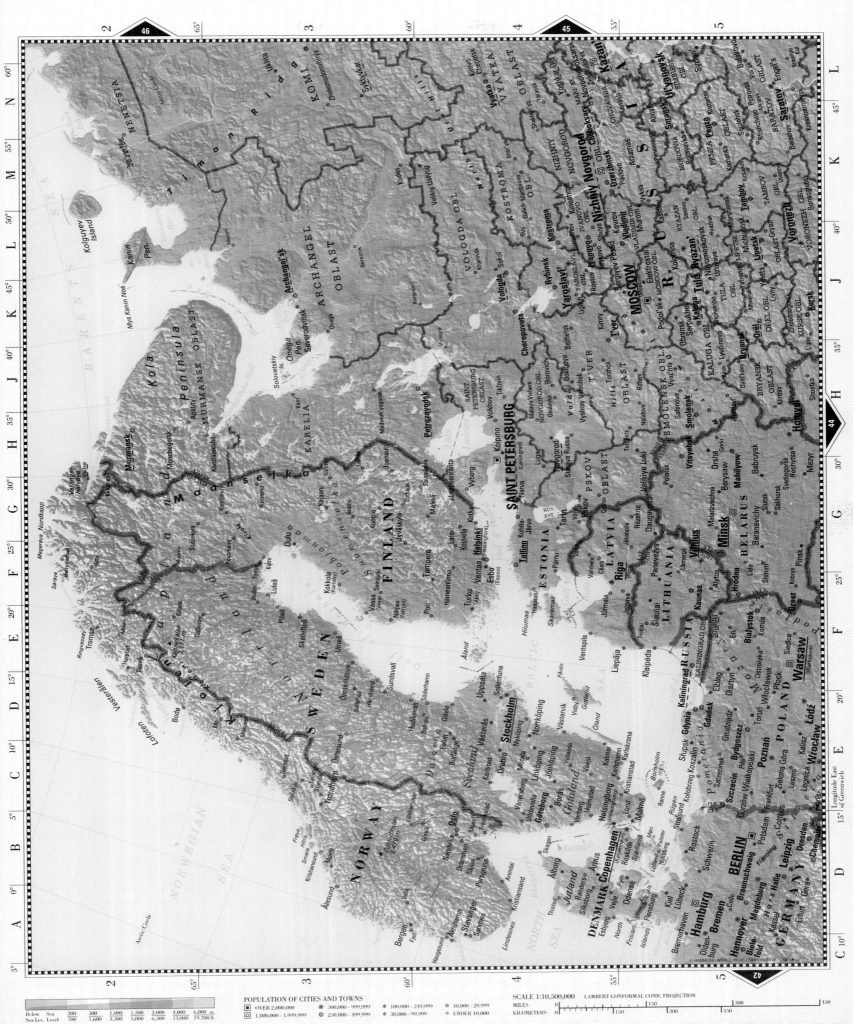

POPULATION OF CITIES AND TOWNS

▣ OVER 2,000,000   ⊙ 500,000 - 999,999   ⊕ 100,000 - 249,999   ○ 10,000 - 29,999
▢ 1,000,000 - 1,999,999   ⊙ 250,000 - 499,999   ⊙ 30,000 - 99,999   ○ UNDER 10,000

SCALE 1:10,500,000   LAMBERT CONFORMAL CONIC PROJECTION

MILES 0   150   300

KILOMETERS 0   150   300   450

© HAMMOND WORLD ATLAS CORPORATION

South Central Europe

Central Eurasia

Russia and Neighboring Countries

RUSSIA
(Administrative divisions are named only when they differ from their respective capitals.)

1. ADYGEA AUT. REP.
2. KARACHAY-CHERKESSIA AUT. REP.
3. KABARDINO-BALKARIA AUT. REP.
4. NORTH OSSETIA AUT. REP.
5. INGUSHETIA AUT. REP.
6. CHECHNYA AUT. REP.
7. DAGESTAN AUT. REP.
8. MORDOVIA AUT. REP.
9. CHUVASHIA AUT. REP.
10. MARI EL AUT. REP.
11. TATARSTAN AUT. REP.
12. BASHKORTOSTAN AUT. REP.
13. UDMURTIA AUT. REP
14. PERMYAKIA AUT. OKRUG
15. KHAKASSIA AUT. REP.
16. UST -ORDA AUT. OKRUG
17. AGA AUT. OKRUG

© HAMMOND WORLD ATLAS CORPORATION

POPULATION OF CITIES AND TOWNS

▪ OVER 2,000,000   ● 500,000 - 999,999   ● 50,000 - 99,999
▫ 1,000,000 - 1,999,999   ● 100,000 - 499,999   ● UNDER 50,000

SCALE 1:21,000,000   LAMBERT CONFORMAL CONIC PROJECTION

MILES   0   300   600   900
KILOMETERS   0   300   600   900

Asia-Physical

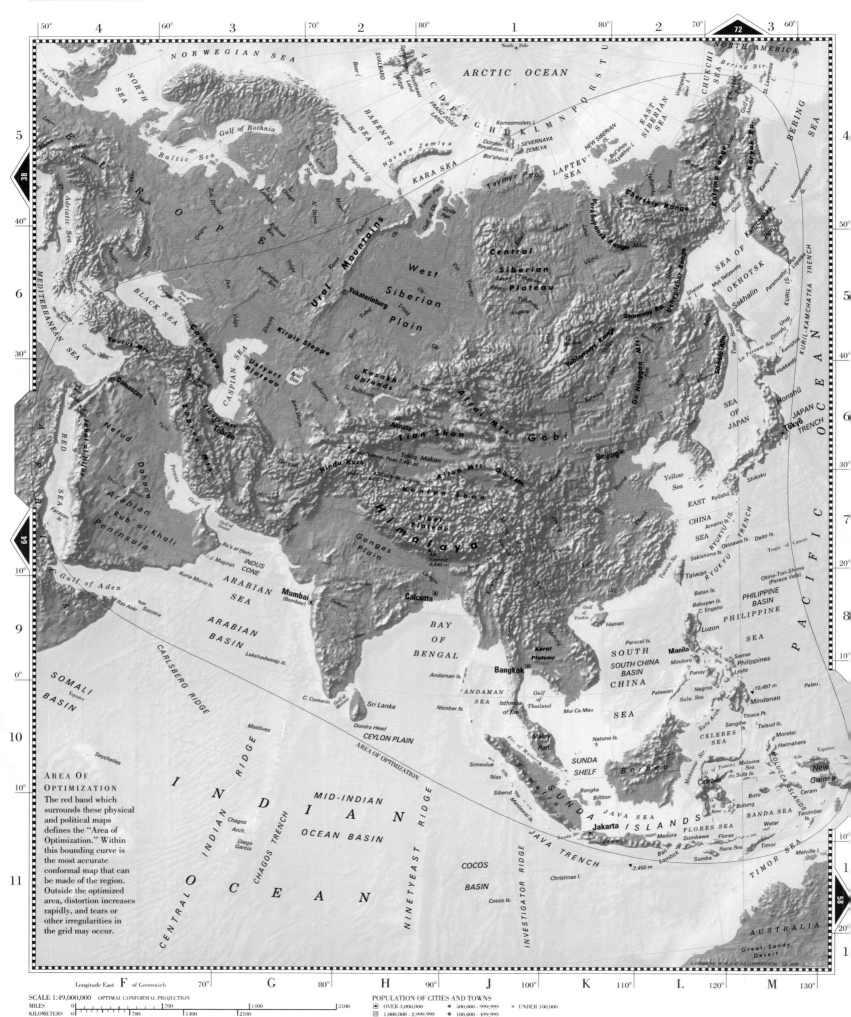

NORWEGIAN SEA

ARCTIC OCEAN

North Pole

NORTH SEA

NORTH AMERICA

SVALBARD

Bear I.

FRANZ-JOSEF LAND

BARENTS SEA

Komsomolets I.

NEW SIBERIAN IS.

CHUKCHI SEA

Bering Str.

BERING SEA

Gulf of Bothnia

Baltic Sea

Novaya Zemlya

October Revolution I.
Bol'shevik I.

SEVERNAYA ZEMLYA

KARA SEA

Taymyr Pen.

LAPTEV SEA

EAST SIBERIAN SEA

Koryak Range

Kamchatka

Cherskiy Range

Kolyma Range

NORTH SEA

EUROPE

Ural Mountains

West Siberian Plain

Central Siberian Plateau

Stanovoy Ra.

SEA OF OKHOTSK

Sakhalin

KURIL-KAMCHATKA TRENCH

Yekaterinburg

MEDITERRANEAN SEA

BLACK SEA

Caucasus

CASPIAN SEA

Kirgiz Steppe

Ustyurt Plateau

Aral Sea

Kazakh Uplands

L. Balkhash

Altai Mts.

Yablonovyy Range

Da Hinggan Mts.

Sikhote-Alin

SEA OF JAPAN

Honshū

Tōkyō

JAPAN TRENCH

Taurus Mts.

Damascus

Elburz Mts.
Tehran
Zagros Mts.

Almaty

Tian Shan

Talda Makan

Gobi

Beijing

Yellow Sea

Shikoku

Kyūshū

Hindu Kush

Pamir
Everest Peak 7,495 m

Altun Mts.
Qilian Mts.

Kunlun Shan

EAST CHINA SEA

Amami Is.

RYUKYU TRENCH

Nefud

Dahana

Arabian Peninsula

Rub' al Khali

RED SEA

Gulf of Oman

Persian Gulf

Himalaya

Tibet Plateau

Everest 8,848 m

Taiwan

Okinawa Is.

Daito Is.

Gulf of Aden

Ra's al Hadd

INDUS CONE

ARABIAN SEA

Ganges Plain

Ganges

Batan Is.

Babuyan Is.
C. Engaño

Tropic of Cancer

Okino-Tori-Shima (Parece Vela)

SOMALI BASIN

ARABIAN BASIN

Mumbai (Bombay)

Calcutta

BAY OF BENGAL

Gulf of Tonkin

Hainan

Luzon

PHILIPPINE BASIN

PHILIPPINE SEA

Equator

Lakshadweep Is.

Narmada

Godavari

Andaman Is.

Korat Plateau

Bangkok

Paracel Is.

SOUTH CHINA SEA

SOUTH CHINA BASIN

Manila

Mindoro

Samar

Philippines

Leyte

CARLSBERG RIDGE

C. Comorin
Gulf of Mannar

Sri Lanka

Nicobar Is.

ANDAMAN SEA

Isthmus of Kra

Gulf of Thailand

Mui Ca Mau

Palawan

Panay

Negros

–10,497 m

Mindanao

Palau I.

Dondra Head

CEYLON PLAIN

AREA OF OPTIMIZATION

Maldives

Simeulue

Nias

Malay Pen.

Str. of Malacca

Natuna Is.

Sulu Arch.

Tinaca Pt.

Sulu Sea

Sangihe Is.

Talaud Is.

Morotai

CELEBES SEA

Halmahera

Seychelles

INDIAN RIDGE

Chagos Arch.
Diego Garcia

MID-INDIAN OCEAN BASIN

SUNDA SHELF

Borneo

Makassar Str.

Celebes

G. of Tomini

Moluca Sea
Sula Is.

MOLUCCA ISLANDS

Buru

Butung

New Guinea

Ceram

NINETYEAST RIDGE

INDIAN OCEAN

CHAGOS TRENCH

COCOS BASIN

Cocos Is.

Christmas I.

INVESTIGATOR RIDGE

Siberut

Mentawai Is.

Sumatra

SUNDA ISLANDS

JAVA TRENCH

Java

Jakarta

Sunda Str.

Bali

Lombok

Bangka
Billiton

JAVA SEA

Madura

Sumbawa

Flores

FLORES SEA

Savu Sea

Sumba

BANDA SEA

Wetar

Tanimbar Is.

Timor

TIMOR SEA

Melville I.

–7,450 m

AUSTRALIA

Great Sandy Desert

AREA OF OPTIMIZATION

The red band which surrounds these physical and political maps defines the "Area of Optimization." Within this bounding curve is the most accurate conformal map that can be made of the region. Outside the optimized area, distortion increases rapidly, and tears or other irregularities in the grid may occur.

Longitude East F of Greenwich

SCALE 1:49,000,000   OPTIMAL CONFORMAL PROJECTION

MILES   0   700   1400   2100
KILOMETERS   0   700   1400   2100

POPULATION OF CITIES AND TOWNS

▣ OVER 3,000,000   ● 500,000 - 999,999   ○ UNDER 100,000
☐ 1,000,000 - 2,999,999   • 100,000 - 499,999

© HAMMOND WORLD ATLAS CORPORATION

Asia - Political

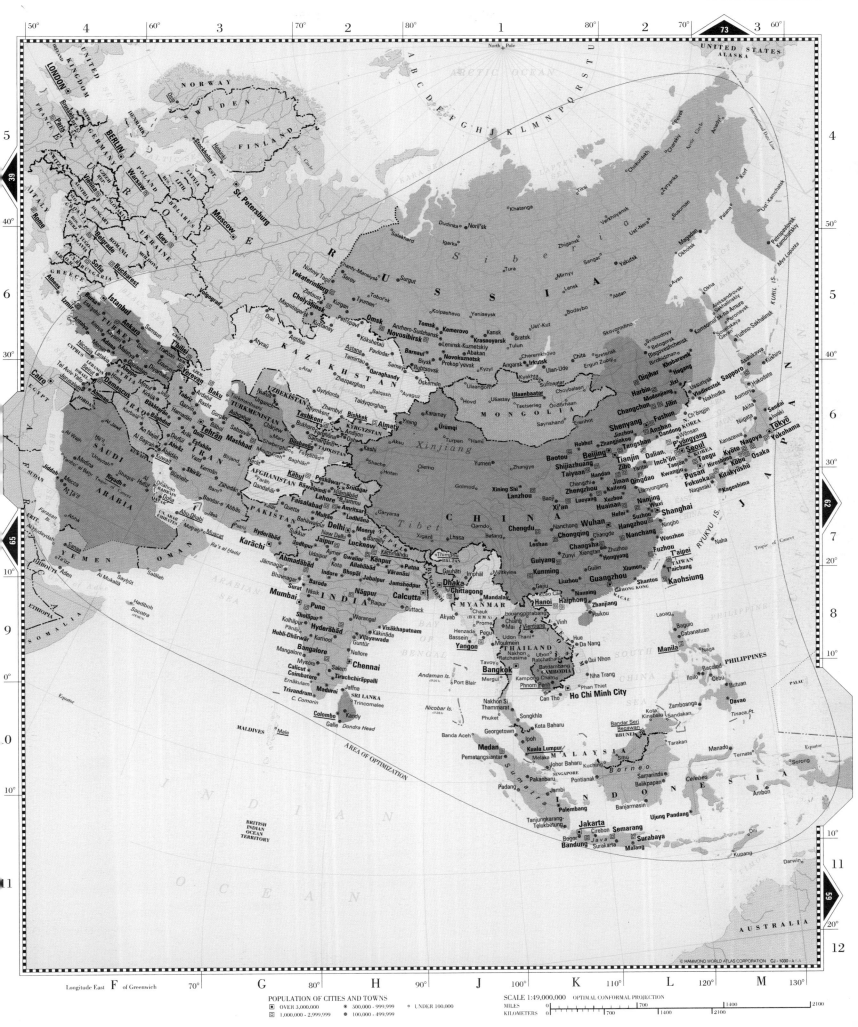

POPULATION OF CITIES AND TOWNS

☐ OVER 3,000,000   ● 500,000 - 999,999   ○ UNDER 100,000

☐ 1,000,000 - 2,999,999   ● 100,000 - 499,999

SCALE 1:49,000,000   OPTIMAL CONFORMAL PROJECTION

MILES 0   700   1400   2100

KILOMETERS 0   1400   2100

Longitude East F of Greenwich

© HAMMOND WORLD ATLAS CORPORATION   CJ - 1030 - A - ASIA

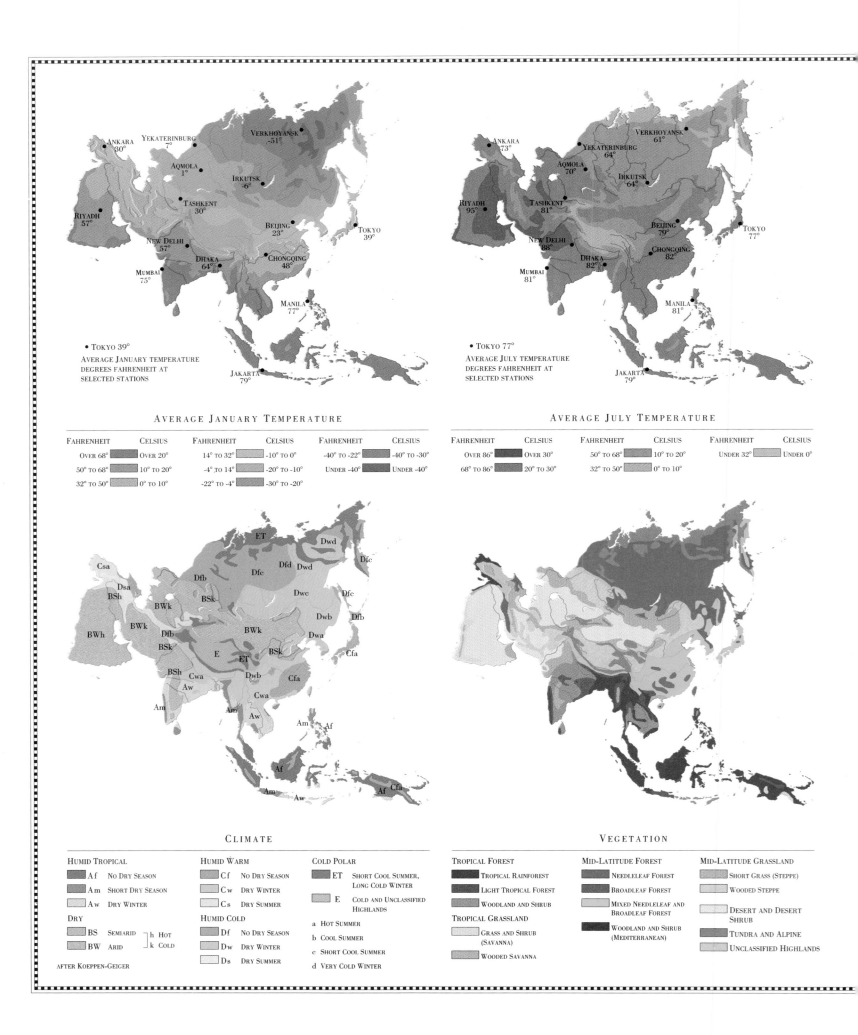

AVERAGE JANUARY TEMPERATURE

• TOKYO 39°
AVERAGE JANUARY TEMPERATURE
DEGREES FAHRENHEIT AT
SELECTED STATIONS

FAHRENHEIT	CELSIUS	FAHRENHEIT	CELSIUS	FAHRENHEIT	CELSIUS
OVER 68°	OVER 20°	14° TO 32°	-10° TO 0°	-40° TO -22°	-40° TO -30°
50° TO 68°	10° TO 20°	-4° TO 14°	-20° TO -10°	UNDER -40°	UNDER -40°
32° TO 50°	0° TO 10°	-22° TO -4°	-30° TO -20°		

AVERAGE JULY TEMPERATURE

• TOKYO 77°
AVERAGE JULY TEMPERATURE
DEGREES FAHRENHEIT AT
SELECTED STATIONS

FAHRENHEIT	CELSIUS	FAHRENHEIT	CELSIUS	FAHRENHEIT	CELSIUS
OVER 86°	OVER 30°	50° TO 68°	10° TO 20°	UNDER 32°	UNDER 0°
68° TO 86°	20° TO 30°	32° TO 50°	0° TO 10°		

CLIMATE

HUMID TROPICAL
- Af NO DRY SEASON
- Am SHORT DRY SEASON
- Aw DRY WINTER

DRY
- BS SEMIARID ⎤ h HOT
- BW ARID ⎦ k COLD

AFTER KOEPPEN-GEIGER

HUMID WARM
- Cf NO DRY SEASON
- Cw DRY WINTER
- Cs DRY SUMMER

HUMID COLD
- Df NO DRY SEASON
- Dw DRY WINTER
- Ds DRY SUMMER

COLD POLAR
- ET SHORT COOL SUMMER, LONG COLD WINTER
- E COLD AND UNCLASSIFIED HIGHLANDS

a HOT SUMMER
b COOL SUMMER
c SHORT COOL SUMMER
d VERY COLD WINTER

VEGETATION

TROPICAL FOREST
- TROPICAL RAINFOREST
- LIGHT TROPICAL FOREST
- WOODLAND AND SHRUB

TROPICAL GRASSLAND
- GRASS AND SHRUB (SAVANNA)
- WOODED SAVANNA

MID-LATITUDE FOREST
- NEEDLELEAF FOREST
- BROADLEAF FOREST
- MIXED NEEDLELEAF AND BROADLEAF FOREST
- WOODLAND AND SHRUB (MEDITERRANEAN)

MID-LATITUDE GRASSLAND
- SHORT GRASS (STEPPE)
- WOODED STEPPE
- DESERT AND DESERT SHRUB
- TUNDRA AND ALPINE
- UNCLASSIFIED HIGHLANDS

Asia - Comparisons

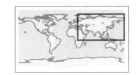

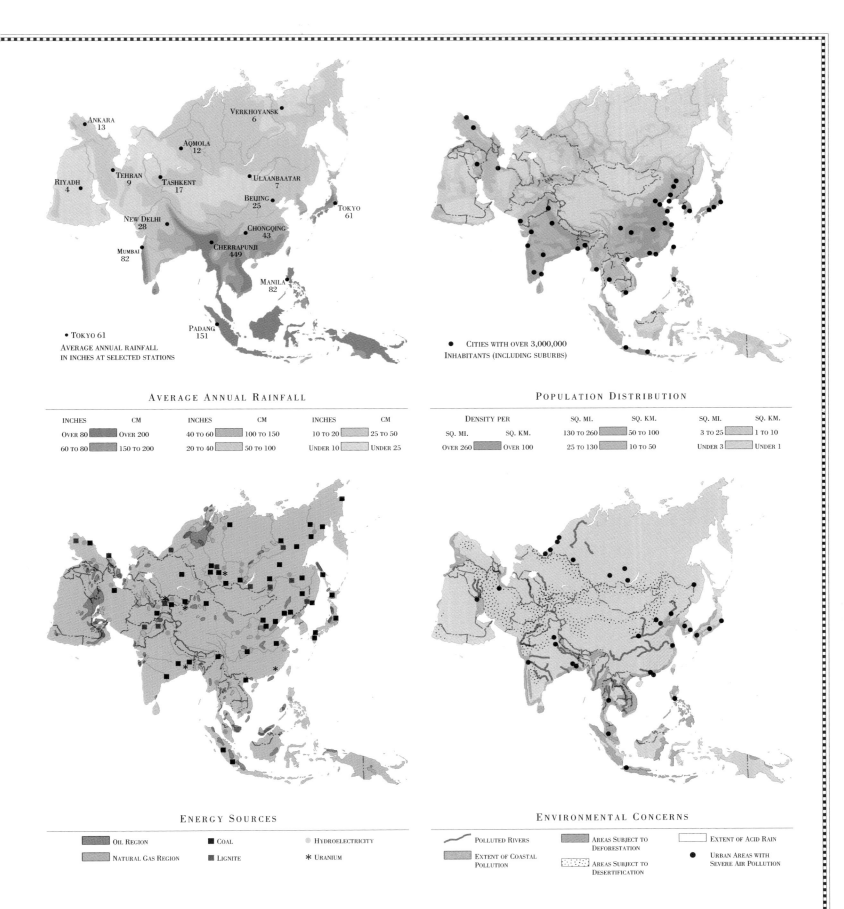

AVERAGE ANNUAL RAINFALL

ANKARA
13

VERKHOYANSK
6

AQMOLA
12

RIYADH
4

TEHRAN
9

TASHKENT
17

ULAANBAATAR
7

BEIJING
25

NEW DELHI
28

CHONGQING
43

CHERRAPUNJI
449

TOKYO
61

MUMBAI
82

MANILA
82

PADANG
151

• TOKYO 61
AVERAGE ANNUAL RAINFALL
IN INCHES AT SELECTED STATIONS

INCHES	CM	INCHES	CM	INCHES	CM
OVER 80	OVER 200	40 TO 60	100 TO 150	10 TO 20	25 TO 50
60 TO 80	150 TO 200	20 TO 40	50 TO 100	UNDER 10	UNDER 25

POPULATION DISTRIBUTION

• CITIES WITH OVER 3,000,000
INHABITANTS (INCLUDING SUBURBS)

DENSITY PER		SQ. MI.	SQ. KM.	SQ. MI.	SQ. KM.
SQ. MI.	SQ. KM.	130 TO 260	50 TO 100	3 TO 25	1 TO 10
OVER 260	OVER 100	25 TO 130	10 TO 50	UNDER 3	UNDER 1

ENERGY SOURCES

▨ OIL REGION		■ COAL		● HYDROELECTRICITY	
▨ NATURAL GAS REGION		■ LIGNITE		✳ URANIUM	

ENVIRONMENTAL CONCERNS

〰 POLLUTED RIVERS	▨ AREAS SUBJECT TO DEFORESTATION	▢ EXTENT OF ACID RAIN
▨ EXTENT OF COASTAL POLLUTION	⋰ AREAS SUBJECT TO DESERTIFICATION	● URBAN AREAS WITH SEVERE AIR POLLUTION

Southwestern Asia

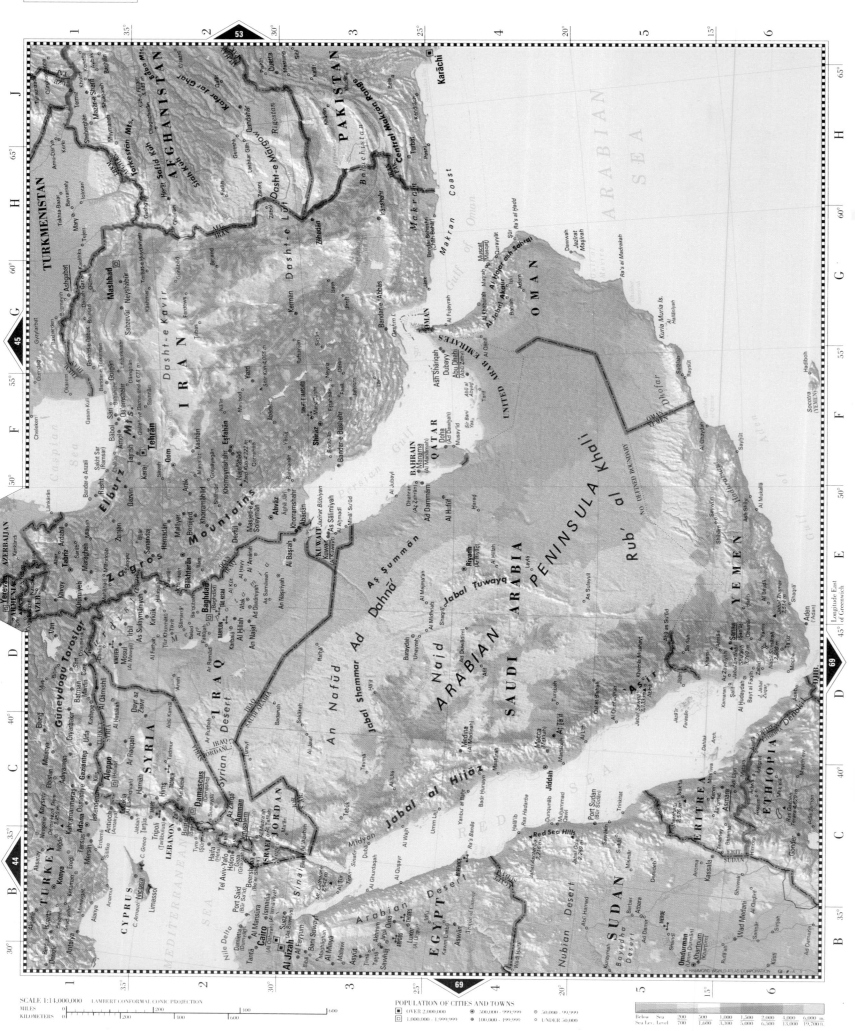

POPULATION OF CITIES AND TOWNS

□ OVER 2,000,000   ● 500,000 - 999,999   ⊕ 50,000 - 99,999
□ 1,000,000 - 1,999,999   ● 100,000 - 199,999   ○ UNDER 50,000

Below   Sea
Sea Lev. Level   200   500   1,000   1,500   2,000   3,000   6,000 m.
700   1,600   3,300   5,000   6,500   13,000   19,700 ft.

Indian Subcontinent

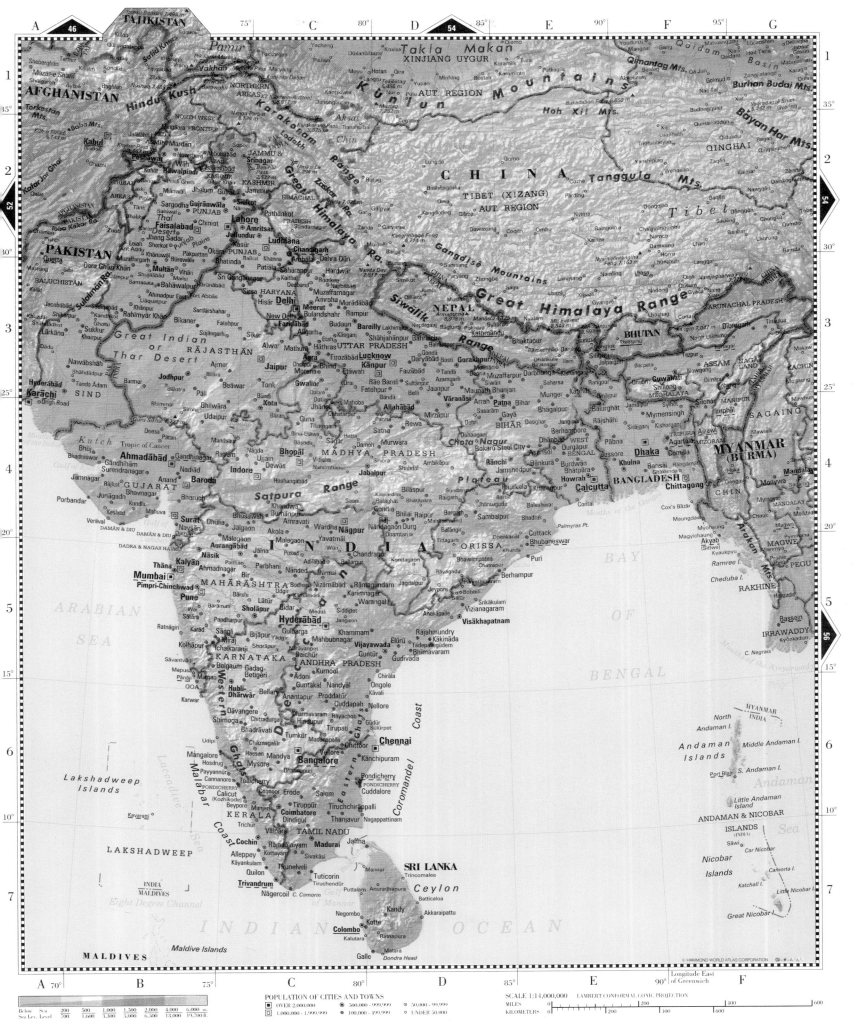

POPULATION OF CITIES AND TOWNS

- ■ OVER 2,000,000
- □ 1,000,000 - 1,999,999
- ● 500,000 - 999,999
- ◉ 100,000 - 199,999
- ○ 50,000 - 99,999
- ○ UNDER 50,000

SCALE 1:14,000,000   LAMBERT CONFORMAL CONIC PROJECTION

MILES   0   100   200   400   600

KILOMETERS   0   200   400   600

Longitude East of Greenwich

K 115° 130° P 47 135° Q 140° R 145° S

45°

RUSSIA

Khabarovsk

Sakhalin Vzmor'ye Dolinsk
Yuzhno-Sakhalinsk
SEA OF
OKHOTSK

Kholmsk
Nevel'sk Korsakov Novikovo
Shebunino Mys Aniva
Occupied by Russia
since 1945, claimed
by Japan.

Etorofu

Sōya-misaki Wakkanai Kunashiri

3

HEILONGJIANG

Yichun

Hegang

Qiqihar
Daqing

Jiamusi
Shuangyashan

Harbin

Asahikawa Kitami

Otaru Obihiro
Sapporo Hokkaidō

Muroran
Hakodate Erimo-misaki

40°

Mudanjiang

Vladivostok

Changchun

JILIN

Aomori Hachinohe
Hirosaki Ōdate
Akita Morioka
Sakata Kamaishi

4

SEA OF
JAPAN

Sado Niigata
Yamagata Ishinomaki
Sendai

LIAONING

Shenyang Fushun

Anshan

NORTH
KOREA

Hamhung

Kimch'aek

Fukushima
Nagaoka Iwaki

35°

Beijing

Tangshan

Tianjin

Dalian

P'yongyang

Seoul

Inch'on

Wonsan

SOUTH
KOREA

Kanazawa
Komatsu Toyama Nagano Utsunomiya
Fukui Gifu Nagoya Mito
Kyōto Shimizu Chiba
Kobe Osaka Hamamatsu
Sakai
Tokyo Yokohama
Fuji

Honshū

Taiyuan

Jinan Zibo

Qingdao

Taejon Taegu

Kwangju Masan
Pusan Ulsan

Okayama Himeji
Hiroshima
Kitakyūshū
Fukuoka
Matsue
Matsuyama
Kōchi

Shikoku

5

Zhengzhou

SHANDONG

YELLOW
SEA

Cheju

Kumamoto
Kagoshima Miyazaki

Kyūshū

30°

Nanjing
Shanghai
Wuxi Suzhou
SHANGHAI

Hangzhou

EAST CHINA
SEA

Amami Is.

25°

Nanchang

Changsha

ZHEJIANG

JIANGXI

Ryukyu Islands

Okinawa

Naha

Tropic of Cancer

PACIFIC

7

T'aipei
T'aichung

TAIWAN

Keelung

Kaohsiung

HONG KONG
MACAU

OCEAN

20°

115° L 120° M 57 125° N 130° P 135° Q
Longitude East
of Greenwich

POPULATION OF CITIES AND TOWNS

■ OVER 2,000,000   ● 500,000 - 999,999   ○ 50,000 - 99,999
□ 1,000,000 - 1,999,999   ◉ 100,000 - 499,999   ○ UNDER 50,000

SCALE 1:14,000,000   LAMBERT CONFORMAL CONIC PROJECTION

MILES   0   200   400   600
KILOMETERS   0   200   400   600

20°

CHINA

Leizhou Pen. Haikang Xuwen
Haiphong (Hai Phong) Nam Dinh Thanh Hoa *Gulf of Tonkin* Dan Xian Wenchang *Hainan*
Maungdaw Pyubbwe Chauk Meiktila Taunggyi *Shan Plateau* Muang Xey Xem Nua Bai Thuong Dongfang **HAINAN** Yulin
Magyichaung Magwe Yenangyaung Magwe SHAN Chiang Rai Louangphrabang Ban Ban Vinh

Akyab (Sittwe) Kyaukpyu
Ramree I. MANDALAY Loikaw *Dai Mae Tho 2,030 m* Nan Muang Pak Lay Phou 2,711 m Quang Tri
Cheduba I. **MYANMAR** KAYAH Chiang Mai Lampang *Doi Inthanon 2,600 m* Muang Phrae **LAOS** *Phou Len 2,711 m* Louangnamtha Quang Tri

2 *Bay* (BURMA) KARAN Phirae Vientiane Udon Thani Muang Khammouan Nakhon Phanom Savannakhet Hue Da Nang
of RAKHINE PEGU *Tenem Range* Tak (Viangchan) Phitsanulok Hoi An
Bengal Henzada **Kho Sawai** Khon Kaen Tam Ky *SOUTH CHINA*
IRRAWADDY **Yangon** Nakhon Sawan **Plateau** Nakhon Phanom Quang Ngai **VIETNAM**
Bassein (Rangoon) Pegu **THAILAND** Ban Muang Kon Tum
C. Negrais MON Nakhon Ratchasima Ubon Ratchathani Pakxe *Ngoc Linh 2,600 m*

15° *Mouths of the Ayeyarwady* Kyonkadun Sara Buri Champasak Muang May Qui Nhon *SEA* Scarb Shoal

53 **MYANMAR INDIA** Tavoy **Bangkok** *Phanom Dongrak Mts* **CAMBODIA** Buon Ma Thuot Tuy Hoa

3 North Andaman I. TENASSERIM (Krung Thep) Chon Buri Battambang Nha Trang
Andaman Islands Palaw Rat Buri Chanthaburi Chang I. Kampong Cham De Lat Cam Ranh Phan Rang
Middle Andaman I. Mergui Chang I. Kut I. CAMBODIA VIETNAM Phan Thiet
S. Andaman I. *Phnum Aoral 1,771 m* Tay Ninh
Port Blair Little Andaman Island *Mergui Archipelago* **Phnom Penh** Kampong Saom (Phnum Penh) Bien Hoa
Chumphon **Ho Chi Minh City** (Saigon)
10° **ANDAMAN & NICOBAR** Long Xuyen My Tho
ISLANDS (INDIA) *Andaman* *Gulf* Phu Quoc I. Can Tho Rach Gia Bac Lieu
Nicobar Islands *Sea* *of* Phangan I. Samui I. *Thailand* Ca Mau Soc Trang *Spratly Islands* (Sovereignty disputed)
Camorta I. Isthmus of Kra Mui Ca Mau Con Son Pa
Car Nicobar Katchall I. Nakhon Si Thammarat Pue Princ
Little Nicobar I. Phuket Trang Songkhla Balabac

4 Great Nicobar I. Hat Yai Yala Bonggi I. MALAYSIA
We I. Sabang Alor Setar Kota Baharu Limbuak Sikuati
Banda Aceh Langkawi I. *Malay* **MALAYSIA** **Gunung Kinabalu 4,101 m** Kampong
Sungai Petani Pinang I. Peninsula Kuala Terengganu Kota Kinabalu Tuaran Sukau
Langsa Georgetown Taiping MAL. INDO. Natuna Is. Kuamut Lahad Datu Mostyn

5° *Strait of Malacca* Ipoh Kuantan **BRUNEI** Miri Pensiangan
Pusat Gayo Mts Telok Anson Natuna Is. Bandar Seri Begawan Lumbia Malinau
Gunung Leuser 3,466 m **Medan** Gunung Pasaman Bunguran I. Crocker Ra. Bunyu I.
Pematangsiantar **Kuala Lumpur** *Malaya* Anambas Is. Gunung Murud 2,438 m Tarakan
Tebingtinggi Shah Alam Subi I. **Sarawak**
Simeulue I. Kelang Seremban Sibu *Iran Mts* Gunung Liangpran 2,240 m

5 Tuangku Birus Melaka Segamat Tioman I. Saretok *Borneo*
Nias I. Sibolga Rupat I. Batu Pahat Keluang Kuching Kapuas Hulu Mts.
Banyak Islands Padangsidempuan Johor Baharu Mendatan Pamangkat MAL. INDO. *Kalimantan*
Pakanbaru **Singapore** Bengkalis I. **SINGAPORE** Tambelan Is. Singkawang Malang
Riau Islands Ngabang Samarinda

0° Equator *Batu Islands* Gunung Pasaman 2,912 m *Lingga* Pontianak *Schwaner Mts* Bukit Raya 2,278 m Balikpapan
Bukittinggi Payakumbuh Rengat *Is.* Sintang Maya I. Singkep I. Palangkaraya
Tanahbala I. Padang *Sumatra* Bangka I. Karimata I. Sampit Barabai
Siberut I. Gunung Kerinci 3,805 m Jambi Muntok Pangkalpinang Banjarmasin *Meratus Mts* Kotabaru

6 *Mentawai Islands* *Barisan Mountains* Tanjungpandan Belitung I. Sebuku I.
Sipura I. Curup **Palembang** Kangean I. Laut I.
Bengkulu Batuaja Menggala
Gunung Dempo 3,159 m *Greater* *Sunda* *Islands*
Kotabumi

5° Enggano I. Tanjungkarang *JAVA SEA* Bawean I. *Lesser*

INDIAN OCEAN Serang **Jakarta** Cirebon Pekalongan Madura Kangean Is.
Panaitan I. Bogor Tegal **Semarang** **Surabaya**
Bandung *Gunung Galunggung 2,958 m* Surakarta Madiun **Malang** Probolinggo
7 Cilacap Yogyakarta Kediri *Bali* *Gunung Agung 3,142 m* Moyo I.
Java *Gunung Kelud 1,676 m* Jember Gunung Agung *Sumbawa*
Gunung Semeru 3,676 m Denpasar Mataram
Lombok Sum

10°

Below Sea 200 500 1,000 1,500 2,000 4,000 6,000 m.
Sea Lev. Level 700 1,600 3,300 5,000 6,500 13,000 19,700 ft.

Southeastern Asia

Australia, New Zealand - Physical

LAMBERT CONFORMAL CONIC PROJECTION
© HAMMOND WORLD ATLAS CORP.

SCALE 1:19,400,000   OPTIMAL CONFORMAL PROJECTION

MILES 0   250   500   750
KILOMETERS 0   250   500   750

POPULATION OF CITIES AND TOWNS

☐ OVER 2,000,000   ☐ 500,000 — 999,999   ○ 50,000 — 99,999
☐ 1,000,000 — 1,999,999   ○ 100,000 — 199,999   ○ UNDER 50,000

AREA OF OPTIMIZATION
The red land which surrounds this map defines the "Area of Optimization." Within this bounding curve is the most accurate conformal map that can be made of the region. Outside the optimized area, distortion increases rapidly, and tears or other irregularities in the grid may occur.

Australia, New Zealand - Political

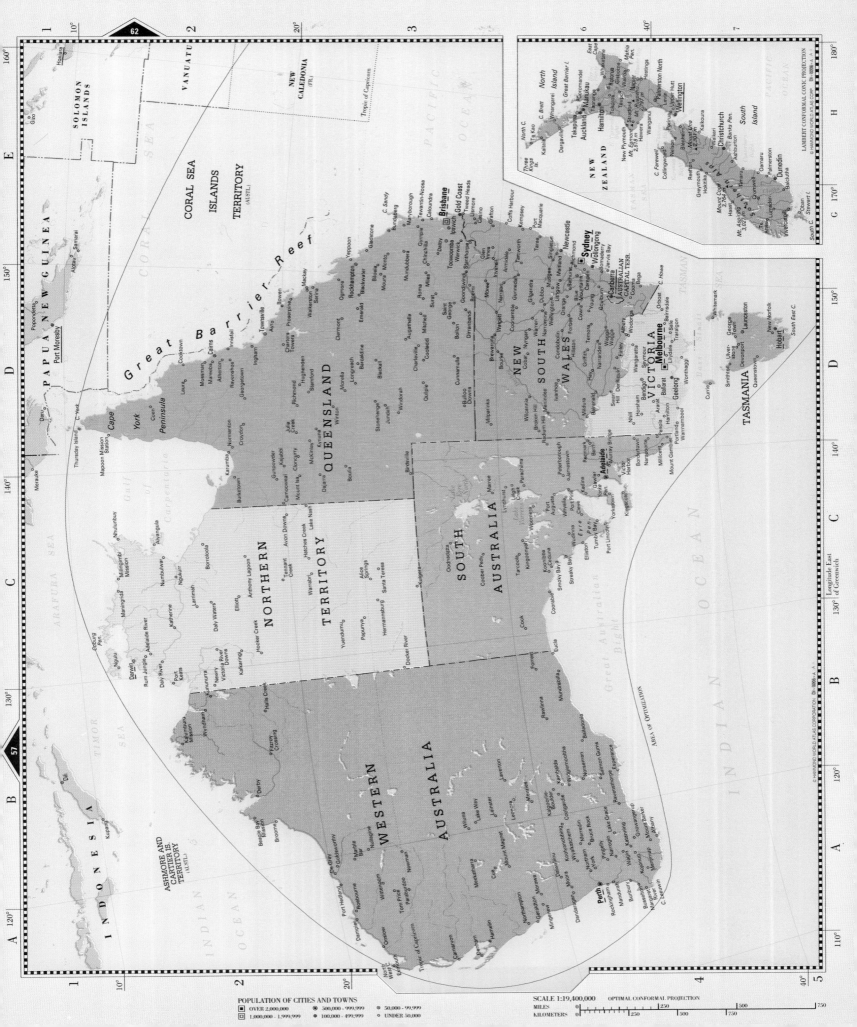

SOLOMON ISLANDS

VANUATU

NEW CALEDONIA (FR.)

CORAL SEA ISLANDS TERRITORY (AUSTL.)

PAPUA NEW GUINEA

INDONESIA

Great Barrier Reef

Cape York Peninsula

Gulf of Carpentaria

ARAFURA SEA

TIMOR SEA

ASHMORE AND CARTIER IS. TERRITORY (AUSTL.)

NORTHERN TERRITORY

QUEENSLAND

WESTERN AUSTRALIA

SOUTH AUSTRALIA

NEW SOUTH WALES

VICTORIA

TASMANIA

AUSTRALIAN CAPITAL TERR.

Brisbane

Sydney
Wollongong
Canberra

Melbourne
Geelong

Adelaide

Perth

Hobart

INDIAN OCEAN

PACIFIC OCEAN

CORAL SEA

TASMAN SEA

Great Australian Bight

AREA OF OPTIMIZATION

NEW ZEALAND

North Island

South Island

Southern Alps

Auckland
Hamilton
Wellington
Christchurch
Dunedin

Mt. Cook 3,764 m
Mt. Egmont 2,518 m
Mt. Aspiring 3,027 m
Mount Una 2,301 m

PACIFIC OCEAN

TASMAN SEA

LAMBERT CONFORMAL CONIC PROJECTION
© HAMMOND WORLD ATLAS CORP.

POPULATION OF CITIES AND TOWNS
▣ OVER 2,000,000 ● 500,000 - 999,999 ◦ 50,000 - 99,999
▢ 1,000,000 - 1,999,999 ● 100,000 - 499,999 ◦ UNDER 50,000

SCALE 1:19,400,000   OPTIMAL CONFORMAL PROJECTION
MILES   0   250   500   750
KILOMETERS   0   250   500   750

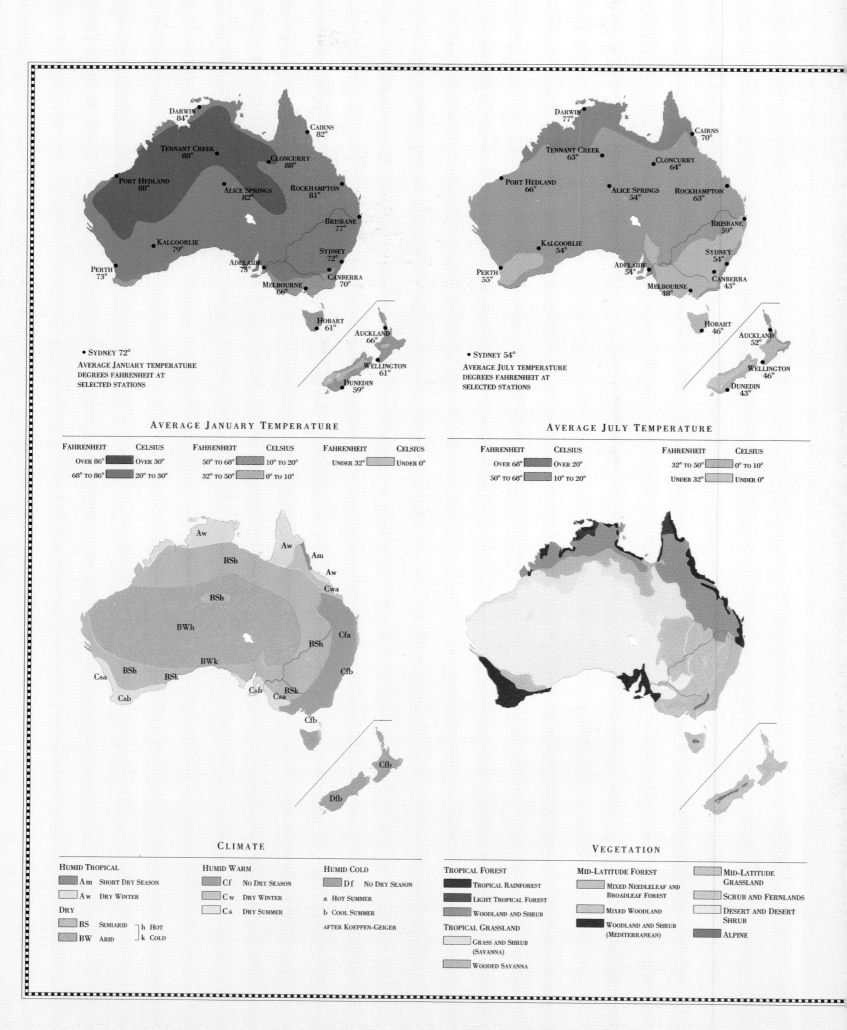

AVERAGE JANUARY TEMPERATURE

DARWIN 84°
CAIRNS 82°
TENNANT CREEK 88°
CLONCURRY 88°
PORT HEDLAND 88°
ALICE SPRINGS 82°
ROCKHAMPTON 81°
BRISBANE 77°
KALGOORLIE 79°
SYDNEY 72°
ADELAIDE 78°
CANBERRA 70°
PERTH 73°
MELBOURNE 66°
HOBART 61°
AUCKLAND 66°
WELLINGTON 61°
DUNEDIN 59°

• SYDNEY 72°
AVERAGE JANUARY TEMPERATURE
DEGREES FAHRENHEIT AT
SELECTED STATIONS

FAHRENHEIT	CELSIUS	FAHRENHEIT	CELSIUS	FAHRENHEIT	CELSIUS
OVER 86°	OVER 30°	50° TO 68°	10° TO 20°	UNDER 32°	UNDER 0°
68° TO 86°	20° TO 30°	32° TO 50°	0° TO 10°		

AVERAGE JULY TEMPERATURE

DARWIN 77°
CAIRNS 70°
TENNANT CREEK 63°
CLONCURRY 64°
PORT HEDLAND 66°
ALICE SPRINGS 54°
ROCKHAMPTON 63°
BRISBANE 59°
KALGOORLIE 54°
SYDNEY 54°
ADELAIDE 54°
CANBERRA 43°
PERTH 55°
MELBOURNE 48°
HOBART 46°
AUCKLAND 52°
WELLINGTON 46°
DUNEDIN 43°

• SYDNEY 54°
AVERAGE JULY TEMPERATURE
DEGREES FAHRENHEIT AT
SELECTED STATIONS

FAHRENHEIT	CELSIUS	FAHRENHEIT	CELSIUS
OVER 68°	OVER 20°	32° TO 50°	0° TO 10°
50° TO 68°	10° TO 20°	UNDER 32°	UNDER 0°

Climate map (upper labels)

Aw, Aw, Am, Aw, BSh, Cwa, BSh, BWh, Cfa, BSh, BWk, Csa, BSh, BSk, Cfb, Csb, BSk, Csa, Cfb, Cfb, Dfb

CLIMATE

HUMID TROPICAL
Am — SHORT DRY SEASON
Aw — DRY WINTER

DRY
BS — SEMIARID   h HOT
BW — ARID   k COLD

HUMID WARM
Cf — NO DRY SEASON
Cw — DRY WINTER
Cs — DRY SUMMER

HUMID COLD
Df — NO DRY SEASON
a HOT SUMMER
b COOL SUMMER

AFTER KOEPPEN-GEIGER

VEGETATION

TROPICAL FOREST
TROPICAL RAINFOREST
LIGHT TROPICAL FOREST
WOODLAND AND SHRUB

TROPICAL GRASSLAND
GRASS AND SHRUB (SAVANNA)
WOODED SAVANNA

MID-LATITUDE FOREST
MIXED NEEDLELEAF AND BROADLEAF FOREST
MIXED WOODLAND
WOODLAND AND SHRUB (MEDITERRANEAN)

MID-LATITUDE GRASSLAND
SCRUB AND FERNLANDS
DESERT AND DESERT SHRUB
ALPINE

Australia, New Zealand - Comparisons

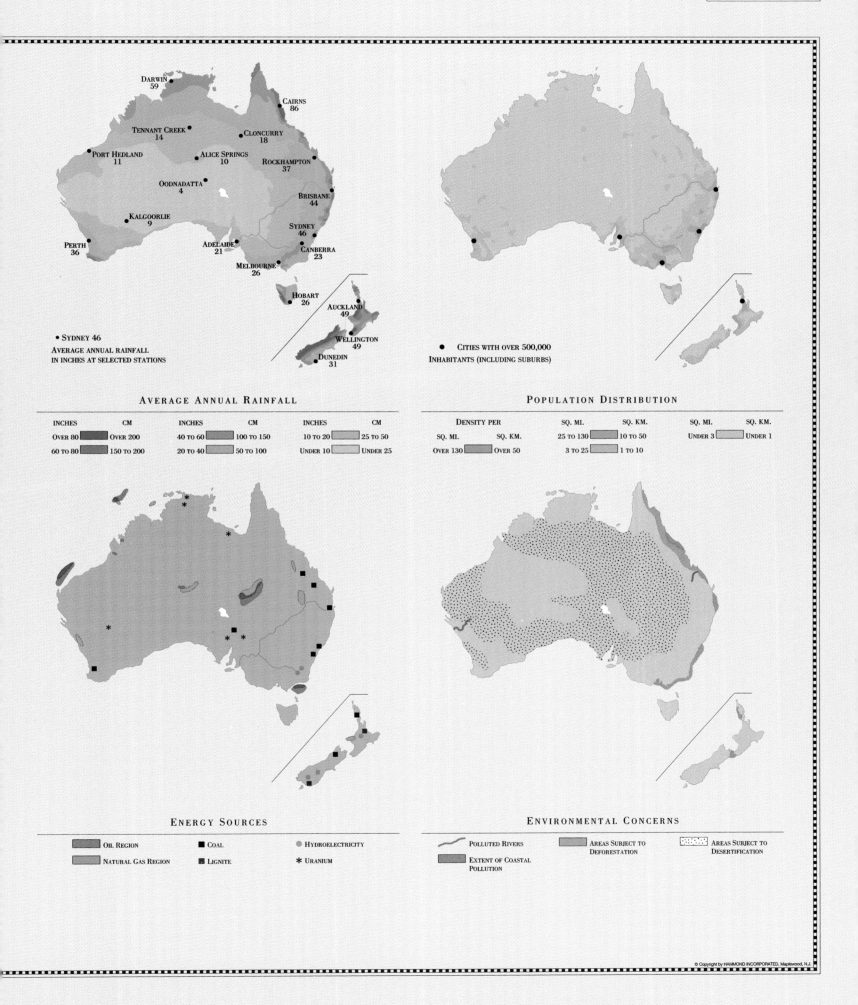

DARWIN 59
CAIRNS 86
TENNANT CREEK 14
CLONCURRY 18
PORT HEDLAND 11
ALICE SPRINGS 10
ROCKHAMPTON 37
OODNADATTA 4
BRISBANE 44
KALGOORLIE 9
SYDNEY 46
PERTH 36
ADELAIDE 21
CANBERRA 23
MELBOURNE 26
HOBART 26
AUCKLAND 49
WELLINGTON 49
DUNEDIN 31

• SYDNEY 46
AVERAGE ANNUAL RAINFALL
IN INCHES AT SELECTED STATIONS

• CITIES WITH OVER 500,000
INHABITANTS (INCLUDING SUBURBS)

AVERAGE ANNUAL RAINFALL

INCHES	CM	INCHES	CM	INCHES	CM
OVER 80	OVER 200	40 TO 60	100 TO 150	10 TO 20	25 TO 50
60 TO 80	150 TO 200	20 TO 40	50 TO 100	UNDER 10	UNDER 25

POPULATION DISTRIBUTION

DENSITY PER							
SQ. MI.	SQ. KM.	SQ. MI.	SQ. KM.	SQ. MI.	SQ. KM.	SQ. MI.	SQ. KM.
OVER 130	OVER 50	25 TO 130	10 TO 50	UNDER 3	UNDER 1		
		3 TO 25	1 TO 10				

ENERGY SOURCES

▬ OIL REGION	■ COAL	● HYDROELECTRICITY	
▬ NATURAL GAS REGION	■ LIGNITE	✳ URANIUM	

ENVIRONMENTAL CONCERNS

∿ POLLUTED RIVERS	▬ AREAS SUBJECT TO DEFORESTATION	⠿ AREAS SUBJECT TO DESERTIFICATION
▬ EXTENT OF COASTAL POLLUTION		

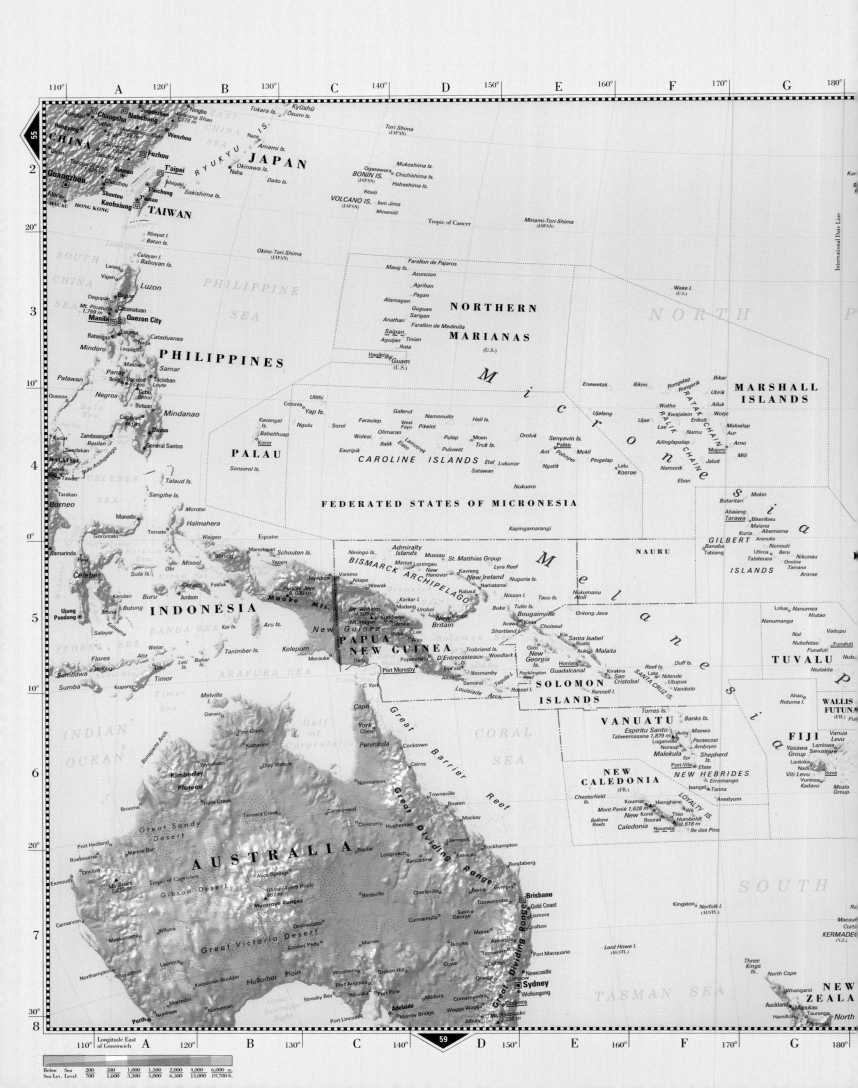

Below Sea 200 500 1,000 1,500 2,000 4,000 6,000 m.
Sea Lev. Level 700 1,600 3,300 5,000 6,500 13,000 19,700 ft.

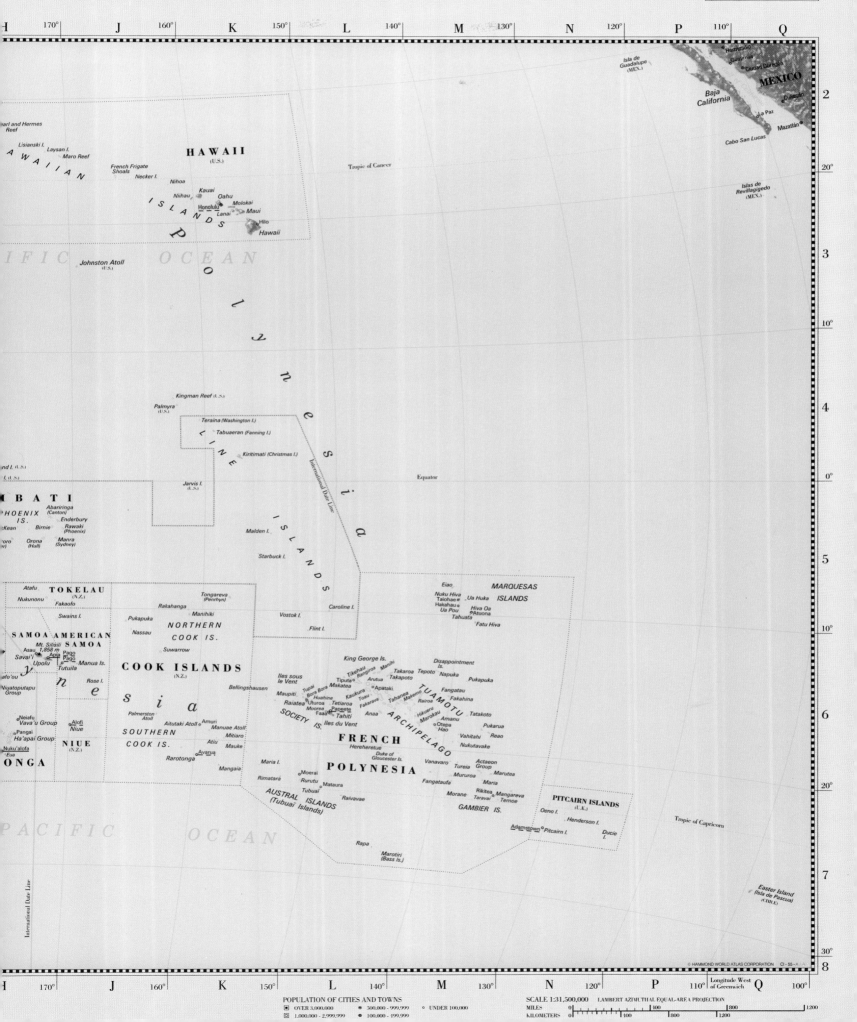

Africa - Physical

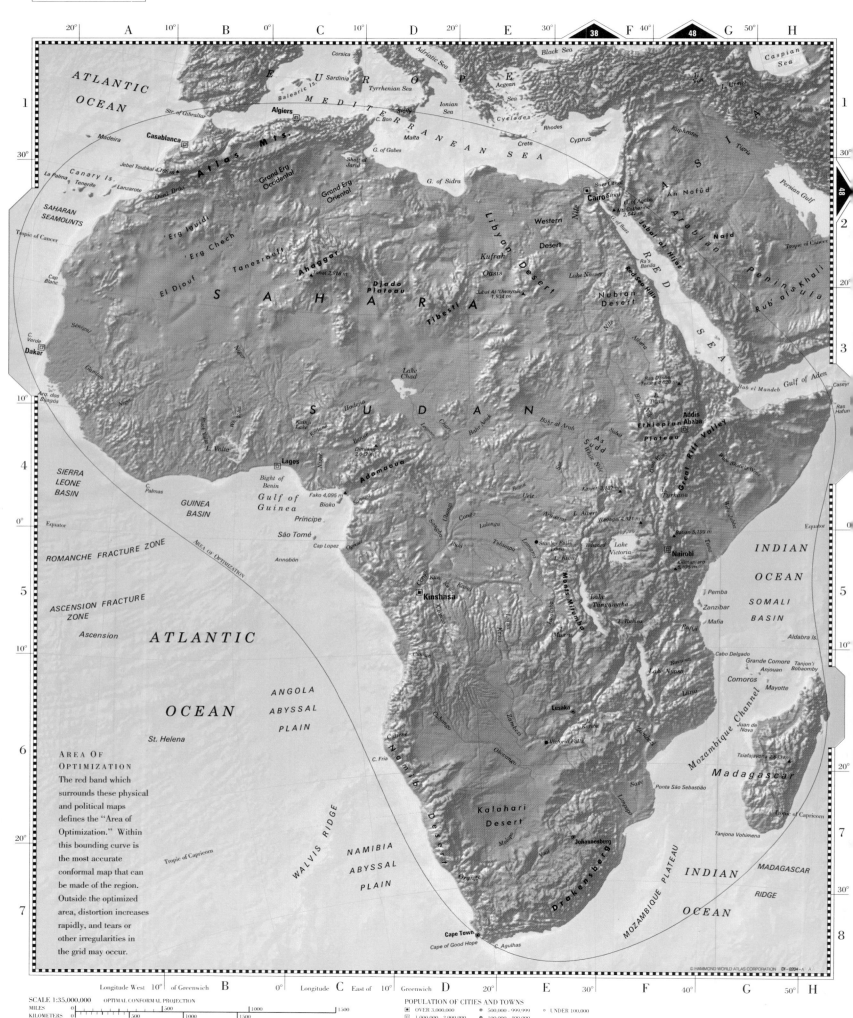

AREA OF OPTIMIZATION
The red band which surrounds these physical and political maps defines the "Area of Optimization." Within this bounding curve is the most accurate conformal map that can be made of the region. Outside the optimized area, distortion increases rapidly, and tears or other irregularities in the grid may occur.

SCALE 1:35,000,000   OPTIMAL CONFORMAL PROJECTION

MILES
KILOMETERS

POPULATION OF CITIES AND TOWNS
■ OVER 3,000,000   ● 500,000 - 999,999   ○ UNDER 100,000
□ 1,000,000 - 2,999,999   ● 100,000 - 499,999

© HAMMOND WORLD ATLAS CORPORATION

Africa - Political

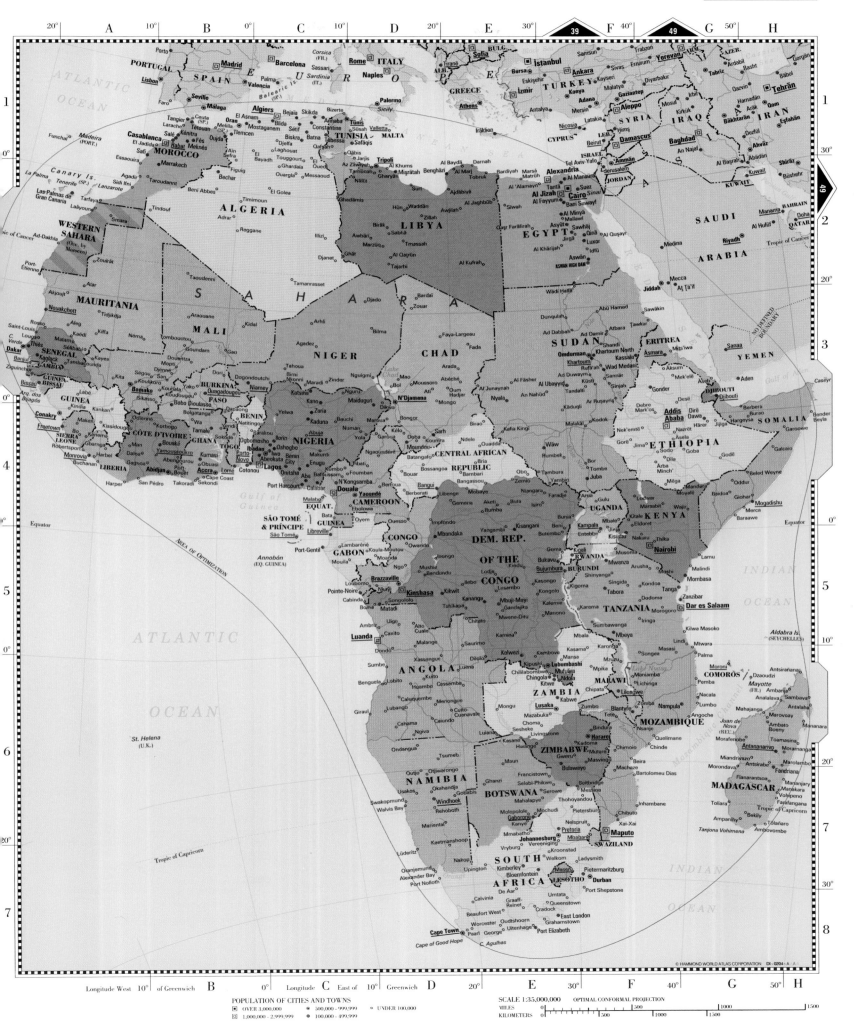

POPULATION OF CITIES AND TOWNS

☐ OVER 3,000,000   ● 500,000 - 999,999   ○ UNDER 100,000

☐ 1,000,000 - 2,999,999   ● 100,000 - 499,999

SCALE 1:35,000,000   OPTIMAL CONFORMAL PROJECTION

MILES

KILOMETERS

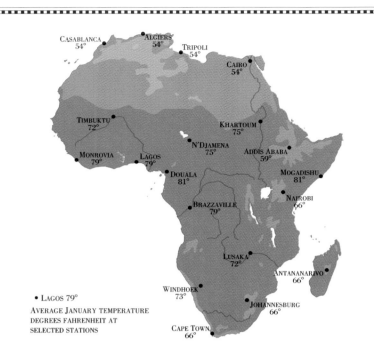

CASABLANCA 54°
ALGIERS 54°
TRIPOLI 54°
CAIRO 54°
TIMBUKTU 72°
KHARTOUM 75°
N'DJAMENA 75°
ADDIS ABABA 59°
MONROVIA 79°
LAGOS 79°
DOUALA 81°
MOGADISHU 81°
BRAZZAVILLE 79°
NAIROBI 66°
LUSAKA 72°
ANTANANARIVO 66°
WINDHOEK 73°
JOHANNESBURG 66°
CAPE TOWN 66°

• LAGOS 79°
AVERAGE JANUARY TEMPERATURE
DEGREES FAHRENHEIT AT
SELECTED STATIONS

AVERAGE JANUARY TEMPERATURE

FAHRENHEIT	CELSIUS	FAHRENHEIT	CELSIUS
OVER 68°	OVER 20°	32° TO 50°	0° TO 10°
50° TO 68°	10° TO 20°	UNDER 32°	UNDER 0°

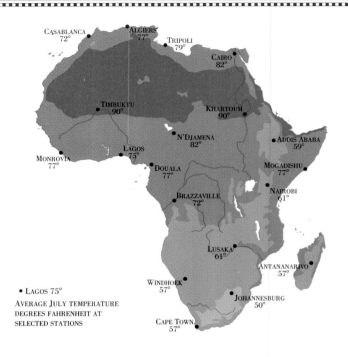

CASABLANCA 72°
ALGIERS 77°
TRIPOLI 79°
CAIRO 82°
TIMBUKTU 90°
KHARTOUM 90°
N'DJAMENA 82°
ADDIS ABABA 59°
MONROVIA 77°
LAGOS 75°
DOUALA 77°
MOGADISHU 77°
BRAZZAVILLE 72°
NAIROBI 61°
LUSAKA 61°
ANTANANARIVO 57°
WINDHOEK 57°
JOHANNESBURG 50°
CAPE TOWN 57°

• LAGOS 75°
AVERAGE JULY TEMPERATURE
DEGREES FAHRENHEIT AT
SELECTED STATIONS

AVERAGE JULY TEMPERATURE

FAHRENHEIT	CELSIUS	FAHRENHEIT	CELSIUS
OVER 86°	OVER 30°	50° TO 68°	10° TO 20°
68° TO 86°	20° TO 30°	UNDER 50°	UNDER 10°

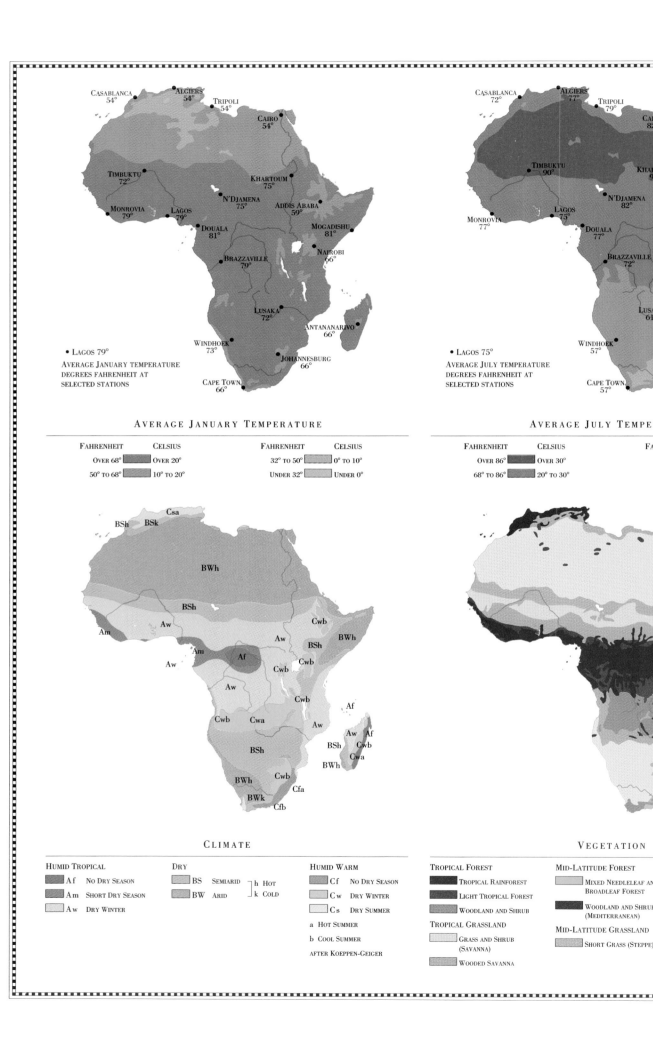

Csa
BSh
BSk
BWh
BSh
Am
Aw
Cwb
Aw
BSh
BWh
Am
Af
Cwb
Aw
Cwb
Aw
Cwb
Af
Cwb
Cwa
Aw
Aw
Af
BSh
Cwb
Cwa
BWh
BWh
Cwb
Cfa
BWk
Cfb

CLIMATE

HUMID TROPICAL		DRY			HUMID WARM	
Af	NO DRY SEASON	BS	SEMIARID	h HOT	Cf	NO DRY SEASON
Am	SHORT DRY SEASON	BW	ARID	k COLD	Cw	DRY WINTER
Aw	DRY WINTER				Cs	DRY SUMMER

a HOT SUMMER
b COOL SUMMER

AFTER KOEPPEN-GEIGER

VEGETATION

TROPICAL FOREST	MID-LATITUDE FOREST	DESERT AND DESERT SHRUB
TROPICAL RAINFOREST	MIXED NEEDLELEAF AND BROADLEAF FOREST	RIVER VALLEY AND OASIS
LIGHT TROPICAL FOREST	WOODLAND AND SHRUB (MEDITERRANEAN)	UNCLASSIFIED HIGHLANDS
WOODLAND AND SHRUB		
TROPICAL GRASSLAND	MID-LATITUDE GRASSLAND	
GRASS AND SHRUB (SAVANNA)	SHORT GRASS (STEPPE)	
WOODED SAVANNA		

Africa - Comparisons

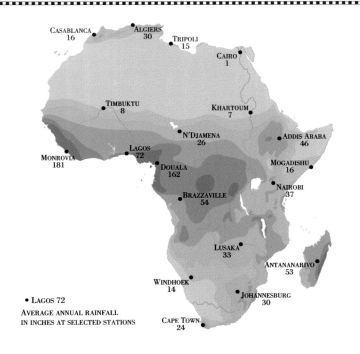

AVERAGE ANNUAL RAINFALL

INCHES	CM	INCHES	CM	INCHES	CM
OVER 80	OVER 200	40 TO 60	100 TO 150	10 TO 20	25 TO 50
60 TO 80	150 TO 200	20 TO 40	50 TO 100	UNDER 10	UNDER 25

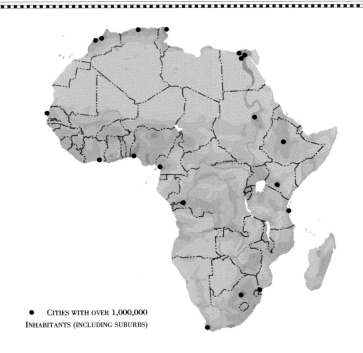

● LAGOS 72
AVERAGE ANNUAL RAINFALL
IN INCHES AT SELECTED STATIONS

● CITIES WITH OVER 1,000,000
INHABITANTS (INCLUDING SUBURBS)

POPULATION DISTRIBUTION

DENSITY PER		SQ. MI.	SQ. KM.	SQ. MI.	SQ. KM.
SQ. MI.	SQ. KM.	130 TO 260	50 TO 100	3 TO 25	1 TO 10
OVER 260	OVER 100	25 TO 130	10 TO 50	UNDER 3	UNDER 1

ENERGY SOURCES

OIL REGION   ■ COAL   ✳ URANIUM

NATURAL GAS REGION   ● HYDROELECTRICITY

ENVIRONMENTAL CONCERNS

POLLUTED RIVERS   AREAS SUBJECT TO DEFORESTATION    EXTENT OF ACID RAIN

EXTENT OF COASTAL POLLUTION    AREAS SUBJECT TO DESERTIFICATION

© Copyright by HAMMOND INCORPORATED, Maplewood, N.J.

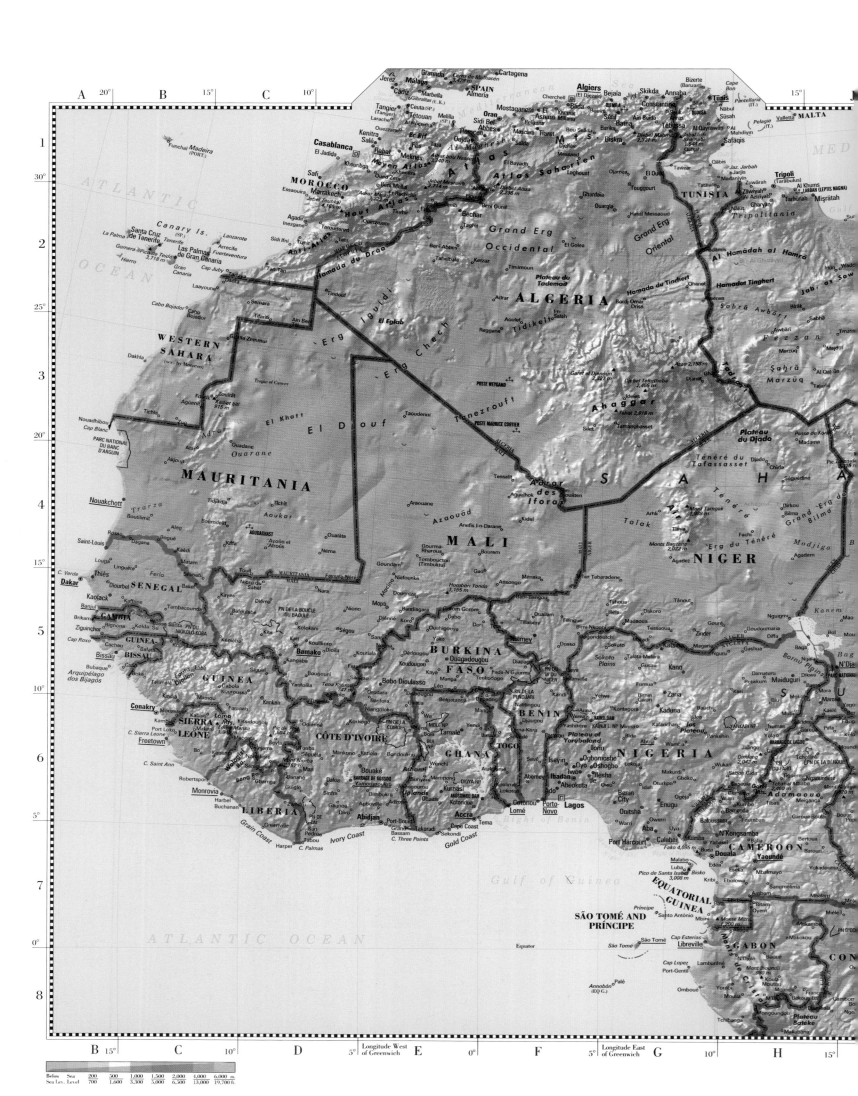

ATLANTIC OCEAN

MED

A 20°   B 15°   C 10°

1
30°
2
25°
3
Tropic of Cancer
20°
4
15°
5
10°
6
5°
7
0°
Equator
8

ATLANTIC OCEAN

Gulf of Guinea

SPAIN

Cartagena

Granada   Cerro de Mulhacén   Algiers (El Djezaïr)   Bizerte (Banzart)   Cape Bon

Málaga   Marbella   Almería   Cherchell   Bejaïa   Jijel   Skikda   Annaba   Tûnis   Pantelleria (IT.)

Cádiz   Gibraltar (U.K.)   Mostaganem   El Asnam   Milana   Bône   Sétif   Aïn Beïda   Constantine   Souk Ahras   SOUSSA   Valletta   MALTA

Tangier (Tanger)   Ceuta (SP.)   Melilla (SP.)   Al Hoceima   Oran   Tlemcen   Mascara   Tiaret   Bou Saâda   Barika   Batna   Tébessa   Al Qayrawan   Al Mahdiyah   Safaqis

Tétouan (Tetuán)   Sidi Bel Abbès   Khemis   Saïda   Djelfa   Biskra   Pelagie (IT.)

MOROCCO

Kenitra   Salé   Rabat   Meknès   Fès   Oujda   Laghouat   El Oued   Tripoli (Tarabulus)   MED

El Jadida   Casablanca   Khouribga   Beni Mellal   Djebel Ksel 2,008 m   Ghardaïa   Touggourt   Al Khums (LEPTIS MAGNA)   Tatawin   Madaniyin   Al Aziziyah   Tarhuna   Misratah

Safi   Essaouira   Marrakech   Adrar bou Nasseur 3,340 m   Djebel Mzarah 2,714 m   Djebel Aïssa 2,236 m   Béchar   Beni Ounif   **TUNISIA**   Qâbis   Jaz. Jarbah   Jarjis   Tripolitania

Agadir   Inezgane   Taroudannt   Ouarzazate   Tinrhir   Taghit   Hassi Messaoud   Nalut   Jabal Nafusah   Gharyan

Jebel Toubkal 4,165 m   Haut Atlas   Tinfou   Grand Erg Occidental   El Golea   Ouargla   Ghadamis   Al Hamadah al Hamra

Tiznit   Anti-Atlas   Tata   Hamada du Drâa   Beni Abbès   Tabelbala   Kerzaz   Timimoun   Al Hadir   Al Ghuzayyil   Awbari

Sidi Ifni   Tan-Tan   Tarfaya   Tindouf   Plateau du Tademaït   Hamada du Tinghert   Hamadat Tinghert   Jab. as Saw

Tarfaya   Cabo Bojador   Semara   Tifariti   Aïn Ben Tili   Adrar   Bordj Omar Driss   In Salah   Ohanet

Canary Is. (SP.)   La Palma   Santa Cruz de Tenerife   Tenerife   Lanzarote   Arrecife   Fuerteventura   Cap Juby   El Eglab   Reggane   Aoulef   Tidikelt   Bîrâk   Sabhā   Fezzan   Tmassa

Gomera   Pico de Teide 3,718 m   Las Palmas de Gran Canaria   Gran Canaria   Laayoune   Erg Iguidi   Erg Chech   Marzuq   Majdul   Marzuq

Hierro   **WESTERN SAHARA** (occ. by Morocco)   Dakhla   Güera Zemmur   Adrar   Zouérat   Kediet Ijill 915 m   Taoudenni   Garet el Djenoun 2,327 m   Djebel Teferedjeba 2,455 m   Azao 2,158 m   Şahrā' Al Qaṭrūn   Tajarhi

ALGERIA   POSTE WEYGAND   Silet   Tamanghasset   Iddles   Tahat 2,918 m   Djanet   Tadjourt

Cabo Bojador   Tichla   Aguenit   El Khatt   POSTE MAURICE CORTIER   Tanezrouft   Ahaggar

Nouadhibou   Cap Blanc   Atâr   Ouadane   El Djouf   ALGERIA MALI   Adrar des Iforas   Aguelhok   SAHARA   Plateau du Djado   Passe de Korizo   Pic Toussidé 3,315 m

PARC NATIONAL DU BANC D'ARGUIN   Akjoujt   Ouarane   Aoukar   Taoudenni   Tessalit   Boughessa   Madama   Chirfa   Séguédine

MAURITANIA   Tidjikja   Tîchît   Araouane   Azaouâd   Kidal   Arhş   Mont Tamgak 1,988 m   Djado   Achegour   Dirkou   Grand Erg de Bilma

Nouakchott   Trarza   Boutilimit   Tidjikja   Aoudaghast   Ayoûn el Atroûs   Ouatâta   Néma   Gourma-Rharous   Anefis In-Darane   Kidal   Talak   Timia   Bilma   Fachi   'Erg du Ténéré   Madjigo   Agadem

Nouâmghâr   Boulmit   Aleg   Bogué   Kiffa   Goundam   Tombouctou (Timbuktu)   Gao   Ménaka   In Tabaradene   Tânout   Agadez   Monts Bagzane 2,022 m

Saint-Louis   Rosso   Dagana   Kaédi   Matam   Nioro du Sahel   Nara   MAURITANIA MALI   Fassala-Néré   Niafounké   Ansongo   NIGER MALI   Tahoua   Dakoro   Nguigmi   Kanem   Mao

C. Verde   Louga   Linguère   Ferlo   Sélibaby   Toulel   Mopti   Hombori Tondo 1,155 m   Bani-Bangou   Filingué   Illéla   Madaoua   Goure   Tessaoua   Zinder   Goudoumaria   Diffa

Dakar   Thiès   Diourbel   MALI   PN DE LA BOUCLE DU BAOULÉ   Djenné   Douentza   Dori   Niamey   Dosso   Birni Nkonni   Maradi   Katsina   Magaria   Gashua   N'Djamena

Kaolack   Kaffrine   Tambacounda   Bakel   Diéma   Nioro   Niono   Ségou   Koro   Bandiagara   Batou Gorou   Tillabéry   Gaya   Dogondoutchi   Sokoto   Zaria   Kano   Potiskum   Damaturu   Maiduguri   Dikwa

SENEGAL   Banjul   Kaffrine   Kayes   Did?ni   Koutiala   San   Dédougou   Yako   Kaya   **BURKINA FASO**   Fada N'Gourma   Diapaga   Sokoto Plains   Talata Mafara   Funtua   Kaduna   Bauchi   Biu   Mora

GAMBIA   Bignona   Kolda   Su   Passe Santa   PN DU NIOKOLO-KOBA   Kita   Bamako   Koulikoro   Dioila   Koutiala   Ouagadougou   **BURKINA FASO**   Ouahigouya   Tenkodogo   PN W DU NIGER   Kandi   Kontagora   Zaria   Kafanchan   Jos   Los Plateau   YANKARI NP   Yola

Brikama   Ziguinchor   Cap Roxo   Bafatá   Kouroussa   Kankan   Bougouni   Yanfolila   Sikasso   Bobo Dioulasso   Léo   Manga   PN D'ARLY   PN DE LA PENDJARI   **NIGERIA**   Pankshin   Numan

Cacheu   **GUINEA-BISSAU**   Gabú   Dabola   Kouroussa   Kangaba   Orodara   Banfora   Bolgatanga   **BENIN**   Djougou   Jalingo   Dimango 2,042 m

BISSAU   Bubaque   Arquipélago dos Bijagós   Boké   Telimélé   Dinguiraye   Faranah   Mandiana   Odienné   Kong   Wa   Tamale   Natitingou   Parakou   Wawa   PN DE LA BÉNOUÉ

GUINEA   Kindia   Dabola   Oualata   Tena Kourou 747 m   Korhogo   Katiola   PN DE LA COMOÉ   Nikki   Oyo   Makurdi   Sabon Gida   Jimeta   Tibati   Ngaoundéré

Conakry   Mamou   Dalaba   Kabala   Kissidougou   Beyla   **CÔTE D'IVOIRE**   Katiola   Bouaké   PN DE LA MARAHOUÉ   Bondoukou   Bui   Bole   MOLE NP   Kaduna   KAINJI L. NP   Minna   Bida   Iseyin   Oyo   Ogbomosho   Ilesha   Benin City   Makurdi   Gboko   Bamenda   **CAMEROON**   Tignère

Kambia   Kabala   Mousoyoro   Mamou   **SIERRA LEONE**   Mani 1,948 m   Man   Séguéla   Tiéroko 1,504 m   Yamoussoukro   Sunyani   Mampong   Wenchi   **GHANA**   Kumasi   Ho   Lomé   **TOGO**   Savé   Abeokuta   **Ibadan**   Ife   Oshogbo   Enugu   Onitsha   Owerri   Kumba   Fumban   Banyo   Mont Oku 2,460 m   Mont Bambouto 2,740 m   Dimlang   Dschang   Bafoussam

Freetown   C. Sierra Leone   Makeni   Bo   Kenema   Mt. Nimba 1,752 m   Danané   Gagnoa   Daloa   Dimbokro   BARRAGE DE KOSSOU   Obuasi   Koforidua   AKOSOMBO DAM   DIGYA NP   Abomey   Porto-Novo   Cotonou   **Lagos**   Sapele   Warri   Aba   Port Harcourt   Calabar   N'Kongsamba   **Douala**   **Yaoundé**   Eséka   Sangmélima   Mbalmayo

C. Saint Ann   Robertsport   Kabala   Bong Range   Gbanga   Guiglo   Guigo   Sinfra   Sinfra   Kumasi   Oda   Atakpamé   Kpalimé   Keta   Cotonou   Bight of Benin   Benin City   Warri   Calabar   Kribi   Malabo   Luba   Pico de Santa Isabel 3,008 m   Bioko   Edéa   Ebolowa   Bitam   Oyem

Monrovia   Harbel   Buchanan   **LIBERIA**   Zwedru   Greenville   PN DE TAÏ   Tabou   Sassandra   San Pedro   Grand-Bassam   Takoradi   Sekondi   Cape Coast   Gold Coast   Porto-Novo   **Accra**   Tema   **EQUATORIAL GUINEA**   **SÃO TOMÉ AND PRÍNCIPE**   Príncipe   Santo António   Mbini   Monte Mitra 1,200 m   Cap Esterias   **Libreville**   **GABON**   Mitzik

Bong Range   Grain Coast   Ivory Coast   C. Palmas   Harper   San Pedro   C. Three Points   Cap Lopez   Port-Gentil   Lambaréné   **CON**

Equator   Annobón (EQ. G.)   Palé   São Tomé   Ombouté   Yombi   Koula-Moutou   Plateau Batéké   Franceville   Moanda

B 15°   C 10°   D 5° Longitude West of Greenwich   E 0°   F 5° Longitude East of Greenwich   G 10°   H 15°

Northern Africa

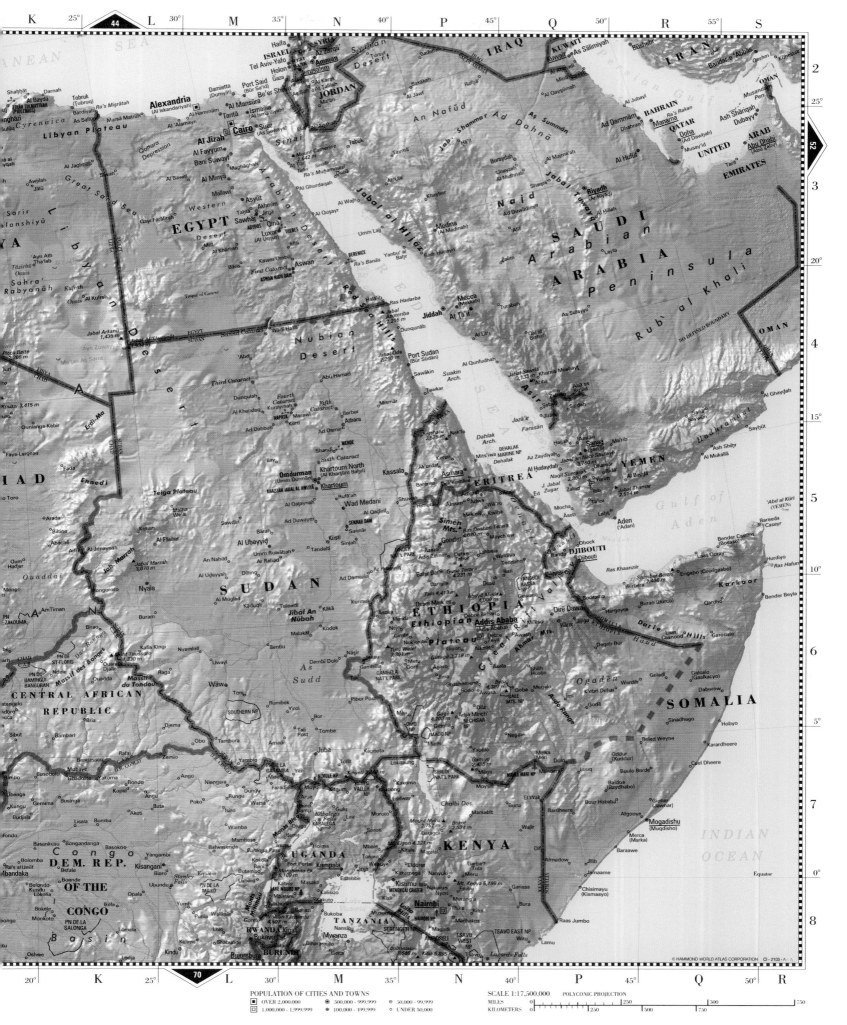

MEDITERRANEAN SEA

ISRAEL
Tel Aviv-Yafo
Holon
Jerusalem
Haifa
SYRIA
Amman
Zarqa
Syrian Desert
IRAQ
KUWAIT
Kuwait
Ash Sha'bīyah
IRAN
Būshehr
Bandar-e 'Abbās
Qeshm

Shahhāt Darnah
Al Baydā'
Tobruk (Tubruq)
Bardiyah Ra's Misrātah
Alexandria (Al Iskandariyah)
Damietta (Dumyāt)
Port Said (Būr Sa'īd)
Ismailia
Cairo
OMAN
Musandam Pen.

LIBYA
Cyrenaica
Libyan Plateau
Al Jizah
Suez
Sinai
JORDAN
An Nafūd
SAUDI
ARABIA
BAHRAIN
Manama
QATAR
Doha (Ad Dawhah)
UNITED ARAB EMIRATES
Abu Dhabi (Abū Zaby)

EGYPT
Western Desert
Qattara Depression
Asyūt
Al Minya
Arabian Desert
Medina (Al Madinah)
Najd
Riyadh (Ar Riyāḍ)

Great Sand Sea
Luxor (Al Uqsur)
THEBES
Aswan
ASWAN HIGH DAM
RED SEA
Mecca (Makkah)
Jiddah
At Tā'if
Arabian Peninsula
Rub' al Khali
OMAN

SUDAN
Nubian Desert
Port Sudan (Būr Sūdān)
YEMEN
Sana
Al Mukallā
Hadramawt
Saybūt

Khartoum
Omdurman (Umm Durmān)
Khartoum North (Al Kharṭūm Baḥrī)
Kassala
Asmara
ERITREA
DJIBOUTI
Djibouti
Gulf of Aden
'Abd al Kūri (YEMEN)
Aden ('Adan)

CHAD
Ennedi
Teiga Plateau
Al Ubayyid
ETHIOPIA
Ethiopian Plateau
Addis Ababa (Ādīs Ābeba)
Dirē Dawa
SOMALIA
Mogadishu (Muqdisho)

CENTRAL AFRICAN REPUBLIC
Jabal Marrah 4,070 m
Nyala
Ras Dashen Terara 4,620 m
Simēn Mts.
Gonder

SUDAN
Jibāl An Nūbah
As Sudd
Juba
UGANDA
Kampala
KENYA
Nairobi
INDIAN OCEAN
Equator

DEM. REP. OF THE CONGO
Congo Basin
Lake Victoria
RWANDA
Kigali
BURUNDI
Bujumbura
TANZANIA
Kibo 5,895 m
Mwanza

POPULATION OF CITIES AND TOWNS
■ OVER 2,000,000 ● 500,000 - 999,999 ◉ 50,000 - 99,999
□ 1,000,000 - 1,999,999 ● 100,000 - 199,999 ○ UNDER 50,000

SCALE 1:17,500,000 POLYCONIC PROJECTION
MILES 0 250 500 750
KILOMETERS 0 250 500 750

Southern Africa

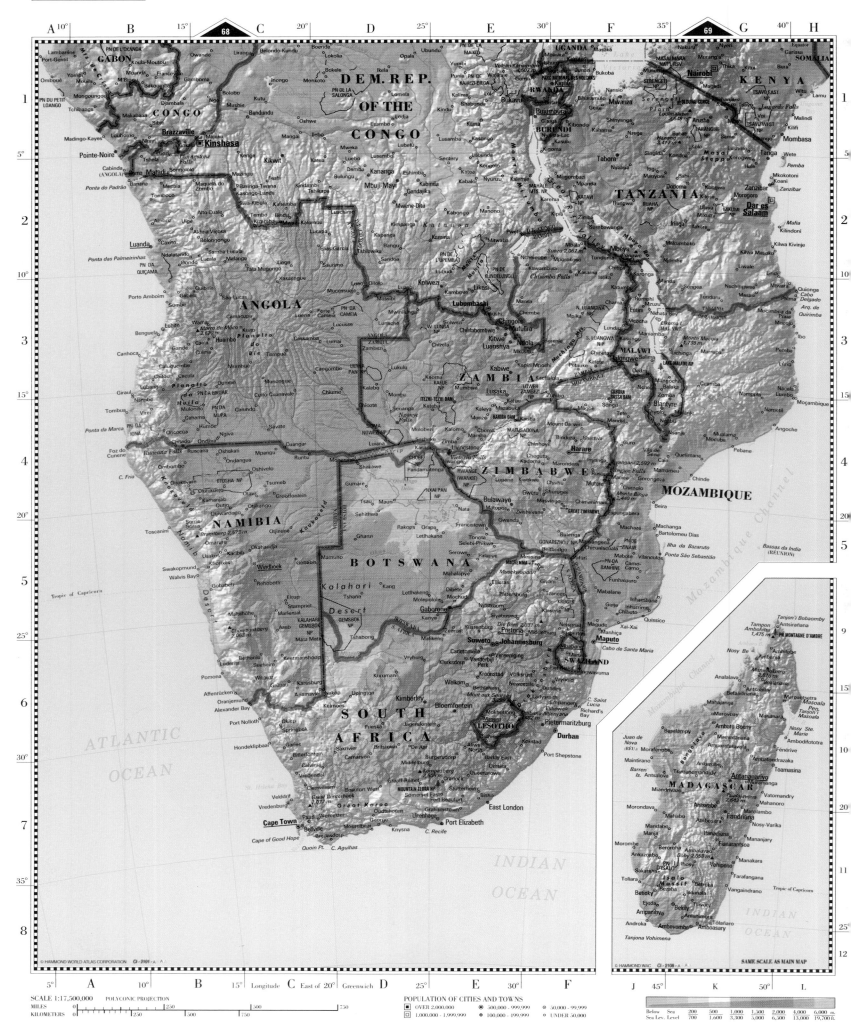

POPULATION OF CITIES AND TOWNS
- ■ OVER 2,000,000
- ◻ 1,000,000 - 1,999,999
- ⬤ 500,000 - 999,999
- ⬤ 100,000 - 199,999
- ● 50,000 - 99,999
- ● UNDER 50,000

SCALE 1:17,500,000   POLYCONIC PROJECTION

MILES

KILOMETERS

SAME SCALE AS MAIN MAP

	Below Sea	200	500	1,000	1,500	2,000	4,000	6,000 m.
	Sea Lev. Level	700	1,600	3,300	5,000	6,500	13,000	19,700 ft.

Arctic Regions, Antarctica

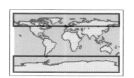

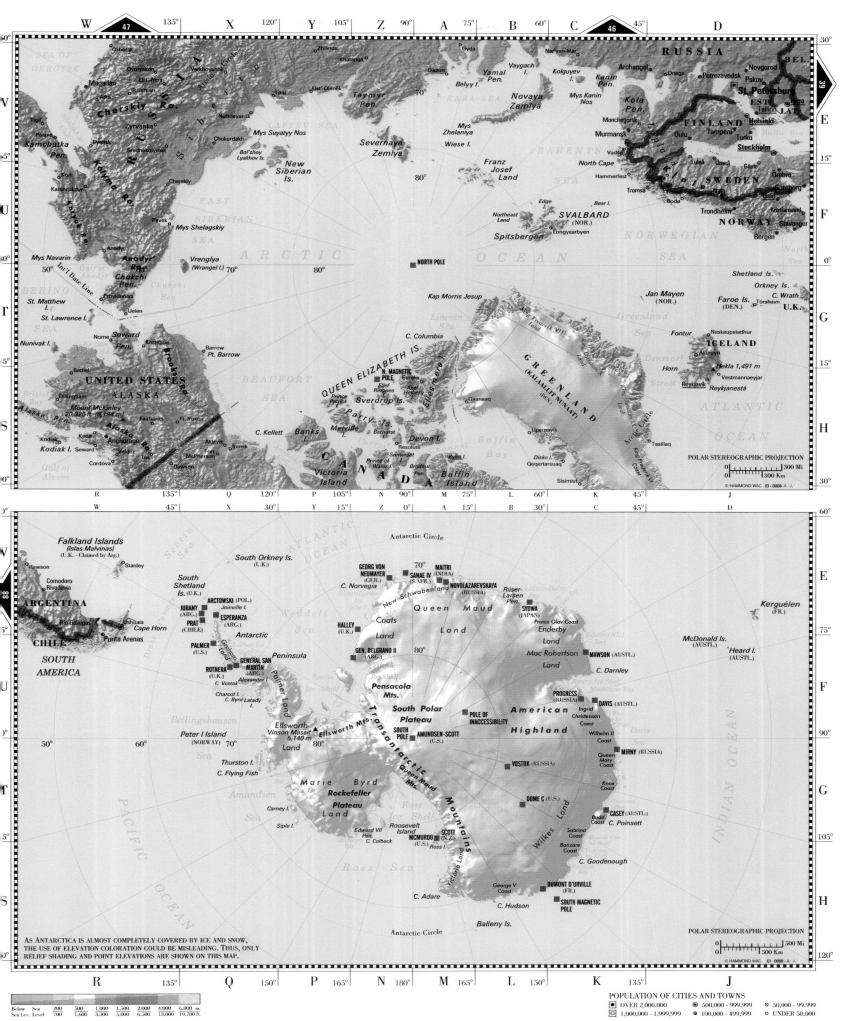

POLAR STEREOGRAPHIC PROJECTION

AS ANTARCTICA IS ALMOST COMPLETELY COVERED BY ICE AND SNOW,
THE USE OF ELEVATION COLORATION COULD BE MISLEADING. THUS, ONLY
RELIEF SHADING AND POINT ELEVATIONS ARE SHOWN ON THIS MAP.

POPULATION OF CITIES AND TOWNS
- ■ OVER 2,000,000
- ◉ 500,000 - 999,999
- ⊙ 50,000 - 99,999
- ▣ 1,000,000 - 1,999,999
- ◎ 100,000 - 499,999
- ○ UNDER 50,000

North America - Physical

AREA OF OPTIMIZATION

The red band which surrounds these physical and political maps defines the "Area of Optimization." Within this bounding curve is the most accurate conformal map that can be made of the region. Outside the optimized area, distortion increases rapidly, and tears or other irregularities in the grid may occur.

SCALE 1:35,000,000

MILES 0   500   1000   1500

KILOMETERS 0   500   1000   1500

POPULATION OF CITIES AND TOWNS
- ⬛ OVER 3,000,000
- ⬛ 1,000,000 - 2,999,999
- ⦿ 500,000 - 999,999
- ● 100,000 - 199,999
- ○ UNDER 100,000

© Hammond World Atlas Corporation   CI - 1076 - A

North America - Political

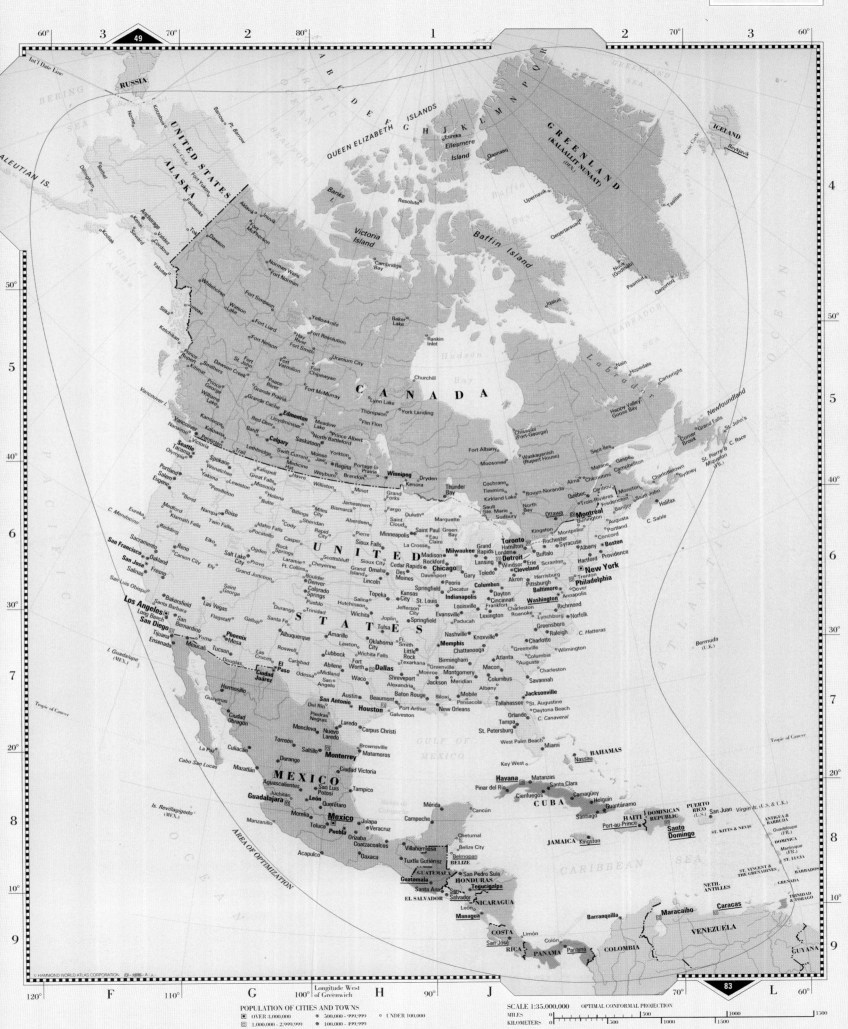

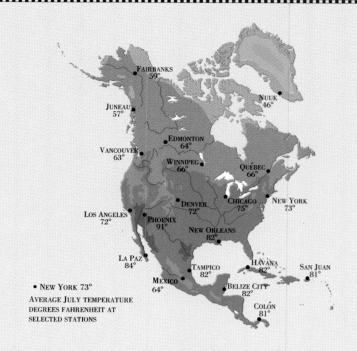

FAIRBANKS -11°
NUUK 18°
JUNEAU 28°
EDMONTON 7°
VANCOUVER 37°
WINNIPEG 0°
QUÉBEC 12°
DENVER 30°
CHICAGO 27°
NEW YORK 34°
LOS ANGELES 55°
PHOENIX 52°
NEW ORLEANS 55°
LA PAZ 63°
TAMPICO 64°
HAVANA 72°
SAN JUAN 75°
MEXICO 54°
BELIZE CITY 73°
COLÓN 81°

• NEW YORK 34°
AVERAGE JANUARY TEMPERATURE
DEGREES FAHRENHEIT AT
SELECTED STATIONS

AVERAGE JANUARY TEMPERATURE

FAHRENHEIT	CELSIUS	FAHRENHEIT	CELSIUS	FAHRENHEIT	CELSIUS
OVER 68°	OVER 20°	14° TO 32°	-10° TO 0°	-40° TO -22°	-40° TO -30°
50° TO 68°	10° TO 20°	-4° TO 14°	-20° TO -10°	UNDER -40°	UNDER -40°
32° TO 50°	0° TO 10°	-22° TO -4°	-30° TO -20°		

FAIRBANKS 59°
NUUK 46°
JUNEAU 57°
EDMONTON 64°
VANCOUVER 63°
WINNIPEG 66°
QUÉBEC 66°
DENVER 72°
CHICAGO 75°
NEW YORK 73°
LOS ANGELES 72°
PHOENIX 91°
NEW ORLEANS 82°
LA PAZ 84°
TAMPICO 82°
HAVANA 82°
SAN JUAN 81°
MEXICO 64°
BELIZE CITY 82°
COLÓN 81°

• NEW YORK 73°
AVERAGE JULY TEMPERATURE
DEGREES FAHRENHEIT AT
SELECTED STATIONS

AVERAGE JULY TEMPERATURE

FAHRENHEIT	CELSIUS	FAHRENHEIT	CELSIUS	FAHRENHEIT	CELSIUS
OVER 86°	OVER 30°	50° TO 68°	10° TO 20°	14° TO 32°	-10° TO 0°
68° TO 86°	20° TO 30°	32° TO 50°	0° TO 10°	UNDER 14°	UNDER -10°

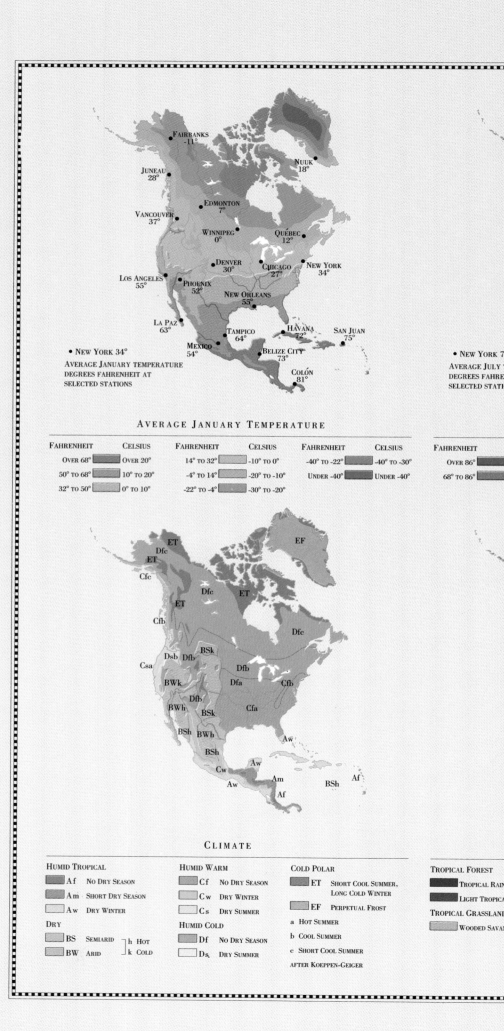
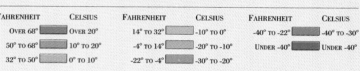
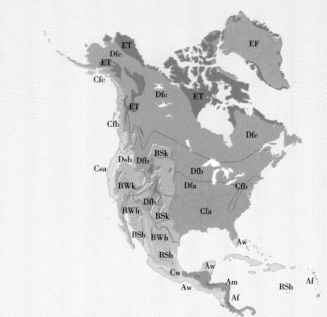

ET
Dfc
ET
Cfc
EF
Dfc
ET
Cfb
ET
Dfc
Csa
Dsb Dfb
BSk
Dfb
BWk
Dfa
Cfb
Dfb
BWh
BSk
Cfa
BSh BWh
BSh
Aw
Cw
Aw
Am
BSh
Af
Aw
Af

CLIMATE

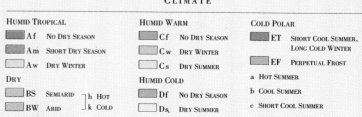

HUMID TROPICAL			HUMID WARM			COLD POLAR	
	Af	NO DRY SEASON		Cf	NO DRY SEASON	ET	SHORT COOL SUMMER, LONG COLD WINTER
	Am	SHORT DRY SEASON		Cw	DRY WINTER	EF	PERPETUAL FROST
	Aw	DRY WINTER		Cs	DRY SUMMER	a	HOT SUMMER
DRY			HUMID COLD			b	COOL SUMMER
	BS	SEMIARID	h HOT		Df	NO DRY SEASON	c	SHORT COOL SUMMER
	BW	ARID	k COLD		Ds	DRY SUMMER		
						AFTER KOEPPEN-GEIGER	

VEGETATION

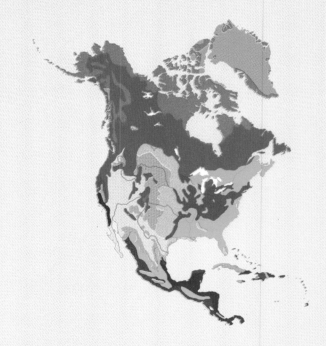

TROPICAL FOREST	MID-LATITUDE FOREST	MID-LATITUDE GRASSLAND
TROPICAL RAINFOREST	NEEDLELEAF FOREST	SHORT GRASS (STEPPE)
LIGHT TROPICAL FOREST	BROADLEAF FOREST	TALL GRASS (PRAIRIE)
TROPICAL GRASSLAND	MIXED NEEDLELEAF AND BROADLEAF FOREST	DESERT AND DESERT SHRUB
WOODED SAVANNA	WOODLAND AND SHRUB (MEDITERRANEAN)	TUNDRA AND ALPINE
		PERMANENT ICE COVER

North America - Comparisons

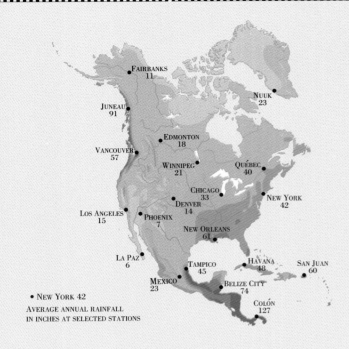

FAIRBANKS
11

NUUK
23

JUNEAU
91

EDMONTON
18

VANCOUVER
57

WINNIPEG
21

QUÉBEC
40

CHICAGO
33

NEW YORK
42

DENVER
14

LOS ANGELES
15

PHOENIX
7

NEW ORLEANS
61

LA PAZ
6

TAMPICO
45

HAVANA
48

SAN JUAN
60

MEXICO
23

BELIZE CITY
74

COLÓN
127

● NEW YORK 42
AVERAGE ANNUAL RAINFALL
IN INCHES AT SELECTED STATIONS

AVERAGE ANNUAL RAINFALL

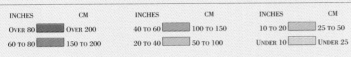

INCHES	CM	INCHES	CM	INCHES	CM
OVER 80	OVER 200	40 TO 60	100 TO 150	10 TO 20	25 TO 50
60 TO 80	150 TO 200	20 TO 40	50 TO 100	UNDER 10	UNDER 25

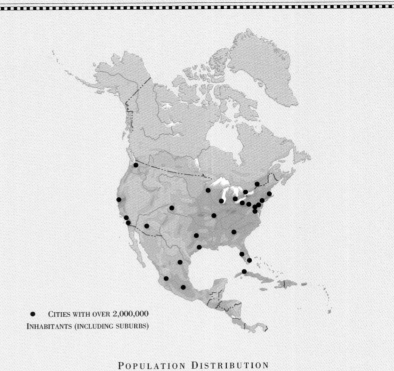

● CITIES WITH OVER 2,000,000
INHABITANTS (INCLUDING SUBURBS)

POPULATION DISTRIBUTION

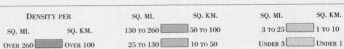

DENSITY PER							
SQ. MI.	SQ. KM.	SQ. MI.	SQ. KM.	SQ. MI.	SQ. KM.		
OVER 260	OVER 100	130 TO 260	50 TO 100	3 TO 25	1 TO 10		
		25 TO 130	10 TO 50	UNDER 3	UNDER 1		

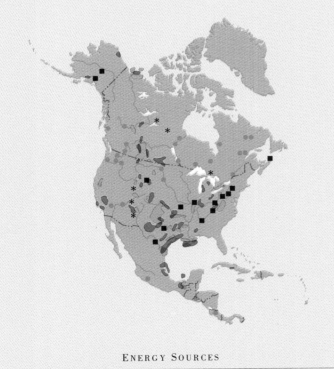

ENERGY SOURCES

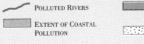

▬ OIL REGION	■ COAL	✳ URANIUM	
▬ NATURAL GAS REGION	● HYDROELECTRICITY		

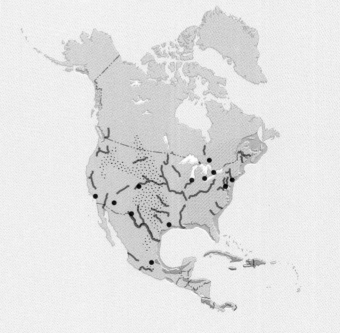

ENVIRONMENTAL CONCERNS

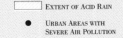

∿ POLLUTED RIVERS	AREAS SUBJECT TO DEFORESTATION	EXTENT OF ACID RAIN
EXTENT OF COASTAL POLLUTION	AREAS SUBJECT TO DESERTIFICATION	● URBAN AREAS WITH SEVERE AIR POLLUTION

POPULATION OF CITIES AND TOWNS

■ OVER 2,000,000   ◨ 500,000 - 999,999   ◉ 50,000 - 99,999
▣ 1,000,000 - 1,999,999   ● 100,000 - 499,999   ○ UNDER 50,000

SCALE 1:14,000,000   LAMBERT CONFORMAL CONIC PROJECTION

MILES   0   200   400
KILOMETERS   0   200   400   600

© HAMMOND WORLD ATLAS CORPORATION

Eastern United States, Southeastern Canada

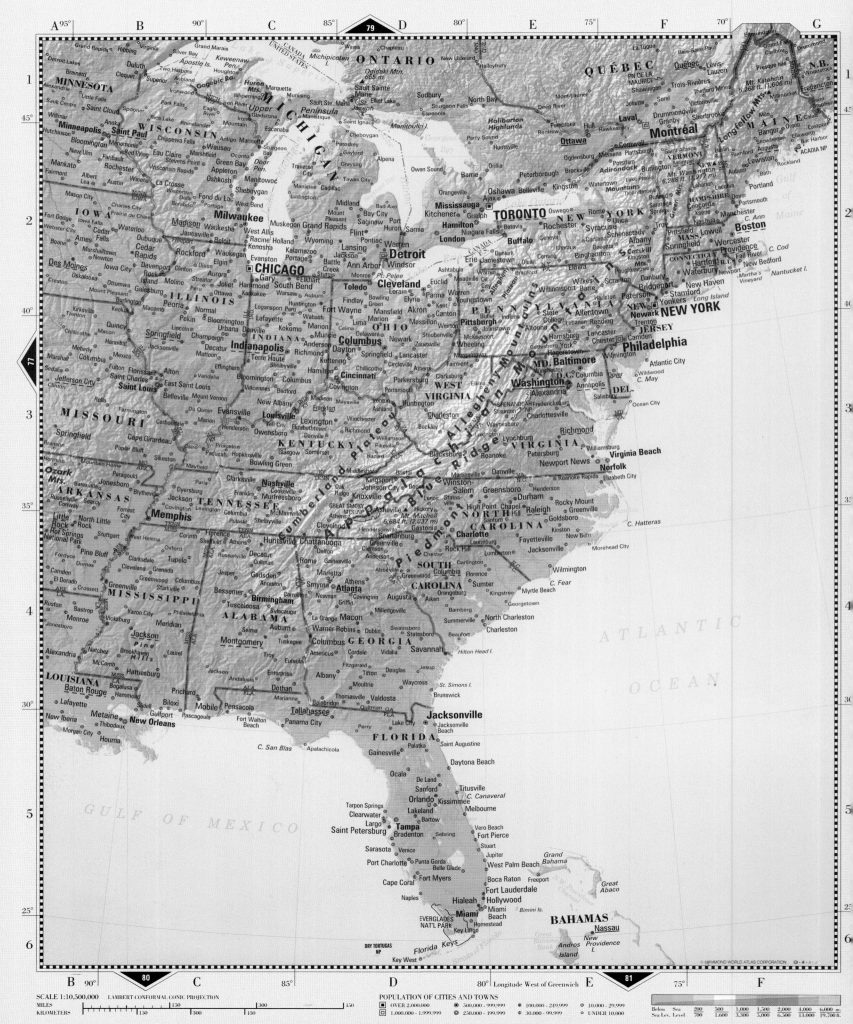

SCALE 1:10,500,000   LAMBERT CONFORMAL CONIC PROJECTION

MILES

KILOMETERS

POPULATION OF CITIES AND TOWNS

■ OVER 2,000,000   ● 500,000 - 999,999   ● 100,000 - 249,999   ○ 10,000 - 29,999
□ 1,000,000 - 1,999,999   ● 250,000 - 199,999   ● 30,000 - 99,999   ○ UNDER 10,000

	Below Sea	200	500	1,000	1,500	2,000	4,000	6,000 m.
	Sea Lev. Level	700	1,600	3,300	5,000	6,500	13,000	19,700 ft.

Canada

POPULATION OF CITIES AND TOWNS

- ■ OVER 2,000,000
- ◉ 500,000 - 999,999
- ◉ 50,000 - 99,999
- ▣ 1,000,000 - 1,999,999
- ● 100,000 - 499,999
- ○ UNDER 50,000

SCALE 1:21,000,000   LAMBERT CONFORMAL CONIC PROJECTION

MILES

KILOMETERS

Mexico, Central America and West Indies

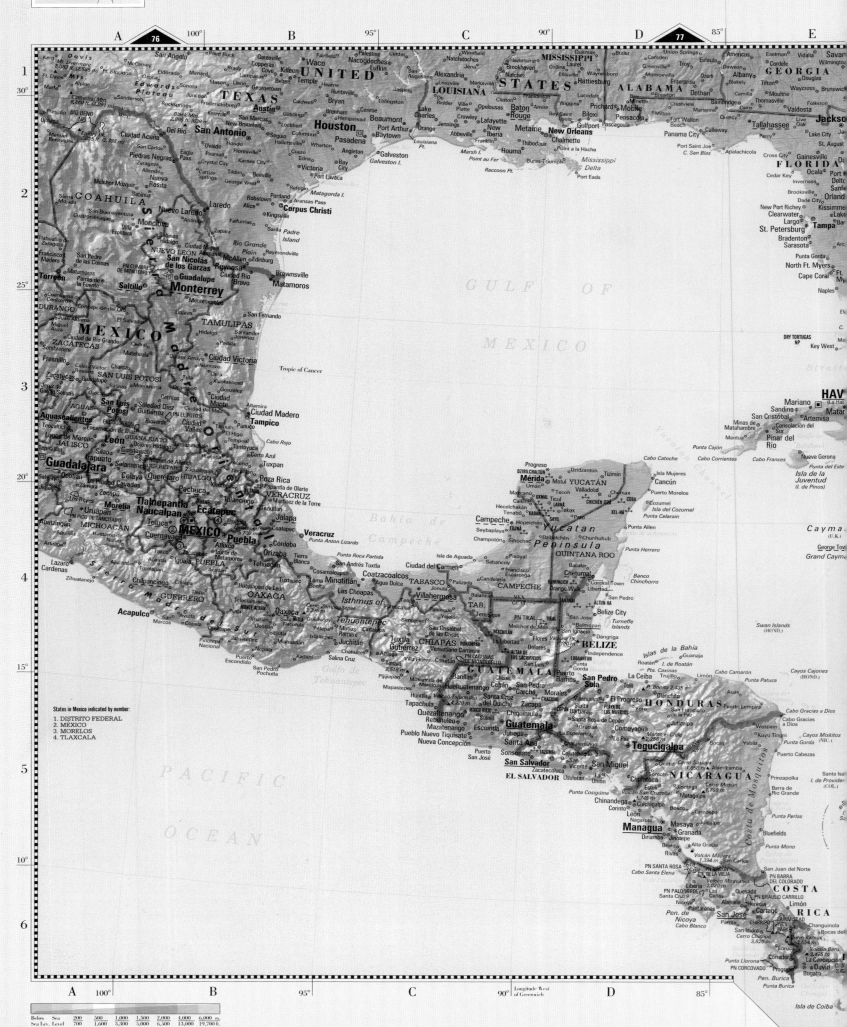

States in Mexico indicated by number:
1. DISTRITO FEDERAL
2. MÉXICO
3. MORELOS
4. TLAXCALA

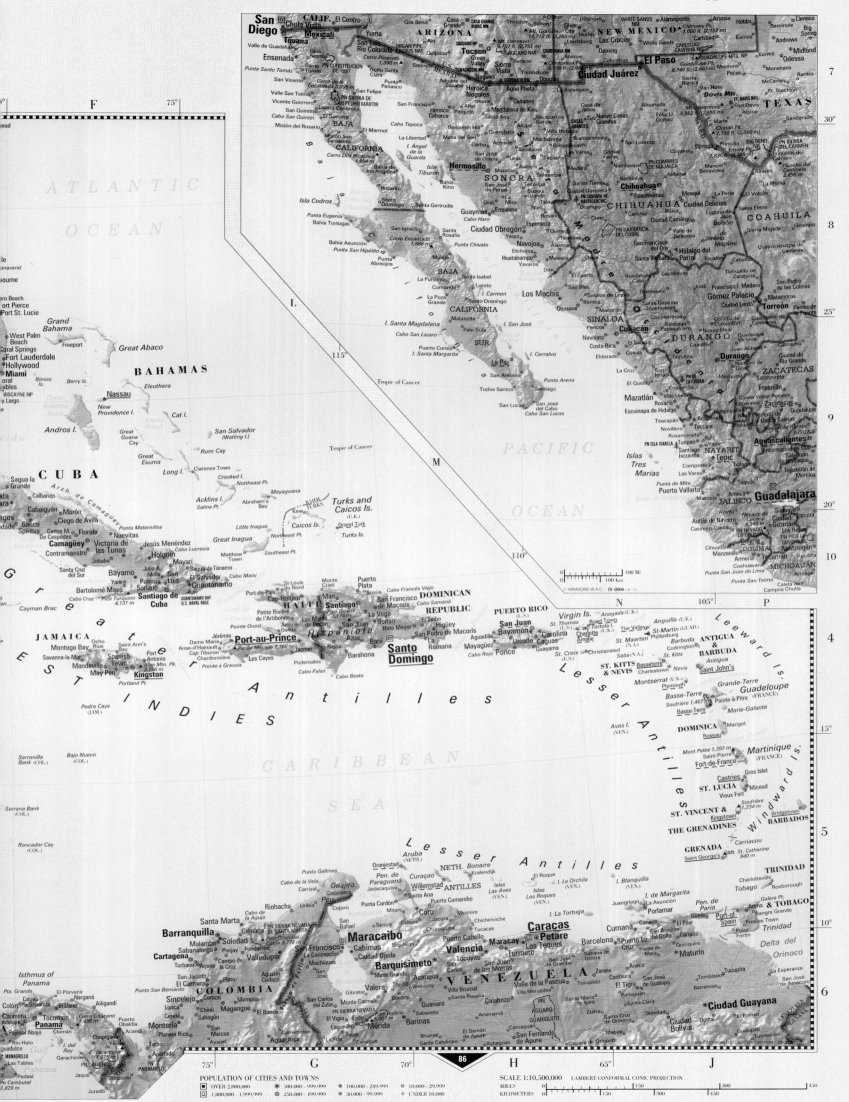

South America - Physical

AREA OF OPTIMIZATION
The red band which surrounds these physical and political maps defines the "Area of Optimization." Within this bounding curve is the most accurate conformal map that can be made of the region. Outside the optimized area, distortion increases rapidly, and tears or other irregularities in the grid may occur.

POPULATION OF CITIES AND TOWNS
■ OVER 3,000,000   ● 500,000 - 999,999   ○ UNDER 100,000
☐ 1,000,000 - 2,999,999   ● 100,000 - 199,999

© HAMMOND WORLD ATLAS CORPORATION   CI-1069-A

SCALE 1:28,000,000   OPTIMAL CONFORMAL PROJECTION
MILES
KILOMETERS

South America - Political

POPULATION OF CITIES AND TOWNS

■ OVER 3,000,000   ● 500,000 - 999,999   ○ UNDER 100,000
▣ 1,000,000 - 2,999,999   ◉ 100,000 - 199,999

SCALE 1:28,000,000   OPTIMAL CONFORMAL PROJECTION

MILES   0   400   800   1200
KILOMETERS   0   400   800   1200

BARRANQUILLA 79°
CARACAS 66°
PARAMARIBO 79°
BOGOTÁ 57°
QUITO 55°
MANAUS 79°
FORTALEZA 81°
LIMA 72°
LA PAZ 52°
BRASÍLIA 73°
ANTOFAGASTA 68°
RÍO DE JANEIRO 79°
ASUNCIÓN 84°
CURITIBA 68°
SANTIAGO 66°
BUENOS AIRES 73°
COMODORO RIVADAVIA 64°
RÍO GRANDE 48°

• LIMA 72°
AVERAGE JANUARY TEMPERATURE
DEGREES FAHRENHEIT AT
SELECTED STATIONS

AVERAGE JANUARY TEMPERATURE

FAHRENHEIT	CELSIUS	FAHRENHEIT	CELSIUS	FAHRENHEIT	CELSIUS
OVER 86°	OVER 30°	50° TO 68°	10° TO 20°	UNDER 32°	UNDER 0°
68° TO 86°	20° TO 30°	32° TO 50°	0° TO 10°		

BARRANQUILLA 82°
CARACAS 70°
PARAMARIBO 81°
BOGOTÁ 57°
QUITO 55°
MANAUS 81°
FORTALEZA 79°
LIMA 59°
LA PAZ 46°
BRASÍLIA 64°
ANTOFAGASTA 55°
RÍO DE JANEIRO 66°
ASUNCIÓN 64°
CURITIBA 55°
SANTIAGO 46°
BUENOS AIRES 52°
COMODORO RIVADAVIA 45°
RÍO GRANDE 34°

• LIMA 59°
AVERAGE JULY TEMPERATURE
DEGREES FAHRENHEIT AT
SELECTED STATIONS

AVERAGE JULY TEMPERATURE

FAHRENHEIT	CELSIUS	FAHRENHEIT	CELSIUS	FAHRENHEIT	CELSIUS
OVER 86°	OVER 30°	50° TO 68°	10° TO 20°	UNDER 32°	UNDER 0°
68° TO 86°	20° TO 30°	32° TO 50°	0° TO 10°		

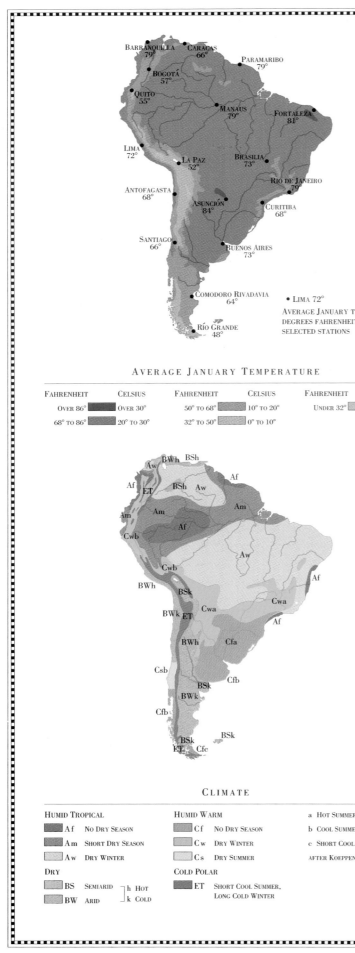

BWh
BSh
Aw
Af
Af
ET
BSh
Aw
Am
Am
Am
Cwb
Af
Aw
Af
Cwb
BWh
BSk
Cwa
BWk
ET
Cwa
Af
BWh
Cfa
Csb
BSk
Cfb
BWk
Cfb
BSk
BSk
ET
Cfc

CLIMATE

HUMID TROPICAL
Af NO DRY SEASON
Am SHORT DRY SEASON
Aw DRY WINTER

DRY
BS SEMIARID ⎤ h HOT
BW ARID ⎦ k COLD

HUMID WARM
Cf NO DRY SEASON
Cw DRY WINTER
Cs DRY SUMMER

COLD POLAR
ET SHORT COOL SUMMER, LONG COLD WINTER

a HOT SUMMER
b COOL SUMMER
c SHORT COOL SUMMER

AFTER KOEPPEN-GEIGER

VEGETATION

TROPICAL FOREST
TROPICAL RAINFOREST
LIGHT TROPICAL FOREST
WOODLAND AND SHRUB

TROPICAL GRASSLAND
GRASS AND SHRUB (SAVANNA)
WOODED SAVANNA

MID-LATITUDE FOREST
NEEDLELEAF FOREST
MIXED NEEDLELEAF AND BROADLEAF FOREST
WOODLAND AND SHRUB (MEDITERRANEAN)

MID-LATITUDE GRASSLAND
SHORT GRASS (STEPPE)
TALL GRASS (PRAIRIE) AND WOODED STEPPE

DESERT AND DESERT SHRUB
TUNDRA AND ALPINE
UNCLASSIFIED HIGHLANDS

South America - Comparisons

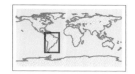

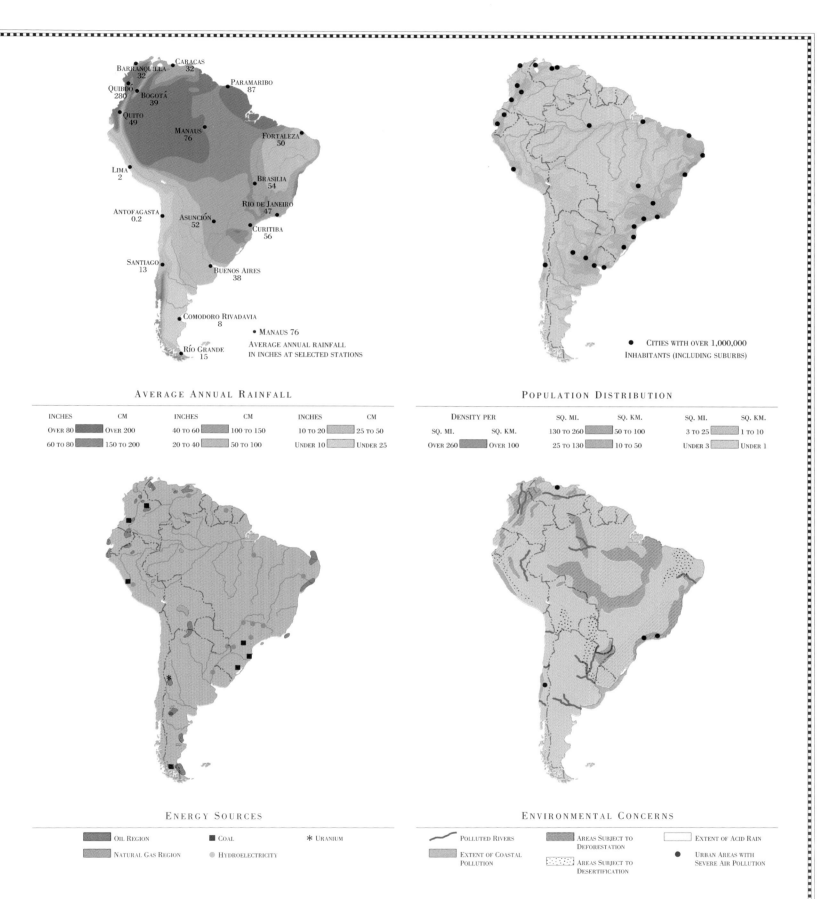

AVERAGE ANNUAL RAINFALL

BARRANQUILLA 32
CARACAS 32
QUIBDÓ 280
BOGOTÁ 39
QUITO 49
PARAMARIBO 87
MANAUS 76
FORTALEZA 50
LIMA 2
BRASILIA 54
RIO DE JANEIRO 47
ANTOFAGASTA 0.2
ASUNCIÓN 52
CURITIBA 56
SANTIAGO 13
BUENOS AIRES 38
COMODORO RIVADAVIA 8
RÍO GRANDE 15

● MANAUS 76
AVERAGE ANNUAL RAINFALL
IN INCHES AT SELECTED STATIONS

INCHES	CM	INCHES	CM	INCHES	CM
OVER 80	OVER 200	40 TO 60	100 TO 150	10 TO 20	25 TO 50
60 TO 80	150 TO 200	20 TO 40	50 TO 100	UNDER 10	UNDER 25

POPULATION DISTRIBUTION

● CITIES WITH OVER 1,000,000
INHABITANTS (INCLUDING SUBURBS)

DENSITY PER		SQ. MI.	SQ. KM.	SQ. MI.	SQ. KM.
SQ. MI.	SQ. KM.	130 TO 260	50 TO 100	3 TO 25	1 TO 10
OVER 260	OVER 100	25 TO 130	10 TO 50	UNDER 3	UNDER 1

ENERGY SOURCES

	OIL REGION	■ COAL	✳ URANIUM
	NATURAL GAS REGION	● HYDROELECTRICITY	

ENVIRONMENTAL CONCERNS

POLLUTED RIVERS	AREAS SUBJECT TO DEFORESTATION	EXTENT OF ACID RAIN
EXTENT OF COASTAL POLLUTION	AREAS SUBJECT TO DESERTIFICATION	● URBAN AREAS WITH SEVERE AIR POLLUTION

ATLANTIC

OCEAN

Totness
Nieuw-
Amsterdam
Paramaribo
Saint-Laurent
du Maroni
Albina
RINAME
Brokopondo
Sinnamary
Kourou
Devil's I.
Iles du Salut
Cottica
Rémire
Cayenne
FRENCH
GUIANA
lana Top
230 m
Saül
Régina
Pointe Béhague
Cabo Orange
Orange
Mts.
Ouaqui
Oiapoque
Calçoene

Tumuc-Humac Mts.

Sa. Lombardo

PN DO
CABO ORANGE

Ilha de Maracá
Amapá
Cabo do Norte

St. Peter and
St. Paul Rocks
(BRAZIL)

Equator

Macapá
Mazagão
I. Janaucu
I. Caviana
I. Mexiana
I. Queimada
Ilha Grande
de Gurupá
Soure
Vigia
Salinópolis
Bragança
Capanema
Ilha de
Marajó
Castanhal
Serra
Javaru
Almeirim
Breves
Belém
Abaetetuba
Igarapé-Miri
Turiaçu
Ilhas de São João
PN DOS LENÇÓIS
MARANHENSES
Rocas
Fernando de Noronha
(BRAZIL)

Orixminá
Óbidos
Alenquer
Monte
Alegre
Portel
Cametá
Mocajuba
Pinheiro
São Luís
Parnaíba
Camocim
Santarém
Paragominas
Penalva
Viana
Rosário
Granja
Sobral
Rapipoca
Caúcaia
Fortaleza

Altamira
Tucuruí
Sa. do Tiracambu
Santa Inês
Itapecuru-Mirim
Pindaré-Mirim
Coroatá
PN DE SETE CIDADES
Coelho
Neto
Tianguá
Ipu
Cascavel

PN DA AMAZÔNIA
(TAPAJOS)
Santa
Luzia
Bacabal
Codó
Caxias
Timon
Piripiri
Campo Maior
Quixeramobim
Boa
Viagem
Canindé
Baturité
Aracati
Areia
Branca
Macau
Itaituba

Sa. do Gurupi
Marabá
Presidente
Dutra
Altos
Teresina
Crateús
Taua
Mombaça
Morada
Nova
Quixadá
Russas
Ceará-Mirim
Mossoró
Natal
Cabo de São Roque

Sa. dos Carajás
Rupiranga
Imperatriz
Barra do
Corda
Grajaú
Teresina
Água
Branca
Acopiara
Icó
Iguatu
Várzea Alegre
Cedro
Sousa
Pombal
Caicó
Currais
Novos
Nova Cruz
Parnamirim
Macaíba

São Félix
do Xingu
Araguatins
Tocantinópolis
Floriano
Colinas
Regeneração
Oeiras
Picos
Araripina
Crato
Juazeiro do
Norte
Ouricuri
Salgueiro
Patos
Santa
Rita
João Pessoa
Bayeux
Guarabira
Campina
Grande
Mamanguape

Serra da
Seringa
Gradaús
Conceição do
Araguaia
Guarai
Balsas
São João
do Piauí
Remanso
Petrolina
Juazeiro
Serra Talhada
Floresta
Arcoverde
Belo Jardim
Vitória de
Santo Antão
Recife
Olinda
Jaboatão
Timbaúba

I   L
Maloca
Sa. do Estrondo
Miracema
do Tocantins
Paraíso do
Tocantins
Porto Nacional
Corrente
Xique-Xique
Irecê
Borborema
Paula Afonso
PN DE PAULO AFONSO
Palmeira dos
Índios
União dos
Palmares
Rio Largo
Arapiraca
Maceió

Alto Floresta
PN DO
ARAGUAIA
Santa
Teresinha
Chapada
dos
Mangabeiras
Barra
Sa. do Tabatinga
Jacobina
Ribeira do
Pombal
Propriá
Penedo
Cícero
Dantas
Itabaiana

PARQUE
NACIONAL
DO XINGU
Sa. dos
Xavantes
Gurupi
Barreiras
Ibotirama
Morro do
Chapéu
Capim
Grosso
Tobias Barreto
Lagarto
Aracaju
Estância

Sinop
Planalto
do
Mato Grosso
Porangatu
Santa
Maria da
Vitória
Santana
Bom Jesus
da Lapa
Riacho de
Santana
Seabra
Serrinha
Esplanada
Alagoinhas
Candeias

ndia
amantina
Nova Xavantina
PN DA CHAPADA
DOS VEADEIROS
Uruaçu
Carinhanha
Caetité
Guanambi
Feira de Santana
Cruz das
Almas
Camaçari
Salvador

Cuiabá
Paxoreo
Ceres
Formosa
Januária
Chapada
Diamantina
Brumado
Jaguaquara
Nazaré
Valença
I. de Tinharé

Rondonópolis
Barra do
Garças
Araguaiana
Goiás
PN DE
BRASÍLIA
Brasília
Taguatinga
Luziânia
Unaí
Espinosa
Monte Azil
Itapetinga
Jequié
Ipiaú
Ubatã
Ubaitaba

Alto Garças
Alto Araguaia
Iporá
Morro Alto
▲ 678 m
Formosa
Morro do
Chapéu
Vitória da
Conquista
Itapetinga
Itabuna
Pau Brasil
Ilhéus

Guiratinga
Mineiros
Jataí
Anápolis
Cristalina
Januária
Montes
Claros
Salinas
Pedra Azul
Canavieiras

Rio Verde de
Mato Grosso
PN DAS EMAS
Goiânia
Pires do
Rio
Paracatu
Pirapora
Bocaiúva
Araçuaí
Itamaraju
PN DE MONTE
PASCOAL

Coxim
Rio Verde
Goiatuba
Catalão
Patos de
Minas
João Pinheiro
Três Marias
Corinto
Diamantina
Itaobim
Jequitinhonha
Nanuque
Prado
Ponta da Baleia

Quirinópolis
Uberlândia
Araguari
Monte
Carmelo
Patrocínio
Curvelo
Pico de Itambé
2.032 m
Sa. do Espinhaço
Teófilo
Otoni
Montanha
Pinheiros

Paranaíba
Ituiutaba
Araxá
Abaeté
Nova Venécia
São Mateus

Jales
Uberaba
Frutal
Sete
Lagoas
Ipatinga
Governador
Valadares
São Gabriel da Palha
Colatina

Campo Grande
Fernandópolis
Aparecida
Franca
Lagoa da
Prata
Contagem
Belo Horizonte
Itabira
Timóteo
Baixo Guandu
Linhares
Vitória

Três Lagoas
São José do
Rio Prêto
Barretos
Bebedouro
Passos
Divinópolis
Conselheiro
Lafaiete
Manhuaçu
Vila Velha
Argolas

Andradina
Catanduva
Ribeirão
Preto
Poços de
Caldas
Alfenas
Varginha
São João
del Rei
Barbacena
Viçosa
Cachoeiro de Itapemirim
Guarapari

Araçatuba
Birigui
Penápolis
Lins
Araraquara
Lavras
Pouso
Coração
Miraí
Itaperuna
Itapemirim

Presidente Epitácio
Dracena
Tupã
São Carlos
Rio Claro
Limeira
Barra Mansa
Juiz de
Fora
Além Paraíba
Campos
Cabo de São Tomé

Presidente
Prudente
Marília
Assis
Baurú
Jaú
Piracicaba
Americana
Volta
Redonda
Nova Friburgo
Macaé

Dourados
Ourinhos
Campinas
Jundiaí
Barbacena
Taubaté
Nova
Iguaçu
Niterói
Petrópolis

Ponta Porã
Sorocaba
São José dos Campos
Rio de Janeiro

Tropic of Capricorn

Naviraí
Paranavaí
Osasco
São Paulo
Santo André
Santos

Maringá
Londrina

ATLANTIC

OCEAN

Ilha da Trindade
(BRAZIL)
Ilhas Martin Vaz
(BRAZIL)

©HAMMOND WORLD ATLAS CORPORATION   CI-2107-A

POPULATION OF CITIES AND TOWNS

■ OVER 2,000,000   ⊙ 500,000 - 999,999   ○ 50,000 - 99,999
□ 1,000,000 - 1,999,999   ⊚ 100,000 - 199,999   ∘ UNDER 50,000

SCALE 1:15,000,000   LAMBERT CONFORMAL CONIC PROJECTION
MILES 0 [____] 200   400   600
KILOMETERS 0 [____] 200   400   600

Southern South America

SCALE 1:15,000,000   LAMBERT CONFORMAL CONIC PROJECTION

MILES

KILOMETERS

POPULATION OF CITIES AND TOWNS

■ OVER 2,000,000   ● 500,000 - 999,999   ⊙ 50,000 - 99,999
□ 1,000,000 - 1,999,999   ◉ 100,000 - 199,999   ○ UNDER 50,000

Population of Major World Cities

The following pages include population figures, given in thousands, for major cities in each country, and for all national capitals, regardless of size. National capitals are indicated with an asterisk (*).

Country / City	Population in thousands
A	
Afghanistan	
Kābul*	1,424
Qandahar	226
Albania	
Tiranë*	244
Algeria	
Algiers*	1,688
Annaba	228
Constantine	450
Oran	599
Andorra	
Andorra la Vella*	16
Angola	
Luanda*	1,530
Antigua and Barbuda	
Saint John's*	22
Argentina	
Avellaneda	347
Bahía Blanca	240
Buenos Aires*	2,961
Córdoba	1,148
General San Martín	408
Lanús	467
La Plata	520
Lomas de Zamora	573
Mar del Plata	512
Morón	642
Qilmes	509
Rosario	895
San Miguel de Tucumán	471
Santa Fé	343
Armenia	
Yerevan*	1,199
Australia	
Adelaide	957
Brisbane	1,146
Canberra*	276
Hobart	127
Melbourne	2,762
Newcastle	262
Perth	1,019
Sydney	3,098
Austria	
Graz	238
Vienna*	1,540
Azerbaijan	
Baku*	1,149
B	
Bahamas	
Nassau*	172
Bahrain	
Manama*	143
Bangladesh	
Chittagong	1,560
Dhaka*	3,638
Khulna	601
Barbados	
Bridgetown*	7
Belarus	
Homyel'	503
Mahilyow	363
Minsk*	1,655
Vitsyebsk	365
Belgium	
Antwerp	468
Brussels*	954
Ghent	230
Liège	195
Belize	
Belmopan*	4
Benin	
Cotonou	537
Porto-Novo*	179
Bhutan	
Thimphu*	30
Bolivia	
Cochabamba	404
La Paz*	711
Santa Cruz	695
Sucre*	131
Bosnia & Herzegovina	
Banja Luka	196
Sarajevo*	529
Botswana	
Gaborone*	175

Country / City	Population in thousands
Brazil	
Aracaju	402
Belém	765
Belo Horizonte	2,206
Brasília*	1,493
Campinas	748
Campo Grande	516
Cuiabá	253
Curitiba	842
Florianópolis	192
Fortaleza	1,027
Goiânia	912
João Pessoa	497
Juiz de Fora	378
Maceió	555
Manaus	1,006
Natal	460
Niterói	401
Nova Iguaçu	562
Osasco	567
Porto Alegre	1,237
Recife	1,297
Ribeirão Preto	416
Rio de Janeiro	5,474
Salvador	2,070
Santo André	518
Santos	416
São Bernardo do Campo	550
São Luís	164
São Paulo	9,394
Teresina	556
Vitória	180
Brunei	
Bandar Seri Begawan*	46
Bulgaria	
Plovdiv	341
Sofia*	1,114
Varna	309
Burkina Faso	
Ouagadougou*	442
Burundi	
Bujumbura*	235
C	
Cambodia	
Phnom Penh*	620
Cameroon	
Douala	1,030
Yaoundé*	654
Canada	
Calgary	768
Edmonton	616
Halifax	114
Hamilton	322
Laval	330
London	326
Mississauga	544
Montréal	1,016
Ottawa*	323
Québec	167
Regina	180
Saskatoon	194
Toronto	654
Vancouver	514
Windsor	198
Winnipeg	618
Cape Verde	
Praia*	62
Central African Republic	
Bangui*	597
Chad	
N'Djamena*	530
Chile	
Antofagasta	227
Concepción	327
Santiago*	4,298
Talcahuano	246
Valparaíso	282
Viña del Mar	304
China	
Anshan	1,215
Baotou	980
Beijing*	5,715
Benxi	767
Changchun	1,698
Changsha	1,077
Chengdu	1,719
Chongqing	2,265

Country / City	Population in thousands
Dalian	1,632
Dandong	525
Daqing	676
Datong	779
Fengcheng	150
Fushun	1,210
Fuxin	623
Fuzhou	890
Guangzhou	2,892
Guiyang	1,009
Handan	798
Hangzhou	1,119
Harbin	2,468
Hefei	733
Hegang	507
Hohhot	654
Huainan	674
Jilin	1,038
Jinan	1,361
Jinzhou	573
Jixi	638
Kaifeng	503
Kunming	1,108
Lanzhou	1,205
Lhasa	99
Liuzhou	602
Luoyang	730
Macau	343
Mudanjiang	562
Nanchang	1,026
Nanjing	2,114
Nanning	723
Ningbo	548
Qingdao	1,317
Qiqihar	1,066
Shanghai	7,551
Shantou	558
Shenyang	3,588
Shijiazhuang	1,065
Suzhou	697
Taiyuan	1,514
Tangshan	1,042
Tianjin	4,521
Ürümqi	1,071
Wuhan	3,177
Wuxi	806
Xi'an	1,954
Xining	559
Xuzhou	795
Yichun	787
Yinchuan	350
Zhangjiakou	525
Zhengzhou	1,139
Zibo	864
Colombia	
Barranquilla	1,000
Bogotá*	5,699
Bucaramanga	403
Cali	1,625
Cartagena	576
Cúcuta	462
Ibagué	336
Manizales	341
Medellín	1,485
Pereira	329
Comoros	
Moroni*	30
Congo, Dem. Rep. of the	
Kananga	372
Kinshasa*	3,800
Lubumbashi	739
Mbuji-Mayi	613
Congo, Rep. of the	
Brazzaville*	938
Pointe-Noire	576
Costa Rica	
San José*	279
Côte d'Ivoire	
Abidjan	1,929
Yamoussoukro*	107
Croatia	
Rijeka	168
Split	200
Zagreb*	868
Cuba	
Camagüey	249
Guantánamo	208
Havana*	2,176

Country / City	Population in thousands
Holguín	242
Santiago de Cuba	430
Cyprus	
Nicosia*	47
Czech Republic	
Brno	390
Ostrava	327
Prague*	1,217
D	
Denmark	
Århus	209
Copenhagen*	467
Djibouti	
Djibouti*	200
Dominica	
Roseau*	6
Dominican Republic	
Santiago de los Caballeros	375
Santo Domingo*	1,609
E	
Ecuador	
Guayaquil	1,513
Quito*	1,113
Egypt	
Alexandria	3,380
Al Jīzah	2,144
Asyūt	321
Cairo*	6,663
Port Said	460
Shubrā al Khaymah	834
Tantā	380
El Salvador	
San Salvador*	415
Equatorial Guinea	
Malabo*	30
Eritrea	
Asmara*	435
Estonia	
Tallinn*	482
Ethiopia	
Addis Ababa*	2,316
F	
Fiji	
Suva*	70
Finland	
Helsinki*	525
Tampere	183
France	
Bordeaux	213
Le Havre	197
Lille	178
Lyon	422
Marseille	808
Nantes	252
Nice	346
Paris*	2,175
Rennes	204
Saint-Étienne	202
Strasbourg	256
Toulouse	366
G	
Gabon	
Libreville*	362
Gambia	
Banjul*	42
Georgia	
T'bilisi*	1,260
Germany	
Berlin*	3,434
Bochum	396
Bonn	292
Bremen	551
Chemnitz	294
Cologne	954
Dortmund	599
Dresden	491
Duisburg	535
Düsseldorf	576
Essen	627
Frankfurt am Main	645
Hamburg	1,652
Hannover	513
Kiel	246
Leipzig	511
Magdeburg	279

Country / City	Population in thousands
Mannheim	310
Munich	1,229
Münster	259
Nürnberg	494
Rostock	237
Saarbrücken	191
Stuttgart	594
Wiesbaden	271
Ghana	
Accra*	954
Kumasi	399
Greece	
Athens*	772
Piraiévs	183
Thessaloníki	384
Grenada	
Saint George's*	5
Guatemala	
Guatemala*	823
Guinea	
Conakry*	950
Guinea-Bissau	
Bissau*	109
Guyana	
Georgetown*	72
H	
Haiti	
Port-au-Prince*	690
Honduras	
San Pedro Sula	287
Tegucigalpa*	577
Hungary	
Budapest*	2,017
Debrecen	212
Miskolc	196
Szeged	175
I	
Iceland	
Reykjavik*	96
India	
Āgra	892
Ahmadābād	2,877
Allahābād	793
Amritsar	709
Aurangābād	573
Bangalore	2,660
Bareilly	587
Bhopāl	1,063
Calcutta	4,400
Chandigarh	504
Chennai (Madras)	3,841
Cochin	565
Coimbatore	816
Cuttack	403
Delhi	7,207
Farīdābād	618
Ghaziābād	454
Guwāhati	584
Gwalior	691
Howrah	950
Hubli-Dhārwār	648
Hyderābād	3,044
Indore	1,092
Jabalpur	742
Jaipur	1,458
Jammu	206
Jamshedpur	461
Jodhpur	666
Jullundur	510
Kalyān	1,015
Kānpur	1,874
Kota	537
Lucknow	1,619
Ludhiāna	1,043
Madurai	941
Meerut	754
Mumbai (Bombay)	9,926
Mysore	481
Nāgpur	1,625
Nāsik	657
New Delhi*	301
Patna	917
Pune (Poona)	1,567
Rānchī	599
Sholāpur	604
Srīnagar	606
Surat	1,499

Country / City	Population in thousands
Thāna	803
Tiruchchirāppalli	387
Trivandrum	524
Vāranāsi	929
Vijayawada	702
Visākhapatnam	752
Indonesia	
Bandung	2,026
Banjarmasin	443
Jakarta*	8,228
Malang	650
Medan	1,685
Padang	477
Palembang	787
Pontianak	397
Semarang	1,004
Surabaya	2,410
Surakarta	504
Ujung Pandang	913
Yogyakarta	412
Iran	
Ahvāz	828
Bākhtarān	666
Eṣfahān	1,221
Karaj	588
Mashhad	1,964
Qom	780
Rasht	374
Shīrāz	1,043
Tabrīz	1,166
Tehrān*	6,750
Zāhedān	420
Iraq	
Al Baṣrah	406
Baghdad*	3,841
Mosul	664
Ireland	
Cork	127
Dublin*	478
Israel	
Jerusalem*	591
Tel Aviv-Yafo	356
Italy	
Bari	341
Bologna	412
Catania	330
Florence	402
Genoa	676
Messina	272
Milan	1,371
Naples	1,025
Palermo	697
Rome*	2,693
Taranto	232
Trieste	231
Turin	962
Venice	85
Verona	253
J	
Jamaica	
Kingston*	104
Japan	
Amagasaki	499
Chiba	829
Fukuoka	1,237
Funabashi	533
Hamakita	811
Hamamatsu	535
Higashi-Ōsaka	518
Hiroshima	1,086
Kagoshima	537
Kawasaki	1,174
Kitakyūshū	1,026
Kōbe	1,477
Kumamoto	579
Kyōto	1,461
Nagoya	2,155
Niigata	486
Okayama	594
Ōsaka	2,624
Sakai	814
Sapporo	1,672
Sendai	918
Shizuoka	472
Tōkyō*	8,164
Toyonaka	410
Utsunomiya	427
Wakayama	397

Country / City	Population in thousands
Yokohama	3,220
Yokosuka	433
Jordan	
Amman*	965
Kazakhstan	
Almaty	1,176
Astana*	277
Öskemen	334
Pavlodar	349
Qaraghandy	596
Semey	342
Shymkent	404
Zhambyl	317
Kenya	
Mombasa	465
Nairobi*	1,346
Kiribati	
Tarawa*	2
Korea, North	
Ch'ŏngjin	754
Hamhŭng	775
P'yŏngyang*	2,639
Wŏnsan	350
Korea, South	
Chŏnju	517
Inch'ŏn	2,203
Kwangju (Kwangju-Jikhalsi)	1,236
Kwangju (Kyŏnggi-Do)	906
Pusan	3,802
Seoul*	10,776
Taegu	2,256
Taejŏn	1,183
Kuwait	
Kuwait*	31
Kyrgyzstan	
Bishkek*	628
Laos	
Vientiane*	377
Latvia	
Riga*	865
Lebanon	
Beirut*	1,000
Lesotho	
Maseru*	109
Liberia	
Monrovia*	421
Libya	
Benghāzī	446
Tripoli*	590
Liechtenstein	
Vaduz*	5
Lithuania	
Kaunas	422
Vilnius*	582
Luxembourg	
Luxembourg*	75
Macedonia, Former Yugoslav Rep. of	
Skopje*	441
Madagascar	
Antananarivo*	676
Malawi	
Blantyre	332
Lilongwe*	234
Malaysia	
Ipoh	383
Kuala Lumpur*	1,145
Maldives	
Male*	55
Mali	
Bamako*	658
Malta	
Valletta*	9
Marshall Islands	
Majuro*	22
Mauritania	
Nouakchott*	390
Mauritius	
Port Louis*	144
Mexico	
Acapulco de Juárez	515
Aguascalientes	440
Chihuahua	516
Ciudad Juárez	790
Culiacán	415
Ecatepec de Morelos	1,218
Guadalajara	1,650
Guadalupe	535
Hermosillo	406
León	758
Mérida	529
Mexicali	439
Mexico*	8,237
Monterrey	1,069
Morelia	428
Netzahualcóyotl	1,255
Puebla de Zaragoza	1,007
Saltillo	421
San Luis Potosí	489
Tijuana	699
Tlalnepantla de Galeana	702
Torreón	439
Veracruz Llave	439
Zapopan	668
Micronesia, Federated States of	
Palikir*	6
Moldova	
Chişinău*	665
Monaco	
Monaco*	27
Mongolia	
Ulaanbaatar*	575
Morocco	
Casablanca	2,541
Fès	508
Marrakech	521
Rabat*	917
Mozambique	
Maputo*	1,007
Myanmar (Burma)	
Mandalay	533
Moulmein	220
Yangon* (Rangoon)	2,513
Namibia	
Windhoek*	147
Nepal	
Kāthmāndu*	421
Netherlands	
Amsterdam*	713
Eindhoven	194
Groningen	169
Rotterdam	590
The Hague*	445
Utrecht	232
New Zealand	
Auckland	346
Christchurch	309
Wellington*	158
Nicaragua	
Managua*	883
Niger	
Niamey*	392
Nigeria	
Abeokuta	387
Abuja*	306
Ibadan	1,295
Ilorin	431
Kano	700
Lagos	1,347
Ogbomosho	660
Oshogbo	441
Port Harcourt	371
Norway	
Bergen	223
Oslo*	489
Oman	
Muscat*	67
Pakistan	
Faisalabad	1,104
Gujrānwāla	659
Hyderābād	752
Islāmābād*	204
Karāchi	5,076
Lahore	2,953
Multān	732
Peshāwar	566
Quetta	286
Rāwalpindi	795
Sargodha	291
Siālkot	302
Palau	
Koror*	9
Panama	
Panamá*	456
Papua New Guinea	
Port Moresby*	193
Paraguay	
Asunción*	547
Peru	
Callao	512
Chiclayo	412
Comas	287
Lima*	376
Trujillo	509
Philippines	
Caloocan	643
Cebu	688
Davao	961
Makati	453
Manila*	1,599
Quezon City	1,677
Zamboanga	464
Poland	
Białystok	268
Bydgoszcz	380
Gdańsk	462
Gdynia	251
Katowice	366
Kraków	746
Łódź	849
Lublin	349
Poznań	587
Szczecin	411
Warsaw*	1,651
Wrocław	641
Portugal	
Lisbon*	818
Porto	330
Qatar	
Doha*	217
Romania	
Braşov	324
Bucharest*	2,068
Cluj-Napoca	329
Constanţa	351
Iaşi	344
Ploieşti	253
Timisoara	334
Russia	
Archangel'sk	410
Astrakhan'	508
Barnaul	595
Bryansk	456
Cheboksary	446
Chelyabinsk	1,130
Groznyy	354
Irkutsk	630
Ivanovo	474
Izhevsk	652
Kazan'	1,086
Kemerovo	513
Khabarovsk	608
Kirov	491
Krasnodar	636
Krasnoyarsk	917
Kursk	434
Lipetsk	466
Magnitogorsk	439
Moscow*	8,527
Murmansk	454
Naberezhnye Chelny	527
Nizhniy Novgorod	1,425
Nizhniy Tagil	431
Novokuznetsk	597
Novosibirsk	1,424
Omsk	1,164
Orenburg	554
Penza	548
Perm'	1,091
Rostov	1,013
Ryazan'	524
Saint Petersburg	4,329
Samara	1,232
Saratov	899
Tol'yatti	682
Tomsk	498
Tula	534
T'ver	449
Tyumen'	491
Ufa	1,092
Ul'yanovsk	664
Vladivostok	637
Volgograd	997
Voronezh	899
Yaroslavl'	628
Yekaterinburg	1,351
Rwanda	
Kigali*	233
Saint Kitts and Nevis	
Basseterre*	13
Saint Lucia	
Castries*	13
Saint Vincent and the Grenadines	
Kingstown*	15
Samoa	
Apia*	32
San Marino	
San Marino*	3
Sao Tome and Principe	
São Tomé*	43
Saudi Arabia	
Jiddah	1,500
Mecca	630
Riyadh*	1,800
Senegal	
Dakar*	1,641
Seychelles	
Victoria*	24
Sierra Leone	
Freetown*	470
Singapore	
Singapore*	3,462
Slovak Republic	
Bratislava*	442
Košice	235
Slovenia	
Ljubljana*	287
Solomon Islands	
Honiara*	30
Somalia	
Mogadishu*	600
South Africa	
Cape Town*	855
Durban	716
Johannesburg	714
Port Elizabeth	303
Pretoria*	526
Soweto	597
Spain	
Alicante	275
Barcelona	1,631
Bilbao	372
Córdoba	316
Granada	271
Las Palmas de Gran Canaria	372
Madrid*	3,041
Málaga	531
Murcia	342
Palma	322
Saragossa	607
Seville	714
Valencia	764
Valladolid	337
Vigo	289
Sri Lanka	
Colombo*	615
Sudan	
Khartoum*	925
Omdurman	229
Suriname	
Paramaribo*	180
Swaziland	
Mbabane*	38
Sweden	
Göteborg	433
Malmö	234
Stockholm*	675
Switzerland	
Bern*	127
Zürich	344
Syria	
Aleppo	1,542
Damascus*	1,549
Ḥimş	558
Taiwan	
Kaohsiung	1,424
Keelung	368
T'aichung	850
T'ainan	706
T'aipei*	2,639
Tajikistan	
Dushanbe*	602
Tanzania	
Dar es Salaam*	1,361
Thailand	
Bangkok*	5,876
Nakhon Ratchasima	278
Togo	
Lomé*	450
Tonga	
Nuku'alofa*	21
Trinidad and Tobago	
Port-of-Spain*	51
Tunisia	
Tūnis*	674
Turkey	
Adana	916
Ankara*	2,559
Antalya	378
Bursa	835
Diyarbakır	381
Eskişehir	413
Gaziantep	603
İstanbul	6,620
İzmir	1,757
Kayseri	421
Konya	513
Malatya	282
Mersin	422
Turkmenistan	
Ashgabat*	407
Tuvalu	
Funafuti*	2
Uganda	
Kampala*	774
Ukraine	
Chernihiv	311
Dniprodzerzhyns'k	287
Dnipropetrovs'k	1,190
Donets'k	1,121
Horlivka	336
Kharkiv	1,622
Kherson	368
Kiev*	2,643
Kryvyy Rih	729
Luhans'k	505
L'viv	807
Makiyivka	426
Mariupol'	523
Mykolayiv	515
Odesa	1,096
Poltava	324
Sevastopol'	356
Simferopol'	357
Sumy	305
Vinnytsya	384
Zaporizhzhya	884
Zhytomyr	299
United Arab Emirates	
Abu Dhabi*	243
Dubayy	266
United Kingdom	
Belfast	295
Birmingham	966
Bradford	289
Bristol	408
Cardiff	272
Coventry	299
Edinburgh	448
Glasgow	618
Kingston upon Hull	311
Leeds	424
Leicester	319
Liverpool	482
London*	6,680
Manchester	403
Nottingham	270
Plymouth	245
Sheffield	432
Stoke-on-Trent	267
Wolverhampton	258
United States	
Albuquerque	385
Atlanta	394
Austin	466
Baltimore	736
Boston	574
Buffalo	328
Charlotte	396
Chicago	2,784
Cincinnati	364
Cleveland	506
Columbus (Ohio)	633
Dallas	1,007
Denver	468
Detroit	1,028
El Paso	515
Fort Worth	448
Fresno	354
Honolulu	365
Houston	1,631
Indianapolis	742
Jacksonville	635
Kansas City (Mo.)	435
Long Beach	429
Los Angeles	3,485
Memphis	610
Miami	359
Milwaukee	628
Minneapolis	368
Nashville	488
New Orleans	497
New York	7,323
Oakland	372
Oklahoma City	445
Omaha	336
Philadelphia	1,586
Phoenix	983
Pittsburgh	370
Portland	437
Sacramento	369
Saint Louis	397
San Antonio	936
San Diego	1,111
San Francisco	724
San Jose	782
Seattle	516
Toledo	333
Tucson	405
Tulsa	367
Virginia Beach	393
Washington, D.C.*	607
Wichita	304
Uruguay	
Montevideo*	1,360
Uzbekistan	
Andijon	297
Namangan	312
Samarqand	370
Tashkent*	2,073
Vanuatu	
Port-Vila*	19
Venezuela	
Barquisimeto	625
Caracas*	1,822
Ciudad Guayana	453
Maracaibo	1,250
Maracay	354
Petare	338
Valencia	904
Vietnam	
Dà Nang	370
Haiphong	450
Hanoi*	1,090
Ho Chí Minh City	2,900
Yemen	
Aden	562
Sanaa*	972
Yugoslavia	
Belgrade*	1,555
Niš	176
Novi Sad	179
Zambia	
Kitwe	247
Lusaka*	982
Ndola	376
Zimbabwe	
Bulawayo	622
Harare*	1,189

Dependency

Country / City	Population in thousands
Puerto Rico (U.S.)	
San Juan	427

Index of the World

This alphabetical list gives countries, cities, regions, political divisions, and physical features for the world. Latitude/longitude coordinates are given for each entry, where possible, followed by the page number for the map on which the entry appears to the best advantage. The entry may be located on other maps as well by the use of the coordinates given. Capitals are designated by asterisks (*).

Index Abbreviations

Afghan.	Afghanistan	E.	East, Eastern	Miss.	Mississippi	N.Y.	New York	S.D.	South Dakota
Ala.	Alabama	El Sal.	El Salvador	Mo.	Missouri	N.Z.	New Zealand	S. Korea	South Korea
Alg.	Algeria	Eng.	England	Mont.	Montana	Okla.	Oklahoma	Sol. Is.	Solomon Islands
Alta.	Alberta	Eq. Guin.	Equatorial Guinea	Mor.	Morocco	Ont.	Ontario	Sp.	Spain, Spanish
Amer.	America	Falk. Is.	Falkland Islands	Moz.	Mozambique	Ore.	Oregon	St. Ste.	Saint, Sainte
arch.	archipelago	Fla.	Florida	mt., mts.	mountain, mountains	Pa.	Pennsylvania	Switz.	Switzerland
Arg.	Argentina	Fr.	France, French	N,. No.	North, Northern	Pak.	Pakistan	Tanz.	Tanzania
Ariz.	Arizona	Ga.	Georgia	Nat'l Pk	National Park	Para.	Paraguay	Tenn.	Tennessee
Ark.	Arkansas	Ger.	Germany	N.B.	New Brunswick	P.E.I.	Prince Edward Island	Terr.	Territory
Austl.	Australia	Guat.	Guatemala	N.C.	North Carolina	pen.	peninsula	Thai.	Thailand
Belg.	Belgium	Ill.	Illinois	N.D.	North Dakota	plat.	plateau	U.K.	United Kingdom
Br. Col.	British Columbia	Ind.	Indiana	Neb.	Nebraska	P.N.G.	Papua New Guinea	Un.	United
Calif.	California	Indon.	Indonesia	Neth.	Netherlands	Port.	Portugal, Portuguese	U.S.	United States
Can.	Canada	isl., isls.	island, islands	Neth. Ant.	Netherlands Antilles	P.R.	Puerto Rico	Va.	Virginia
CAfr.	Central African Republic	Kans.	Kansas	Nev.	Nevada	prom.	promontory	Ven.	Venezuela
chan.	channel	Kazak.	Kazakhstan	New Cal.	New Caledonia	prov.	province, provincial	Vt.	Vermont
Col.	Colombia	Ky.	Kentucky	Newf.	Newfoundland	Qué.	Québec	W.	West, Western
Colo.	Colorado	La.	Louisiana	N.H.	New Hampshire	Rep.	Republic	Wash.	Washington
Conn.	Connecticut	Lux.	Luxembourg	Nic.	Nicaragua	res.	reservoir	Wis.	Wisconsin
C.R.	Costa Rica	Man.	Manitoba	N.J.	New Jersey	R.I.	Rhode Island	W. Va.	West Virginia
Czech Rep.	Czech Republic	Mart.	Martinique	N. Korea	North Korea	Rom.	Romania	Wyo.	Wyoming
D.C.	District of Columbia	Mass.	Massachusetts	N.M.	New Mexico	S., So.	South, Southern	Yugo.	Yugoslavia
Del.	Delaware	Md.	Maryland	No. Ire.	Northern Ireland	S. Afr.	South Africa	Zim.	Zimbabwe
Den.	Denmark	Mex.	Mexico	N.S.	Nova Scotia	Sask.	Saskatchewan		
Dom. Rep.	Dominican Republic	Mich.	Michigan	N.W. Terrs.	Northwest Territories (Canada)	S.C.	South Carolina		
D.R. Congo	Democratic Republic of the Congo	Minn.	Minnesota			Scot.	Scotland		

A

NAME	LATITUDE	LONGITUDE	PAGE
Aberdeen, Scot.	57° 09′ N	02° 06′ W	42
Abidjan, Côte d'Ivoire	05 20 N	04 01 W	68
Abilene, Texas	32 28 N	99 43 W	76
Abu Dhabi,* United Arab Emirates	24 28 N	54 22 E	52
Abuja,* Nigeria	67 20 N	09 05 E	68
Acapulco, Mex.	16 51 N	99 55 W	80
Accra,* Ghana	05 33 N	00 12 W	68
Aconcagua (mt.)	32 45 S	70 14 W	88
Adana, Turkey	37 00 N	35 15 E	44
Ad Dahna' (desert)	27 30 N	45 00 E	52
Addis Ababa,* Ethiopia	09 01 N	38 45 E	69
Adelaide, Austl.	34 55 S	138 37 E	59
Aden, Yemen	12 45 N	45 05 E	52
Adirondack (mts.)	44 00 N	74 00 W	78
Adrar de Iforas (plat.)	20 00 N	02 00 E	68
Adriatic (sea)	42 50 N	15 40 E	44
Aegean (sea)	40 23 N	25 00 E	44
Afghanistan	34 00 N	65 00 E	49
Agra, India	27 10 N	78 08 E	53
Aguascalientes, Mex.	21 53 N	102 18 W	80
Agulhas (cape)	34 51 S	19 59 E	70
Ahaggar (mts.)	23 00 N	05 00 E	68
Ahmadabad, India	23 00 N	72 44 E	53
Ahvāz, Iran	31 19 N	48 42 E	52
Aklavik, N.W. Terrs.	68 12 N	135 00 W	79
Akron, Ohio	41 05 N	81 31 W	78
Alabama (state), U.S.	33 00 N	87 00 W	78
Åland (isls.)	60 15 N	20 00 E	43
Alaska (gulf)	59 00 N	145 00 W	76
Alaska (pen.)	57 00 N	158 00 W	76
Alaska (range)	63 00 N	151 00 W	76
Alaska (state), U.S.	65 00 N	154 00 W	76
Albania	41 00 N	20 00 E	44
Albany (river)	52 16 N	81 30 W	79
Albany,* N.Y.	42 39 N	73 45 W	78
Albert (lake)	01 45 N	31 00 E	69
Alberta (prov.), Canada	54 00 N	115 00 W	79
Albuquerque, N.M.	35 05 N	106 39 W	76
Aleppo, Syria	36 12 N	37 10 E	52
Aleutian (isls.)	52 00 N	175 00 W	76
Alexandria, Egypt	31 12 N	29 55 E	69
Alexandria, La.	31 18 N	92 27 W	77
Algeria	30 00 N	04 00 E	68
Algiers,* Alg.	36 45 N	03 04 E	68
Alicante, Spain	38 21 N	00 29 W	42
Al Jīsah, Egypt	30 01 N	31 13 E	69
Allahabad, India	25 30 N	81 58 E	69
Allentown, Pa.	40 37 N	75 29 W	77
Almaty, Kazak.	43 15 N	76 57 E	54
Alps (mts.)	46 40 N	10 00 E	42
Alsace (region)	48 30 N	07 35 E	42
Altai (mts.)	47 00 N	92 00 E	54
Altun (mts.)	37 30 N	88 00 E	54
Amarillo, Texas	35 13 N	101 50 W	76
Amazon (river)	00 00	49 00 W	87
American Highland (upland)	72 30 S	78 00 E	71
American Samoa	14 20 S	170 00 W	63
Amherst, N.S.	45 50 N	64 12 W	79
Amman,* Jordan	31 57 N	35 56 E	52
Amritsar, India	31 45 N	74 58 E	53
Amsterdam,* Neth.	52 20 N	04 50 E	42
Amu Darya (river)	43 40 N	59 01 E	46
Amundsen (sea)	72 00 S	109 00 W	71
Amur (river)	52 56 N	141 10 E	55
Anadyr' (mts.)	67 00 N	176 00 E	47
Anatolia (region)	39 00 N	30 00 E	44
Anchorage, Alaska	61 10 N	149 55 W	76
Andaman (isls.)	12 00 N	92 45 E	53
Andes (mts.)	27 00 S	69 00 W	82
Andorra	42 34 N	01 35 E	42
Angara (river)	56 05 N	101 48 E	47
Angola	12 00 S	17 00 E	70
Ankara,* Turkey	39 55 N	32 52 E	44
Annapolis,* Md.	38 58 N	76 30 W	78
Ann Arbor, Mich.	42 17 N	83 45 W	78
Anshan, China	41 08 N	122 59 E	55
Antananarivo,* Madagascar	18 54 S	47 30 E	70
Antarctic (pen.)	69 30 S	65 00 W	71
Anticosti (isl.)	49 30 N	63 00 W	79
Antigua and Barbuda	17 05 N	61 48 W	81
Antwerp, Belg.	51 20 N	04 25 E	42
Apennines (mts.)	43 00 N	13 00 E	44
Apia,* Samoa	13 56 S	171 45 W	63
Appalachian (mts.)	40 00 N	78 00 W	78
Appleton, Wis.	44 16 N	88 25 W	78
Aqaba (gulf)	29 30 N	35 05 E	52
Aqtōbe, Kazakhstan	50 17 N	57 10 E	45
Arafura (sea)	09 00 S	134 00 E	57
Arakan (mts.)	19 00 N	94 00 E	53
Aral (sea)	44 46 N	60 00 E	45
Ararat (mt.)	39 42 N	44 18 E	45
Aras (river)	39 56 N	48 20 E	45
Archangel'sk, Russia	64 34 N	40 32 E	43
Ardennes (region)	50 10 N	05 30 E	42
Arequipa, Peru	16 24 S	71 33 W	86
Argentina	35 00 S	65 00 W	88
Århus, Den.	56 11 N	10 15 E	43
Arizona (state), U.S.	34 00 N	112 00 W	76
Arkansas (river)	33 48 N	91 07 W	77
Arkansas (state), U.S.	34 45 N	92 30 W	77
Armenia	40 15 N	45 00 E	45
Aruba (isl.) Neth.	12 30 N	69 58 W	81
Ascension (isl.)	07 57 S	14 22 W	12
Asheville, N.C.	35 35 N	82 33 W	77
Ashgabat,* Turkmenistan	37 57 N	58 23 E	45
Asir (region)	18 00 N	42 00 E	52
Asmara,* Eritrea	15 20 N	38 57 E	69
Astana,* Kazakhstan	51 10 N	71 30 E	62
Astrakhan', Russia	46 21 N	48 03 E	69
Asunción,* Para.	25 16 S	57 40 W	88
Atacama (desert)	24 00 S	70 00 W	88
Atatürk (res.)	37 30 N	38 30 E	44
Athabasca (lake)	59 20 N	109 00 W	79
Athabasca (river)	58 30 N	111 00 W	79
Athens, Ga.	33 57 N	83 23 W	78
Athens,* Greece	37 59 N	23 44 E	44
Atlanta,* Georgia	33 45 N	84 24 W	78
Atlantic City, N.J.	39 21 N	74 27 W	78
Atlas (mts.)	34 00 N	00 01 W	68
Attu (isl.)	52 55 N	172 55 E	76
Auckland, N.Z.	36 53 S	174 45 E	61
Augsburg, Germany	48 20 N	10 53 E	42
Augusta, Ga.	33 28 N	81 58 W	78
Augusta,* Maine	44 19 N	69 46 W	78
Austin,* Texas	30 16 N	97 45 W	77
Australia	25 00 S	135 00 E	59
Australian Capital Terr.	35 18 S	149 07 E	59
Austria	47 15 N	14 00 E	42
Axel Heiberg (isl.)	79 00 N	90 00 W	79
Ayeyarwady (river)	23 19 N	96 00 E	53
Azerbaijan	40 30 N	48 00 E	45
Azores (isls.)	38 30 N	28 00 W	12
Azov (sea)	46 00 N	37 00 E	44

B

NAME	LATITUDE	LONGITUDE	PAGE
Baffin (bay)	74° 00′ N	68° 00′ W	79
Baffin (isl.)	68 30 N	70 00 W	79
Baghdad,* Iraq	33 21 N	44 24 E	52
Bahamas	24 00 N	76 00 W	81
Bahrain	26 00 N	50 40 E	52
Baja California (pen.)	28 00 N	114 00 W	81
Bakersfield, Calif.	35 22 N	119 01 W	76
Bākhtarān, Iran	34 19 N	47 04 E	52
Baku,* Azerbaijan	40 23 N	49 51 E	45
Balaton (lake)	46 50 N	17 50 E	44
Balearic (isls.)	39 30 N	03 00 E	42
Bali (isl.)	08 30 S	115 30 E	56
Balkan (mts.)	43 15 N	23 00 E	44
Balkhash (lake)	46 00 N	74 00 E	54
Baltic (sea)	56 30 N	19 00 E	43
Baltimore, Md.	39 17 N	76 37 W	78
Bamako,* Mali	12 38 N	07 59 W	68
Banaba (isl.)	00 52 S	169 35 E	62
Banda (sea)	06 00 S	128 00 E	57
Bandar Seri Begawan,* Brunei	04 55 N	114 55 E	56
Bandung, Indon.	06 56 S	107 36 E	56
Bangalore, India	12 59 N	77 28 E	53
Bangka (isl.)	02 22 S	106 08 E	56
Bangkok,* Thai.	13 45 N	100 30 E	56
Bangladesh	23 30 N	90 00 E	53
Bangor, Maine	44 48 N	68 46 W	78
Bangui,* CAfr.	04 22 N	18 36 E	69
Bangweulu (lake)	11 00 S	29 45 E	70
Banjul,* Gambia	13 28 N	16 35 W	68
Banks (isl.)	73 00 N	122 00 W	79
Baotou, China	40 40 N	109 59 E	55
Barbados	13 10 N	59 30 W	81
Barcelona, Spain	41 38 N	02 10 E	42
Barents (sea)	70 00 N	45 00 E	46
Bari, Italy	41 07 N	16 52 E	44
Barisan (mts.)	03 00 S	102 15 E	56
Barkly Tableland (plat.)	18 00 S	136 00 E	59
Baroda, India	22 18 N	73 12 E	53
Barquisimeto, Ven.	10 04 N	69 19 W	86
Barranquilla, Col.	10 59 N	74 50 W	86
Basel, Switz.	47 35 N	07 32 E	42
Bass (strait)	40 15 S	146 00 E	61
Bathurst, N.B.	47 36 N	65 39 W	79
Baton Rouge,* La.	30 27 N	91 11 W	78
Battle Creek, Mich.	42 19 N	85 11 W	78
Baykal (lake)	54 00 N	109 00 E	47
Beaufort (sea)	71 00 N	140 00 W	79
Beaumont, Texas	30 05 N	94 06 W	77
Beersheba, Israel	31 14 N	34 47 E	52
Beijing (Peking),* China	39 56 N	116 24 E	55
Beira, Moz.	19 50 S	34 50 E	70
Beirut,* Lebanon	33 55 N	35 30 E	52
Belarus	53 00 N	28 00 E	43
Belém, Brazil	01 28 S	48 27 W	87
Belfast,* No. Ire.	54 35 N	05 55 W	42
Belgium	50 45 N	04 30 E	42
Belgrade,* Yugo.	44 48 N	20 29 E	44
Belitung (isl.)	02 54 S	107 58 E	56
Belize	17 00 N	88 45 W	80
Belle Isle (strait)	51 30 N	56 30 W	79
Bellingshausen (sea)	69 00 S	81 00 E	71
Belmopan,* Belize	17 15 N	88 47 W	80
Belo Horizonte, Brazil	19 56 S	43 57 W	87
Bengal (bay)	18 00 N	90 00 E	53
Benghazi, Libya	32 07 N	20 03 E	69
Benin	09 00 N	02 00 E	68
Benin, Bight of (bay)	05 00 N	04 00 E	68
Ben Nevis (mt.)	56 48 N	04 59 W	42
Bergen, Norway	60 25 N	05 20 E	43
Bering (sea)	55 00 N	180 00	47
Bering (strait)	67 00 N	170 00 W	76
Berkeley, Calif.	37 52 N	122 16 W	76
Berlin,* Germany	52 30 N	13 20 E	42
Bermuda	32 20 N	64 40 W	73
Bern,* Switz.	47 00 N	07 30 E	42
Bhopāl, India	23 16 N	77 24 E	53
Bhutan	27 15 N	90 00 E	53
Bialystok, Poland	53 09 N	23 09 E	44
Bikini (isl.)	11 37 N	165 33 E	62
Bilbao, Spain	43 16 N	03 05 W	42
Biloxi, Miss.	30 24 N	88 53 W	78
Binghamton, N.Y.	42 06 N	75 55 W	78
Birmingham, Ala.	33 31 N	86 49 W	78
Birmingham, Eng.	52 30 N	01 55 W	42
Biscay (bay)	45 00 N	05 00 W	42
Bishkek,* Kyrgyzstan	42 54 N	74 36 E	54
Bismarck (arch.)	04 00 S	150 00 E	62
Bismarck,* N.D.	46 48 N	100 47 W	76
Bissau,* Guinea-Bissau	11 51 N	15 35 W	68
Bitterroot (mts.)	46 30 N	114 25 W	76
Black (sea)	42 30 N	35 00 E	44
Black Hills (mts.)	44 00 N	103 30 W	76

NAME	LATITUDE	LONGITUDE	PAGE
Blanc (mt.)	45 50 N	06 51 E	42
Blantyre, Malawi	15 49 S	35 00 E	70
Bloemfontein, S. Afr.	29 07 S	26 14 E	70
Bloomington, Ill.	40 29 N	88 59 W	78
Bloomington, Ind.	39 10 N	86 32 W	78
Blue Nile (river)	15 37 N	32 31 E	69
Bogotá,* Col.	04 36 N	74 05 W	86
Boise,* Idaho	43 37 N	116 12 W	76
Bolivia	16 00 S	64 00 W	86
Bologna, Italy	44 30 N	11 20 E	42
Bonaire (isl.), Neth. Ant.	12 12 N	68 15 W	81
Bonifacio (strait)	41 18 N	09 15 E	42
Bonn, Germany	50 44 N	07 06 E	42
Boothia (pen.)	70 00 N	95 00 W	79
Bordeaux, France	44 50 N	00 35 W	42
Borneo (isl.)	00 00	113 00 E	56
Bornholm (isl.)	55 10 N	15 00 E	43
Bosnia and Herzegovina	44 00 N	18 00 E	44
Bosporus (strait)	41 15 N	29 10 E	44
Boston,* Mass.	42 21 N	71 03 W	78
Bothnia (gulf)	62 00 N	20 00 E	43
Botou, China	38 05 N	116 30 E	55
Botswana	22 00 S	24 00 E	70
Bougainville (isl.)	06 10 S	155 15 E	62
Bouvet (isl.)	54 26 S	03 24 E	12
Bozeman, Mont.	45 41 N	111 02 W	76
Bradford, Eng.	53 47 N	01 45 W	42
Brahmaputra (river)	29 30 N	95 00 E	53
Brăila, Rom.	45 15 N	27 58 E	44
Brandon, Man.	49 50 N	99 57 W	79
Brasília,* Brazil	15 47 S	47 55 W	87
Braşov, Romania	45 39 N	25 37 E	44
Bratislava,* Slovakia	48 09 N	17 07 E	44
Braunschweig, Germany	52 22 N	10 42 E	42
Brazil	14 00 S	50 00 W	83
Brazos (river)	28 57 N	95 18 W	77
Brazzaville,* Congo	04 17 S	15 14 E	70
Bremen, Germany	53 10 N	08 40 E	42
Brescia, Italy	45 30 N	10 15 E	42
Bridgeport, Conn.	41 11 N	73 12 W	78
Bridgetown,* Barbados	13 06 N	59 37 W	81
Brisbane, Austl.	27 25 S	153 05 E	59
Bristol (bay)	57 45 N	160 00 W	76
Bristol, Eng.	51 28 N	02 35 W	42
Britanny (region)	48 00 N	03 00 W	42
British Columbia (prov.), Canada..	55 00 N	125 00 W	79
British Indian Ocean Terr.	06 00 S	72 00 E	13
Brno, Czech Rep.	49 10 N	16 30 E	42
Brooks (mts.)	68 30 N	153 00 W	76
Brownsville, Texas	25 54 N	97 30 W	77
Brunei	04 30 N	115 00 E	56
Brussels,* Belg.	50 50 N	04 22 E	42
Bryan, Texas	30 40 N	96 22 W	77
Bucharest,* Rom.	44 25 N	26 06 E	44
Budapest,* Hungary	47 30 N	19 10 E	44
Buenos Aires,* Arg.	34 36 S	58 26 W	88
Buffalo, N.Y.	42 53 N	78 52 W	78
Bujumbura,* Burundi	03 23 S	29 22 E	70
Bulgaria	42 30 N	25 30 E	44
Burgundy (region)	47 00 N	05 00 E	42
Burkina Faso	12 00 N	01 30 W	68
Burlington, Vt.	44 28 N	73 12 W	78
Burma	20 00 N	96 00 E	49
Bursa, Turkey	40 11 N	29 04 E	44
Burundi	03 30 S	30 00 E	70
Bydgoszcz, Poland	53 50 N	27 35 E	42

C

NAME	LATITUDE	LONGITUDE	PAGE
Caatingas (region)	07° 00′ N	43° 00′ W	87
Cádiz, Spain	36 32 N	06 18 W	42
Cagliari, Italy	39 13 N	09 07 E	42
Cairo,* Egypt	30 03 N	31 15 E	69
Calcutta, India	22 30 N	88 30 E	53
Calgary, Alta.	51 01 N	114 05 W	79
Cali, Col.	03 28 N	76 30 W	86
California (gulf)	28 00 N	112 00 W	81
California (state), U.S.	37 00 N	120 00 W	76
Callao, Peru	12 03 S	77 10 W	86
Camagüey, Cuba	21 53 N	77 55 W	81
Cambodia	12 00 N	105 00 E	56
Cameroon	05 00 N	13 00 E	68
Campbellton, N.B.	48 00 N	66 40 W	79
Campeche (bay)	20 00 N	93 00 W	80
Canada	60 00 N	100 00 W	79
Canadian (river)	35 28 N	95 04 W	76
Canary (isls.)	28 00 N	16 00 W	68
Canaveral (cape)	28 27 N	80 32 W	77
Canberra,* Austl.	35 18 S	149 07 E	61
Cannes, France	43 33 N	07 01 E	42
Cantabrica (mts.)	43 15 N	05 00 W	42
Canton (Guangzhou), China	23 07 N	113 15 E	55
Canton, Ohio	40 48 N	81 23 W	78
Cape Town,* S. Afr.	33 57 S	18 28 E	70
Cape Verde	16 00 N	24 00 W	12
Cape York (pen.)	13 00 S	142 30 E	59
Caprivi Strip (region)	18 00 S	23 00 E	70
Caracas,* Ven.	10 30 N	66 55 W	86
Cardiff,* Wales	51 30 N	03 12 W	42
Caribbean (sea)	15 00 N	75 00 W	81
Caroline (isls.)	08 00 N	150 00 E	62
Carpathian (mts.)	48 00 N	23 00 E	44
Carpentaria (gulf)	15 00 S	139 00 E	59
Carson City,* Nev.	39 10 N	119 45 W	76
Cartegena, Spain	37 36 N	00 59 W	42
Casablanca, Mor.	33 36 N	07 38 W	68
Cascades (mts.)	45 00 N	122 00 W	76
Casper, Wyo.	42 51 N	106 19 W	76
Caspian (sea)	42 00 N	50 00 E	44
Catalonia (region)	41 15 N	02 00 E	42
Caucasus (mts.)	42 30 N	45 00 E	45
Cayenne,* Fr. Guiana	04 56 N	52 20 W	87
Cayman (isls.)	19 30 N	80 40 W	80
Cebu, Philippines	10 18 N	123 54 E	57
Cebu (isl.)	10 18 N	123 54 E	57
Cedar Rapids, Iowa	42 00 N	91 41 W	78
Celebes (isl.)	02 00 S	121 00 E	57
Central African Republic	06 00 N	20 00 E	69
Ceuta, Spain	35 52 N	05 20 W	68
Ceylon (Sri Lanka)	07 00 N	81 00 E	53
Chad	15 00 N	18 00 E	69
Chad (lake)	13 15 N	14 30 E	68
Champaign, Ill.	40 07 N	88 14 W	78
Champlain (lake)	44 30 N	73 20 W	78
Changchun, China	43 53 N	125 18 E	55
Chang (Yangtze) (river)	31 48 N	121 10 E	55
Changsha, China	28 12 N	112 59 E	55
Channel (isls.)	49 30 N	02 30 W	42
Chaozhou, China	23 40 N	116 38 E	55
Charleston, S.C.	32 47 N	79 56 W	78
Charleston,* W. Va.	38 21 N	81 38 W	78
Charlotte, N.C.	35 14 N	80 51 W	78
Charlottesville, Va.	38 02 N	78 30 W	78
Charlottetown,* P.E.I.	46 14 N	63 08 W	79
Chattanooga, Tenn.	35 03 N	85 19 W	78
Chelyabinsk, Russia	55 10 N	61 24 E	45
Chelyuskin (cape)	77 45 N	104 30 E	47
Chemnitz, Germany	50 40 N	12 55 E	42
Chengdu, China	30 40 N	104 04 E	54
Chesapeake (bay)	38 35 N	76 25 W	78
Chennai (Madras), India	13 05 N	80 15 E	53
Cheshskaya (bay)	67 30 N	47 00 E	43
Chesterfield Inlet, Nunavut	63 40 N	91 45 W	79
Cheyenne,* Wyo.	41 08 N	104 49 W	76
Chibougamau, Qué.	49 55 N	74 22 W	79
Chicago, Ill.	41 52 N	87 38 W	78
Chicoutimi, Qué.	48 30 N	71 00 W	79
Chidley (cape)	60 23 N	64 26 W	79
Chihuahua, Mex.	28 38 N	106 05 W	81
Chile	32 00 S	71 00 W	83
Chilliwack, Br. Col.	49 10 N	121 57 W	76
Chiloé (isl.)	42 00 S	74 00 W	88
Chimborazo (mt.)	01 28 S	78 48 W	86
China	35 00 N	105 00 E	54
Chişinău,* Moldova	47 00 N	28 50 E	44
Chittagong, Bangladesh	22 15 N	91 55 E	53
Chongqing, China	29 34 N	106 35 E	54
Chonos (arch.)	45 00 S	74 00 W	88
Christchurch, N.Z.	43 32 S	172 39 E	59
Christmas (isl.)	10 30 S	105 40 E	13
Chuckchi (pen.)	66 00 N	175 00 W	47
Churchill (river)	58 47 N	94 11 W	79
Churchill, Man.	58 46 N	94 10 W	79
Cimarron (river)	36 07 N	96 30 W	76
Cincinnati, Ohio	39 06 N	84 31 W	78
Ciudad Guayana, Ven.	08 22 N	62 40 W	86
Ciudad Juárez, Mex.	31 44 N	106 29 W	81
Cleveland, Ohio	41 30 N	81 42 W	78
Clipperton (isl.)	10 13 N	109 10 W	12
Cluj-Napoca, Romania	46 45 N	23 36 E	44
Coast Ranges (mts.)	42 00 N	123 15 W	76
Cocos (isls.)	05 31 N	87 00 W	13
Cod (cape)	42 04 N	70 10 W	78
Cologne, Germany	51 00 N	07 00 E	42
Colombia	05 00 N	74 00 W	86
Colombo,* Sri Lanka	06 55 N	79 50 E	53
Colorado (river), Arg.	39 51 S	62 08 W	88
Colorado (river), U.S., Mexico	31 49 N	114 45 W	76
Colorado (river), U.S., Texas	28 52 N	96 02 W	76
Colorado (state), U.S.	39 00 N	105 30 W	76
Colorado Springs, Colo.	38 50 N	104 49 W	76
Columbia (river)	46 15 N	123 40 W	76
Columbia, Mo.	38 57 N	92 20 W	78
Columbia,* S.C.	34 00 N	81 02 W	78
Columbus, Ga.	32 28 N	84 59 W	78
Columbus,* Ohio	39 58 N	83 00 W	78
Comorin (cape)	07 37 N	77 28 E	53
Comoros	12 00 S	44 00 E	65
Conakry,* Guinea	09 31 N	13 42 W	68
Concepción, Chile	36 50 S	73 01 W	88
Concord,* N.H.	43 12 N	71 32 W	78
Congo, Rep. of the	00 00	15 00 E	65
Congo (basin)	00 00	22 00 E	69
Congo, Dem. Rep. of the	02 00 S	24 00 E	65
Congo (river)	06 05 S	12 20 E	70
Connecticut (state), U.S.	41 38 N	72 45 W	78
Constantine, Alg.	36 23 N	06 38 E	68
Cook (isls.)	20 00 S	158 00 W	63
Cook (mt.)	43 36 S	170 08 E	59
Cook (strait)	41 15 S	174 30 E	59
Copenhagen,* Denmark	55 40 N	12 35 E	43
Coral (sea)	14 00 S	156 00 E	59
Córdoba, Arg.	31 25 S	64 10 W	88
Córdoba, Spain	37 54 N	04 46 W	42
Corfu (isl.)	39 38 N	19 56 E	44
Corinth (gulf)	38 19 N	22 04 E	44
Cork, Ireland	51 55 N	08 30 W	42
Corner Brook, Newf.	48 57 N	57 56 W	79
Cornwall, Ont.	45 01 N	74 44 W	79
Coromandel Coast	13 00 N	80 15 E	53
Corpus Christi, Texas	27 48 N	97 24 W	77
Corsica (isl.)	42 00 N	09 00 E	42
Corvallis, Ore.	44 34 N	123 16 W	76
Costa del Sol (coast)	36 30 N	04 00 W	42
Costa Rica	10 00 N	84 00 W	80
Côte d'Ivoire	07 00 N	05 00 W	68
Coventry, Eng.	52 25 N	01 33 W	42
Cranbrook, Br. Col.	49 31 N	115 46 W	79
Crete (isl.)	35 15 N	25 00 E	44
Crimea (pen.)	45 00 N	34 00 E	44
Croatia	45 30 N	16 00 E	44
Cuba	22 00 N	80 00 W	81
Curaçao (isl.), Neth. Ant.	12 11 N	69 00 W	81
Curitiba, Brazil	25 25 S	49 15 W	88
Cyclades (isls.)	37 00 N	75 00 E	44
Cyprus	35 00 N	33 00 E	52
Czech Republic	49 00 N	17 00 E	44
Czectochowa, Poland	50 49 N	19 06 E	44

D

NAME	LATITUDE	LONGITUDE	PAGE
Da Hinggan (mts.)	48° 30′ N	120° 00′ E	55
Dakar,* Senegal	14 40 N	17 28 W	68
Dalian, China	38 55 N	121 39 E	55
Dallas, Texas	32 47 N	96 48 W	77
Damascus,* Syria	33 35 N	36 28 E	52
Damavand (mt.)	35 57 N	52 08 E	52
Da Nang, Vietnam	16 04 N	108 13 E	56
Danube (river)	45 20 N	29 40 E	44
Dardanelles (strait)	40 07 N	26 23 E	44
Dar es Salaam,* Tanzania	06 48 S	39 17 E	70
Darling (river)	32 00 S	142 57 E	59
Darwin, Austl.	12 27 S	130 50 E	59
Davao, Philippines	07 18 N	125 25 E	57
Davenport, Iowa	41 31 N	90 34 W	78
Davis (strait)	66 30 N	58 00 W	79
Dawson, Yukon Terr.	64 04 N	139 25 W	79
Dayton, Ohio	39 46 N	84 12 W	78
Daytona Beach, Fla.	29 13 N	81 01 W	78
Dead (sea)	31 30 N	35 30 E	52
Death Valley Nat'l Park, U.S.	37 00 N	117 07 W	76
Debrecen, Hungary	47 32 N	21 38 E	44
Deccan (plat.)	17 00 N	78 00 E	53
Delaware (state), U.S.	39 00 N	75 30 W	78
Delgado (cape)	10 41 S	40 38 E	70
Delhi, India	28 29 N	77 15 E	53
Denmark	56 00 N	10 30 E	43
Denver,* Colo.	39 45 N	104 59 W	76
Des Moines,* Iowa	41 35 N	93 37 W	78
Detroit, Mich.	42 20 N	83 03 W	78
Devon (isl.)	75 00 N	86 00 W	79
Dezhneva (cape)	66 05 N	169 40 W	47
Dhaka,* Bangladesh	23 45 N	90 25 E	53
Diego Garcia (isl.)	07 36 S	72 28 E	13
Dinaric Alps (mts.)	43 30 N	17 00 E	44
District of Columbia, U.S.	38 54 N	77 01 W	78
Diyarbakir, Turkey	37 55 N	40 14 E	44
Djibouti	12 00 N	43 00 E	69
Djibouti,* Djibouti	11 35 N	43 09 E	69
Dnipropetrovs'k, Ukraine	48 27 N	35 01 E	44
Dnipro (river)	46 30 N	32 36 E	44
Dnister (river)	46 20 N	30 18 E	44
Doğukaradeniz (mts.)	40 30 N	39 00 E	44
Doha,* Qatar	25 17 N	51 32 E	52
Dominica	15 25 N	61 20 W	81
Dominican Republic	19 00 N	70 00 W	81
Don (river)	47 04 N	39 18 E	44
Donets (river)	47 36 N	40 54 E	44
Donets'k, Ukraine	48 00 N	37 48 E	44
Dortmund, Germany	51 30 N	07 30 E	42
Douala, Cameroon	04 03 N	09 37 E	68
Douro (river)	41 09 N	08 39 W	42
Dover (strait)	51 00 N	01 30 E	42
Dover,* Del.	39 09 N	75 32 W	78
Drake (passage)	60 00 S	67 00 W	88
Dresden, Germany	51 10 N	13 45 E	42
Dublin,* Ire.	53 20 N	06 10 W	42
Dubrovnik, Croatia	42 38 N	18 07 E	44
Duluth, Minn.	46 47 N	92 06 W	78
Dundee, Scot.	56 30 N	02 58 W	42
Durango, Mex.	24 02 N	104 40 W	81
Durban, S. Afr.	29 51 S	31 00 E	70
Durham, N.C.	35 59 N	78 54 W	78
Dushanbe,* Tajikistan	38 33 N	68 48 E	46
Düsseldorf, Germany	51 20 N	06 40 E	42
Dvina, Northern (river)	64 32 N	40 37 E	46

E

NAME	LATITUDE	LONGITUDE	PAGE
East China (sea)	30° 00′ N	125° 00′ E	55
Easter (isl.)	27 08 S	109 25 W	63
Eastern Ghats (mts.)	17 30 N	83 00 E	53
East London, S. Afr.	33 01 S	27 55 E	70
Eau Claire, Wis.	44 49 N	91 30 W	78
Ebro (river)	40 43 N	00 54 E	42
Ecatepec, Mex.	19 35 N	99 04 W	80
Ecuador	01 00 S	79 00 W	86
Edinburgh,* Scot.	55 55 N	03 10 W	42
Edmonton,* Alta.	53 32 N	113 30 W	79
Edmundston, N.B.	47 22 N	68 20 W	79
Edward (lake)	00 20 S	29 35 E	69
Edwards (plat.)	30 30 N	101 00 W	76
Efate (isl.)	17 40 S	168 23 E	62
Egypt	27 00 N	30 00 E	69
Elbe (river)	53 30 N	09 45 E	42
Elbert (mt.)	39 07 N	106 26 W	76
El'brus (mt.)	43 21 N	42 26 E	45
Elburz (mts.)	36 00 N	52 00 E	52
Ellesmere (isl.)	79 00 N	82 00 W	79
El Paso, Texas	31 45 N	106 29 W	76
El Salvador	13 30 N	89 00 W	80
Enewetak (isl.)	11 11 N	162 21 E	62
England, U.K.	53 00 N	01 00 W	42
English (chan.)	50 00 N	02 30 W	42
Equatorial Guinea	01 30 N	10 00 E	68
Erie (lake)	42 20 N	81 00 W	78
Erie, Pa.	42 07 N	80 05 W	78
Eritrea	15 00 N	40 00 E	69
Erzgebirge (mts.)	50 30 N	13 00 E	42
Esfahān, Iran	32 40 N	51 38 E	52
Espíritu Santo (isl.)	15 15 S	166 55 E	62
Essen, Germany	51 30 N	07 00 E	42
Estonia	59 00 N	26 00 E	43
Ethiopia	10 00 N	40 00 E	69
Eugene, Ore.	44 03 N	123 06 W	76
Euphrates (river)	38 00 N	39 05 E	52
Evansville, Ind.	37 58 N	87 34 W	78
Everest (mt.)	27 58 N	87 05 E	53
Everglades Nat'l Park, U.S.	25 15 N	81 00 W	77
Eyre (lake)	28 30 S	137 15 E	59

F

NAME	LATITUDE	LONGITUDE	PAGE
Fairbanks, Alaska	64° 51′ N	147° 43′ W	76
Faisalabad, Pak.	31 25 N	73 05 E	53
Falkland (isls.)	52 00 S	59 00 W	88
Fall River, Mass.	41 42 N	71 09 W	78
Fargo, N.D.	46 52 N	96 48 W	77
Faroe (isls.)	62 00 N	07 00 W	39
Fayetteville, Ark.	36 04 N	94 09 W	77
Fayetteville, N.C.	35 03 N	78 52 W	78
Ferrara, Italy	44 50 N	11 40 E	42
Fezzan (region)	27 00 N	14 00 E	68
Fiji	17 00 S	179 00 E	62
Finisterre (cape)	42 53 N	09 16 W	42
Finland	64 00 N	26 00 E	43
Finland (gulf)	60 00 N	27 00 E	43
Flin Flon, Man.-Sask.	54 46 N	101 53 W	79
Flint, Mich.	43 01 N	83 42 W	78
Florence, Italy	43 46 N	11 13 E	42
Flores (isl.)	08 30 S	121 00 E	57
Flores (sea)	05 39 S	119 54 E	56
Florida (keys)	24 44 N	81 00 W	78
Florida (state), U.S.	28 00 N	82 00 W	78
Former Yugoslav Republic of Macedonia	42 00 N	21 26 E	44
Fortaleza, Brazil	03 41 S	38 33 W	87

NAME	LATITUDE	LONGITUDE	PAGE
Fort Collins, Colo.	40 35 N	105 05 W	76
Fort-de-France,* Mart.	14 36 N	61 05 W	81
Fort Frances, Ont.	48 37 N	93 25 W	79
Fort McMurray, Alta.	56 44 N	111 23 W	79
Fort Myers, Fla.	26 38 N	81 52 W	78
Fort Nelson, Br. Col.	58 49 N	122 36 W	79
Fort Smith, Ark.	35 23 N	94 26 W	77
Fort Smith, N.W. Terrs.	60 00 N	112 00 W	79
Fort Wayne, Ind.	41 04 N	85 08 W	78
Fort Worth, Texas	32 45 N	97 20 W	77
Foxe (basin)	68 00 N	78 00 W	79
France	47 00 N	02 00 E	42
Frankfort,* Ky.	38 12 N	84 53 W	78
Frankfurt, Germany	50 10 N	08 30 E	42
Franz Josef Land (isls.)	81 00 N	51 00 E	46
Fraser (river)	49 08 N	123 10 W	79
Fredericton,* N.B.	45 57 N	66 38 W	79
Freetown,* Sierra Leone	08 29 N	13 13 W	68
French Guiana	04 00 N	53 00 W	87
French Polynesia	15 00 S	140 00 W	63
Fresno, Calif.	36 44 N	119 47 W	76
Fukuoka, Japan	33 35 N	130 24 E	55
Funafuti,* Tuvalu	08 31 S	179 08 E	62
Fundy (bay)	45 00 N	66 00 W	79
Fushun, China	41 52 N	123 53 E	55
Fuzhou, China	26 05 N	119 19 E	55

G

NAME	LATITUDE	LONGITUDE	PAGE
Gabon	00° 00′	12° 00′ E	68
Gaborone,* Botswana	24 40 S	25 54 E	70
Gainesville, Fla.	29 39 N	82 20 W	78
Galápagos (isls.)	00 15 S	90 00 W	12
Galaţi, Romania	45 26 N	28 03 E	44
Galveston, Texas	29 18 N	94 48 W	77
Gambia	13 30 N	15 30 W	68
Gäncä, Azerbaijan	40 40 N	46 22 E	45
Ganges (river)	26 00 N	80 15 E	53
Garonne (river)	45 01 N	00 36 W	42
Gary, Ind.	41 35 N	87 20 W	77
Gaspé (pen.)	48 30 N	65 00 W	79
Gaziantep, Turkey	37 05 N	37 22 E	44
Gdańsk, Poland	54 20 N	18 30 E	43
Gdynia, Poland	54 32 N	18 33 E	43
Geneva (lake)	46 25 N	06 25 E	42
Geneva, Switzerland	46 12 N	06 10 E	42
Genoa, Italy	44 25 N	08 55 E	42
Georgetown,* Guyana	06 49 N	58 10 W	68
Georgetown, Malaysia	05 25 N	100 19 E	56
Georgia	42 00 N	43 00 E	45
Georgia (state), U.S.	32 30 N	83 15 W	78
Georgian (bay)	45 15 N	80 45 W	79
Germany	51 00 N	10 00 E	42
Ghana	07 00 N	01 00 W	68
Ghent, Belgium	51 10 N	03 40 E	42
Gibraltar (strait)	35 55 N	05 35 W	42
Gibraltar	36 08 N	05 22 W	42
Gijón, Spain	43 32 N	05 40 W	42
Glacier Nat'l Park, U.S.	48 35 N	114 00 W	76
Glasgow, Scot.	55 50 N	04 10 W	42
Gobi (desert)	43 00 N	110 00 E	54
Godavari (river)	19 00 N	79 00 E	53
Godwin Austen (K2) (mt.)	35 53 N	76 30 E	53
Goiânia, Brazil	16 40 S	49 16 W	87
Good Hope (cape)	34 21 S	18 29 E	70
Göteborg, Sweden	57 43 N	11 58 E	43
Gotland (isl.)	57 45 N	18 45 E	43
Grampians (mts.)	56 45 N	04 30 W	42
Granada, Spain	37 11 N	03 36 W	42
Gran Chaco (region)	24 00 S	62 00 W	88
Grand Canyon Nat'l Park, U.S.	36 03 N	112 08 W	76
Grande Prairie, Alta.	55 10 N	118 48 W	79
Grand Falls, Newf.	48 56 N	55 40 W	79
Grand Forks, N.D.	47 52 N	97 03 W	77
Grand Rapids, Mich.	42 58 N	85 40 W	78
Graz, Austria	47 00 N	15 30 E	42
Great Australian Bight (bay)	33 00 S	130 00 E	59
Great Barrier (reef)	16 00 S	145 50 E	59
Great Bear (lake)	66 00 N	121 00 W	79
Great Britain (isl.)	54 00 N	02 00 W	42
Great Dividing Range (mts.)	35 00 S	149 35 E	59
Great Indian (desert)	28 00 N	73 00 E	53
Great Rift (valley)	09 00 N	41 00 E	69
Great Salt (lake)	41 05 N	112 30 W	76
Great Sandy (desert)	20 00 S	124 00 E	59
Great Slave (lake)	61 00 N	114 00 W	79
Great Victoria (desert)	27 00 S	130 00 E	59
Greater Antilles (isls.)	18 00 N	74 00 W	81
Greece	39 00 N	23 00 E	44
Greeley, Colo.	40 25 N	101 41 W	76
Green Bay, Wis.	44 31 N	88 00 W	78
Greenland (isl.)	70 00 N	40 00 W	73
Greensboro, N.C.	36 04 N	79 47 W	78
Greenland (sea)	75 00 N	15 00 W	71
Greenville, S.C.	34 51 N	82 24 W	78
Grenada	12 05 N	61 40 W	81
Grenoble, France	45 10 N	05 43 E	42
Guadalajara, Mex.	20 40 N	103 20 W	81
Guadalcanal (isl.)	09 40 S	160 15 E	62
Guadalupe (isl.)	29 11 N	118 17 W	73
Guadarrama (mts.)	41 00 N	03 30 W	42
Guadeloupe (isl.)	16 15 N	61 35 W	81
Guajira (pen.)	11 30 N	72 45 W	86
Guam (isl.)	13 30 N	144 47 E	62
Guangzhou, China	23 07 N	113 15 E	55
Guatemala	15 30 N	90 15 W	80
Guatemala,* Guat.	14 37 N	90 31 W	80
Guayaquil, Ecuador	02 12 S	79 53 W	86
Guernsey (isl.)	49 27 N	02 33 W	42
Guiana Highlands (plat.)	05 00 N	60 00 W	86
Guinea	10 00 N	11 00 W	68
Guinea (gulf)	03 00 N	04 00 E	68
Guinea-Bissau	11 50 N	15 00 W	68
Guwāhati, India	26 10 N	91 45 E	53
Guyana	05 00 N	59 00 W	86

H

NAME	LATITUDE	LONGITUDE	PAGE
Hadhramaut (region)	16° 00′ N	51° 00′ E	52
Hagåtña ,* Guam	13 29 N	144 47 E	62
Hague, The,* Netherlands	52 05 N	04 20 E	42
Haifa, Israel	32 50 N	35 00 E	52
Hainan (isl.)	19 00 N	110 00 E	55
Haiphong, Vietnam	20 52 N	106 41 E	55
Haiti	19 00 N	72 30 W	81
Halifax,* N.S.	44 40 N	63 36 W	79
Halle, Germany	51 30 N	12 00 E	42
Halmahera (isl.)	01 30 N	128 00 E	57
Hamburg, Germany	53 30 N	10 00 E	42
Hamilton, Ohio	39 24 N	84 33 W	78
Hamilton, Ont.	43 12 N	79 50 W	79
Hangzhou, China	30 17 N	120 10 E	55
Hannover, Germany	52 20 N	09 30 E	42
Hanoi,* Vietnam	21 02 N	105 50 E	54
Happy Valley-Goose Bay, Newf.	53 18 N	60 23 W	79
Harare,* Zim.	17 50 S	31 03 E	70
Harbin, China	45 42 N	126 36 E	55
Harrisburg,* Pa.	40 16 N	76 53 W	78
Hartford,* Conn.	41 46 N	72 41 W	78
Hatteras (cape)	35 13 N	75 31 W	78
Havana,* Cuba	23 08 N	82 24 W	80
Hawaii (isl.)	19 30 N	155 30 W	76
Hawaii (state), U.S.	21 00 N	00 10 E	76
Hay River, N.W. Terrs.	60 51 N	115 42 W	79
Heard (isl.)	53 07 S	73 20 E	71
Hebrides (isls.)	57 20 N	07 00 W	42
Hecate (strait)	53 20 N	131 00 W	79
Helena,* Mont.	46 36 N	112 02 W	76
Helmand (river)	31 00 N	64 00 E	53
Helsingborg, Sweden	56 07 N	12 45 E	43
Helsinki,* Finland	60 12 N	25 00 E	43
Herāt, Afghan.	34 20 N	62 12 E	52
Hermosillo, Mex.	29 04 N	110 58 W	81
Hijāz (region)	24 30 N	39 00 E	52
Himalaya (mts.)	28 00 N	81 00 E	53
Hindu Kush (mts.)	35 45 N	70 30 E	53
Hiroshima, Japan	34 24 N	132 25 E	55
Hiva Oa (isl.)	09 46 S	139 00 W	63
Hobart, Austl.	42 52 S	147 18 E	59
Ho Chi Minh City, Vietnam	10 47 N	106 41 E	56
Hokkaido (isl.)	43 00 N	143 00 E	55
Homyel', Belarus	52 25 N	31 00 E	43
Honduras	15 00 N	87 00 W	80
Hong Kong	22 15 N	114 10 E	55
Honiara,* Sol. Is.	09 25 S	160 00 E	62
Honolulu,* Hawaii	21 18 N	157 51 W	76
Honshu (isl.)	36 00 N	137 00 E	55
Horn (cape)	55 59 S	67 16 W	88
Houston, Texas	29 45 N	95 22 W	77
Howrah, India	22 35 N	82 20 E	53
Hrodna, Belarus	53 41 N	23 50 E	44
Huang (river)	38 06 N	118 24 E	55
Hudson (bay)	59 00 N	86 00 W	79
Hudson (strait)	61 30 N	72 00 W	79
Hue, Vietnam	16 29 N	107 34 E	56
Hull, Eng.	53 45 N	00 20 W	42
Hull, Qué.	45 26 N	75 44 W	79
Hungary	47 00 N	19 00 E	44
Huntington, W. Va.	38 25 N	82 27 W	78
Huntsville, Ala.	34 44 N	86 35 W	78
Huron (lake)	44 30 N	82 30 W	78
Hyderabad, India	17 15 N	78 30 E	53
Hyderabad, Pak.	25 28 N	68 35 E	53

I

NAME	LATITUDE	LONGITUDE	PAGE
Ilbadan, Nigeria	07° 23′ N	03° 54′ E	68
Ibiza (isl.)	39 00 N	01 25 E	42
Iceland	65 00 N	19 00 W	39
Idaho (state), U.S.	44 00 N	114 00 W	76
Iliamna (lake)	59 30 N	155 00 W	76
Illinois (state), U.S.	40 00 N	89 15 W	78
Inch'on, S. Korea	36 51 N	127 26 E	55
India	23 00 N	80 00 E	53
Indiana (state), U.S.	40 00 N	86 00 W	78
Indianapolis,* Ind.	39 46 N	86 10 W	78
Indonesia	05 00 S	120 00 E	56
Indore, India	22 40 N	75 58 E	53
Indus (river)	33 00 N	71 30 E	53
Inner Mongolia (region)	42 00 N	110 00 E	55
Inuvik, N.W. Terrs.	68 21 N	133 43 W	79
Ionian (sea)	38 00 N	19 00 E	44
Iowa (state), U.S.	42 00 N	93 30 W	77
Iowa City, Iowa	41 40 N	91 32 W	78
Iqaluit,* Nunavut	63 45 N	68 31 W	79
Iran	33 00 N	55 00 E	52
Iraq	33 00 N	44 00 E	52
Ireland	53 00 N	08 00 W	42
Irish (sea)	53 40 N	04 30 W	42
Irkutsk, Russia	52 16 N	104 20 E	47
Irtysh (river)	61 02 N	68 47 E	46
Ishevsk, Russia	56 51 N	53 14 E	45
Islamabad,* Pakistan	33 42 N	73 10 E	53
Israel	32 00 N	35 00 E	52
Istanbul, Turkey	41 10 N	29 00 E	44
Itaipu (res.)	25 00 S	54 30 W	88
Italy	42 00 N	13 00 E	39
Ivanovo, Russia	57 00 N	40 59 E	43
Iwo Jima (isl.)	24 47 N	141 20 E	62
Izmir, Turkey	38 25 N	27 10 E	44

J

NAME	LATITUDE	LONGITUDE	PAGE
Jackson,* Miss.	32° 18′ N	90° 11′ W	78
Jacksonville, Fla.	30 20 N	81 40 W	78
Jaipur, India	26 55 N	75 49 E	53
Jakarta,* Indonesia	06 10 S	106 50 E	56
Jamaica	18 15 N	77 30 W	81
James (bay)	53 00 N	80 30 W	79
Jan Mayen (isl.)	71 00 N	08 30 W	39
Japan	38 00 N	138 00 E	55
Japan (sea)	40 00 N	135 00 E	55
Java (isl.)	07 00 S	110 00 E	56
Java (sea)	05 00 S	110 00 E	56
Jayapura, Indon.	02 32 S	140 42 E	57
Jefferson City,* Mo.	38 36 N	92 12 W	78
Jersey (isl.)	49 13 N	02 07 W	42
Jerusalem,* Israel	31 46 N	35 14 E	52
Jidda, Saudi Arabia	21 29 N	39 12 E	52
Jilin, China	43 51 N	126 33 E	55
Jinan, China	36 40 N	117 00 E	55
Johannesburg, S. Afr.	26 12 S	28 03 E	70
Johnston (isl.)	16 44 N	169 31 W	63
Jonquière, Qué.	48 25 N	71 15 W	79
Jordan	31 00 N	37 00 E	52
Joshua Tree Nat'l Park, U.S.	33 55 N	115 56 W	76
Juan de Fuca (strait)	49 15 N	123 30 W	79
Juan Fernández (isls.)	33 36 S	78 55 W	12
Juneau,* Alaska	58 18 N	134 25 W	76
Jura (mts.)	47 10 N	07 00 E	42
Jutland (pen.)	56 00 N	09 00 E	43
Juventud (isl.)	21 40 N	82 50 W	80

K

NAME	LATITUDE	LONGITUDE	PAGE
Kabul,* Afghan.	34° 31′ N	69° 00′ E	52
Kahoolawe (isl.)	20 33 N	156 37 W	76
Kaifeng, China	34 48 N	114 21 E	55
Kalaallit Nunaat (Greenland) (isl.)	70 00 N	40 00 W	73
Kalahari (desert)	23 00 S	22 00 E	70
Kalamazoo, Mich.	42 17 N	85 35 W	78
Kalimantan (region)	01 00 S	113 00 E	56
Kalyān, India	19 15 N	73 09 E	53
Kama (river)	55 10 N	49 20 E	45
Kamchatka (pen.)	56 00 N	160 00 E	47
Kamloops, Br. Col.	50 40 N	120 20 W	79
Kampala,* Uganda	00 19 N	32 35 E	69
Kampuchea (Cambodia)	12 00 N	105 00 E	56
Kananga, D.R. Congo	05 54 S	22 25 E	70
Kanazawa, Japan	36 34 N	136 39 E	55
Kanin (pen.)	67 30 N	45 00 E	43
Kano, Nigeria	12 00 N	08 31 E	68
Kanpur, India	26 28 N	80 21 E	53
Kansas (state), U.S.	38 30 N	98 30 W	76
Kansas City, Kans.	39 06 N	94 38 W	77
Kansas City, Mo.	39 05 N	94 35 W	77
Kaohsiung, China	22 38 N	120 17 E	55
Kara (sea)	72 00 N	62 00 E	46
Karachi, Pak.	24 55 N	67 00 E	53
Karaganda, Kazakhstan	49 50 N	73 10 E	47
Karakoram (mts.)	36 00 N	77 00 E	53
Karakumy (desert)	41 30 N	58 00 E	45
Karlsruhe, Germany	49 00 N	08 28 E	42
Kasai (river)	03 10 S	16 11 E	70
Kassel, Germany	51 20 N	09 15 E	42
Kathmandu,* Nepal	27 45 N	85 25 E	53
Katowice, Poland	50 16 N	19 00 E	44
Kattegat (strait)	57 00 N	11 30 E	43
Kauai (isl.)	22 05 N	159 30 W	76
Kaunas, Lithuania	54 54 N	23 54 E	43
Kavir, Dasht-e (desert)	35 00 N	55 00 E	52
Kawasaki, Japan	35 30 N	139 47 E	55
Kazakhstan	48 00 N	67 00 E	46
Kazan', Russia	55 45 N	49 08 E	45
Kelowna, Br. Col.	49 54 N	119 29 W	79
Kemerovo, Russia	55 20 N	86 05 E	47
Kenora, Ont.	49 46 N	94 28 W	79
Kentucky (lake)	37 00 N	88 16 W	78
Kentucky (state), U.S.	37 30 N	85 00 W	78
Kenya	00 00	38 00 E	69
Kenya (mt.)	00 08 S	37 18 E	69
Kerguélen (isls.)	49 00 S	69 00 E	13
Khabarovsk, Russia	48 30 N	135 06 E	55
Kharkiv, Ukraine	50 00 N	36 15 E	44
Khartoum,* Sudan	15 35 N	32 33 E	69
Khulna, Bangladesh	22 48 N	89 33 E	53
Kiel, Germany	54 20 N	10 10 E	42
Kiev,* Ukraine	50 27 N	30 32 E	44
Kigali,* Rwanda	01 57 S	30 04 E	70
Kilimanjaro (mt.)	03 04 S	37 21 E	70
Kimberley, S. Afr.	28 43 S	24 46 E	70
Kimberley (plat.)	16 00 S	127 00 E	59
Kingston,* Jamaica	18 00 N	76 48 W	81
Kingston, Ont.	44 10 N	76 44 W	79
Kinshasa,* D.R. Congo	04 19 S	15 23 E	70
Kirgiz Steppe (grassland)	49 30 N	57 00 E	45
Kiribati	00 00	175 00 E	62
Kitakyushu, Japan	33 53 N	130 50 E	55
Kjölen (mts.)	65 00 N	15 00 E	43
Knoxville, Tenn.	35 58 N	83 55 W	78
Kobe, Japan	34 41 N	135 10 E	55
Kodiak (isl.)	57 30 N	153 30 W	76
Kola (pen.)	67 20 N	37 00 E	43
Kolguyev (isl.)	68 30 N	49 00 E	43
Kolyma (mts.)	63 00 N	160 00 E	47
Kolyma (river)	69 30 N	161 12 E	47
Komandorskiye (isls.)	55 00 N	167 00 E	47
Konya, Turkey	37 52 N	32 31 E	44
Korea, North	40 00 N	127 00 E	55
Korea, South	37 30 N	128 00 E	55
Koror,* Palau	07 20 N	134 28 E	62
Kosciusko (mt.)	36 28 S	148 16 E	59
Kota Kinabalu, Malaysia	05 59 N	116 04 E	56
Kraków, Poland	50 05 N	19 55 E	44
Krasnodar, Russia	45 02 N	39 00 E	44
Krasnoyarsk, Russia	56 02 N	92 48 E	46
Krishna (river)	15 57 N	80 59 E	53
Krung Thep (Bangkok),* Thailand	13 45 N	100 30 E	56
Kryvyy Rih, Ukraine	47 55 N	33 21 E	44
Kuala Lumpur,* Malaysia	03 09 N	101 42 E	56
Kuching, Malaysia	01 34 N	111 22 E	56
Kugluktuk, Nunavut	67 50 N	115 05 W	79
Kumamoto, Japan	32 48 N	130 43 E	55
Kumasi, Ghana	06 41 N	01 37 W	68
Kunming, China	25 04 N	102 41 E	54
Kunlun (mts.)	36 00 N	90 00 E	54
Kura (river)	39 24 N	49 19 E	45
Kuril (isls.)	45 00 N	150 00 E	47
Kutch (Kachchh), Rann of (salt lake)	24 00 N	70 00 E	53
Kuwait	29 30 N	47 45 E	52
Kuwait,* Kuwait	29 20 N	48 02 E	52
Kwajalein (isl.)	08 43 N	167 44 E	62
Kyoto, Japan	34 58 N	135 45 E	55
Kyrgyzstan	41 00 N	75 00 E	46
Kyushu (isl.)	33 00 N	131 00 E	55

L

NAME	LATITUDE	LONGITUDE	PAGE
Labrador (region)	54° 00′ N	60° 00′ W	79
Laccadive, (sea)	11 00 N	73 00 E	53
Ladoga (lake)	61 00 N	31 00 E	43

NAME	LATITUDE	LONGITUDE	PAGE
Lafayette, Ind.	40 25 N	86 53 W	78
Lagos, Nigeria	06 27 N	03 25 E	68
Lahore, Pak.	31 37 N	74 18 E	53
Lake of the Woods (lake)	49 30 N	94 30 W	79
Lancaster (sound)	74 15 N	84 00 W	79
Lancaster, Pa.	40 02 N	76 18 W	78
Land's End (prom.)	50 05 N	05 30 W	42
Languedoc (region)	43 00 N	03 00 E	42
Lansing,* Mich.	42 44 N	84 33 W	78
Lanzhou, China	36 03 N	103 41 E	54
Laos	19 00 N	103 00 E	49
La Paz,* Bolivia	16 29 S	68 09 W	86
La Pérouse (strait)	45 45 N	142 00 E	55
La Plata (river)	36 00 S	55 00 W	88
Lapland, (region)	68 00 N	23 00 E	43
Laptev (sea)	76 00 N	126 00 E	47
Laramie, Wyo.	41 19 N	105 35 W	76
Las Cruces, N.M.	32 18 N	106 46 W	76
Las Palmas, Canary Is., Spain	28 06 N	15 24 W	65
Las Vegas, Nev.	36 10 N	115 09 W	76
Latvia	57 00 N	24 00 E	43
Lausanne, Switz.	46 31 N	06 37 E	42
Laval, Qué.	45 36 N	73 45 W	77
Lebanon	33 45 N	35 45 E	52
Leeds, Eng.	53 50 N	01 25 W	42
Leeward, (isls.)	18 00 N	61 00 W	81
Le Havre, France	49 25 N	00 10 E	42
Leipzig, Germany	51 20 N	12 20 E	42
Lena (river)	72 00 N	127 00 E	47
León, Mex.	21 07 N	101 40 W	80
Lesotho	29 15 S	28 15 E	70
Lesser Antilles, (isls.)	12 00 N	67 00 W	81
Lésvos (Lesbos) (isl.)	39 20 N	26 15 E	44
Lethbridge, Alta.	49 42 N	112 50 W	79
Lexington, Ky.	38 03 N	84 30 W	78
Leyte (isl.)	10 50 N	125 00 E	57
Lhasa, China	29 39 N	91 06 E	54
Liard (river)	61 50 N	121 19 W	79
Liberia	06 00 N	09 00 W	68
Libreville,* Gabon	00 24 N	09 27 E	68
Libya	27 00 N	17 30 E	69
Libyan (desert)	28 00 N	25 00 E	69
Liechtenstein	47 10 N	09 32 E	42
Liège, Belgium	50 40 N	05 35 E	42
Ligurian, (sea)	43 00 N	09 00 E	42
Lille, France	50 40 N	03 00 E	42
Lilongwe,* Malawi	13 59 S	33 47 E	70
Lima, Ohio	40 44 N	84 06 W	78
Lima,* Peru	12 03 S	77 03 W	86
Limpopo (river)	25 12 S	33 31 E	70
Lincoln,* Neb.	40 49 N	96 42 W	77
Line, (isls.)	04 00 S	155 00 W	63
Linz, Austria	48 18 N	14 15 E	42
Lion (gulf)	43 00 N	03 45 E	42
Lisbon,* Port.	38 43 N	09 10 W	42
Lithuania	55 00 N	24 00 E	43
Little Rock,* Ark.	34 45 N	92 17 W	78
Liverpool, Eng.	53 28 N	02 55 W	42
Livorno, Italy	43 33 N	10 19 E	42
Ljubljana,* Slovenia	46 03 N	14 31 E	44
Llanos (plain)	14 00 N	70 00 W	86
Lloydminster, Alta.-Sask.	53 17 N	110 00 W	79
Łódź, Poland	51 46 N	19 25 E	44
Logan (mt.)	60 34 N	140 24 W	79
Logan, Utah	41 44 N	111 50 W	76
Loire (river)	47 20 N	02 00 E	42
Lomas de Zamora, Arg.	34 46 S	58 24 W	88
Lombok (isl.)	08 48 S	115 52 E	56
Lomé,* Togo	06 07 N	01 14 E	68
London,* Eng.	51 30 N	00 07 W	42
London, Ont.	43 02 N	81 30 W	79
Long (isl.)	40 45 N	73 00 W	78
Long Beach, Calif.	33 47 N	118 11 W	76
Longview, Tex.	32 29 N	94 44 W	77
Lopatka (cape)	50 52 N	156 40 E	47
Lorraine (region)	49 00 N	06 00 E	42
Los Angeles, Calif.	34 03 N	118 14 W	76
Louisiana (state), U.S.	31 00 N	92 30 W	77
Louisville, Ky.	38 15 N	85 46 W	78
Lowell, Mass.	42 38 N	71 19 W	78
Loyalty (isls.)	21 00 S	168 00 E	62
Luanda,* Angola	08 49 S	13 14 E	70
Lubbock, Texas	33 35 N	101 50 W	76
Lübeck, Germany	53 50 N	10 40 E	42
Lubumbashi, D.R. Congo	11 40 S	27 28 E	70
Lucknow, India	26 46 N	80 59 E	53
Ludhiāna, India	30 54 N	75 51 E	53
Lusaka,* Zambia	15 25 S	28 18 E	70
Luxembourg	49 45 N	06 10 E	42
Luxembourg,* Lux.	49 35 N	06 12 E	42
Luzon (isl.)	15 00 N	121 00 E	57
L'viv, Ukraine	49 51 N	24 02 E	44
Lynchburg, Va.	37 25 N	79 08 W	78
Lyon, France	45 40 N	04 40 E	42

M

NAME	LATITUDE	LONGITUDE	PAGE
Maanselkä (mts.)	66° 30´ N	29° 00´ E	43
Macau,* Macau	22 12 N	113 33 E	55
Maceió, Brazil	09 40 S	35 44 W	87
Mackenzie (river)	68 00 N	134 00 W	79
Macon, Ga.	32 50 N	83 38 W	77
Madagascar	18 00 S	47 00 E	70
Madeira (isl.)	32 45 N	17 00 W	68
Madeira (river)	03 23 S	58 45 W	86
Madeleine (isls.)	47 26 N	61 44 W	79
Madison,* Wis.	43 04 N	89 23 W	78
Madrid,* Spain	40 25 N	03 42 W	42
Madura (isl.)	07 00 S	113 00 E	54
Madurai, India	09 55 N	78 15 E	53
Magdalena (river)	11 06 N	75 00 W	86
Magdeburg, Germany	52 10 N	11 40 E	42
Magellan (strait)	54 00 S	71 00 W	88
Magnitogorsk, Russia	53 28 N	59 00 E	46
Maine (state), U.S.	45 30 N	69 00 W	78
Majorca (isl.)	39 35 N	03 00 E	42
Majuro,* Marshall Is.	07 04 N	171 12 E	62
Makassar (strait)	03 57 S	119 32 E	56
Malabar Coast	12 50 N	75 00 E	53
Malabo,* Eq. Guin.	03 45 N	08 46 E	68
Malacca (strait)	03 10 N	100 45 E	56
Málaga, Spain	36 43 N	04 25 W	42

NAME	LATITUDE	LONGITUDE	PAGE
Malang, Indonesia	07 59 S	112 37 E	56
Malatya, Turkey	38 21 N	38 19 E	44
Malawi	13 30 S	34 30 E	70
Malay (pen.)	05 00 N	102 00 E	56
Malaysia	04 00 N	102 00 E	56
Maldives	04 00 N	73 00 E	49
Mali	17 30 N	04 00 W	68
Malmö, Sweden	55 35 N	13 00 E	43
Malta	35 55 N	14 23 E	44
Man (isl.)	54 15 N	04 30 W	42
Managua,* Nic.	12 08 N	86 18 W	80
Manaus, Brazil	03 08 S	60 01 W	86
Manchester, Eng.	53 30 N	02 13 W	42
Manchester, N.H.	42 60 N	71 28 W	78
Mandab, Bab al (strait)	12 39 N	43 26 E	52
Mandalay, Myanmar	21 59 N	96 05 E	53
Manicouagan (res.)	51 24 N	68 44 W	79
Manila,* Philippines	14 36 N	120 59 E	57
Manitoba (lake)	50 30 N	98 20 W	79
Manitoba (prov.), Canada	55 00 N	97 00 W	79
Manitoulin (isl.)	45 50 N	82 25 W	79
Mannar (gulf)	08 00 N	79 00 E	53
Mannheim, Germany	49 30 N	08 28 E	42
Maputo,* Moz.	25 58 S	32 35 E	70
Maracaibo (lake)	09 20 N	71 30 W	86
Maracaibo, Venez.	10 38 N	71 38 W	86
Marajó (isl.)	01 00 S	50 00 W	87
Marañón (river)	04 30 S	73 26 W	86
Margarita (isl.)	11 00 N	64 00 W	86
Marie Byrd Land (region)	80 00 S	120 00 W	71
Mariupol', Ukraine	47 05 N	37 36 E	44
Marmara (sea)	40 42 N	28 12 E	44
Marquesas (isls.)	09 00 S	139 30 W	63
Marrakech, Morocco	31 38 N	08 00 W	68
Marsala, Italy	37 48 N	12 26 E	42
Marseille, France	43 18 N	05 23 E	42
Marshall Islands	09 00 N	168 00 E	62
Martinique (isl.)	14 40 N	61 00 W	81
Maryland (state), U.S.	39 00 N	76 30 W	78
Mashhad, Iran	36 18 N	59 36 E	52
Massachusetts (state), U.S.	42 20 N	72 00 W	78
Massif Central (plat.)	45 00 N	03 00 E	42
Mato Grosso (plat.)	14 30 S	54 00 W	87
Maui (isl.)	20 48 N	156 20 W	76
Mauna Loa (mt.)	19 29 N	155 36 W	76
Mauritania	20 00 N	11 00 W	68
Mauritius	20 15 S	57 30 E	13
Mayotte (isl.)	13 00 S	45 00 E	65
Mazār-e Sharif, Afghan.	36 42 N	67 06 E	52
McAllen, Tex.	26 12 N	98 14 W	77
M'Clintock (chan.)	71 30 N	103 00 W	79
McKinley (mt.)	63 04 N	151 00 W	76
Mecca, Saudi Arabia	21 29 N	39 45 E	52
Medan, Indon.	03 35 N	98 40 E	56
Medellín, Col.	06 15 N	75 34 W	86
Medicine Hat, Alta.	50 02 N	110 41 W	79
Mediterranean (sea)	40 00 N	10 00 E	42
Mekong (river)	16 00 N	105 00 E	56
Melanesia (isls.)	10 00 S	160 00 E	62
Melbourne, Fla.	28 05 N	80 36 W	78
Melbourne, Austl.	37 50 S	145 00 E	59
Melville (isl.)	75 30 N	112 00 W	79
Memphis, Tenn.	35 09 N	90 03 W	78
Mendocino (cape)	40 27 N	124 26 W	76
Mendoza, Arg.	32 53 S	68 49 W	88
Mérida, Mex.	20 58 N	89 37 W	80
Mesopotamia (region)	34 00 N	44 00 E	52
Meuse (river)	51 49 N	05 01 E	42
Mexico	22 00 N	102 00 W	80
Mexico (gulf)	25 00 N	90 00 W	80
Mexico,* Mex.	19 26 N	99 08 W	80
Miami, Fla.	25 47 N	80 12 W	78
Michigan (lake)	44 00 N	87 00 W	78
Michigan (state), U.S.	44 00 N	85 00 W	78
Micronesia	12 00 N	154 00 E	62
Micronesia, Fed. States of	08 00 N	150 00 E	62
Midway (isls.)	28 15 N	177 20 W	62
Milan, Italy	45 30 N	09 10 E	42
Milwaukee, Wis.	43 02 N	87 54 W	78
Minami-Tori-Shima (isl.)	24 20 N	154 00 E	62
Mindanao (isl.)	08 00 N	125 00 E	57
Mindoro (isl.)	12 50 N	121 10 E	57
Minneapolis, Minn.	44 59 N	93 16 W	78
Minnesota (state), U.S.	46 30 N	94 30 W	77
Minorca (isl.)	40 00 N	04 00 E	42
Minsk,* Belarus	53 50 N	27 35 E	44
Miskolc, Hungary	48 10 N	20 50 E	44
Mississippi (river)	29 10 N	89 16 W	78
Mississippi (state), U.S.	33 00 N	89 45 W	78
Missoula, Mont.	46 52 N	114 00 W	76
Missouri (river)	38 50 N	90 10 W	77
Missouri (state), U.S.	38 30 N	92 30 W	77
Mitchell (mt.)	35 46 N	82 16 W	78
Mobile, Ala.	30 42 N	88 03 W	78
Modesto, Calif.	37 38 N	121 00 W	76
Mogadishu,* Somalia	02 03 N	45 20 E	69
Mojave (desert)	35 00 N	117 00 W	76
Moldova	47 00 N	29 00 E	44
Molokai (isl.)	21 08 N	157 00 W	76
Moluccas (isls.)	02 30 S	129 00 E	57
Mona (passage)	18 15 N	68 00 W	81
Monaco	43 44 N	07 25 E	42
Moncton, N.B.	46 05 N	64 46 W	79
Mongolia	47 00 N	102 00 E	54
Monrovia,* Liberia	06 19 N	10 48 W	68
Montana (state), U.S.	47 00 N	110 00 W	76
Montenegro (rep.), Yugo.	42 30 N	19 15 E	44
Monterrey, Mex.	25 45 N	100 20 W	80
Montevideo,* Uruguay	34 53 S	56 10 W	88
Montgomery,* Ala.	32 23 N	86 19 W	78
Montpelier,* Vt.	44 16 N	72 35 W	78
Montréal, Qué.	45 35 N	73 40 W	79
Montserrat	16 44 N	62 10 W	81
Moose Jaw, Sask.	50 24 N	105 33 W	79
Morelia, Mex.	19 42 N	101 07 W	80
Morena (mts.)	38 30 N	05 00 W	42
Morocco	33 00 N	07 00 W	68
Morón, Arg.	34 39 S	58 37 W	88
Moscow (Moskva),* Russia	55 45 N	37 35 E	43
Moscow (upland)	55 00 N	33 00 E	43
Mosquitos (coast)	13 00 N	88 00 W	80
Mozambique	18 00 S	35 00 E	70
Mozambique (channel)	22 00 S	38 00 E	70
Multān, Pakistan	30 11 N	71 29 E	53
Mumbai (Bombay), India	19 00 N	72 48 E	53

NAME	LATITUDE	LONGITUDE	PAGE
Muncie, Ind.	40 11 N	85 23 W	78
Munich (München), Germany	48 10 N	11 30 E	42
Murcia, Spain	37 43 N	01 08 W	42
Murmansk, Russia	68 58 N	33 05 E	43
Murray (river)	35 33 S	144 00 E	59
Muscat,* Oman	23 37 N	58 35 E	52
Muskegon, Mich.	43 14 N	86 15 W	78
Myanmar (Burma)	20 00 N	96 00 E	49
Mykolayiv, Ukraine	46 58 N	32 00 E	44

N

NAME	LATITUDE	LONGITUDE	PAGE
Naberezhnye Chelny, Russia	55° 42´ N	52° 19´ E	45
Nafūd (desert)	28 00 N	41 00 E	52
Nagoya, Japan	35 10 N	137 55 E	55
Nagpur, India	21 15 N	79 12 E	53
Nairobi,* Kenya	01 17 S	36 49 E	69
Najd (region)	25 00 N	43 00 E	52
Namib (desert)	23 00 S	14 00 E	70
Namibia	23 00 S	17 00 E	70
Nanchang, China	28 40 N	115 53 E	55
Nancy, France	48 40 N	06 10 E	42
Nanjing, China	32 03 N	118 48 E	55
Nantes, France	47 15 N	01 30 W	42
Nantucket (isl.)	41 16 N	70 05 W	78
Naples, Italy	40 51 N	14 15 E	42
Nashville,* Tenn.	36 10 N	86 47 W	78
Nassau,* Bahamas	25 05 N	77 21 W	81
Nasser (lake)	24 00 N	32 50 E	69
Naucalpan, Mex.	19 28 N	99 14 W	80
Nauru	00 32 S	166 56 E	62
N'Djamena,* Chad	12 07 N	15 04 E	68
Nebraska (state), U.S.	41 30 N	100 00 W	76
Negrais (cape)	16 02 N	94 12 E	56
Negro (river), Arg.	41 02 S	62 47 W	88
Negro (river), Brazil	03 10 S	59 55 W	68
Negros (isl.)	10 00 N	123 00 E	57
Nelson (river)	57 00 N	92 38 W	79
Nepal	28 00 N	84 00 E	53
Netherlands	52 00 N	05 30 E	42
Netherlands Antilles	12 10 N	69 00 W	81
Nevada (state), U.S.	39 00 N	117 00 W	76
Nevis (isl.)	17 10 N	62 38 W	81
Newark, N.J.	40 44 N	74 10 W	78
New Bedford, Mass.	41 38 N	70 55 W	78
New Britain (isl.)	05 55 S	150 20 E	62
New Brunswick (prov.), Canada	46 30 N	66 45 W	79
New Caledonia (isl.)	21 30 S	165 30 E	62
Newcastle, Austl.	32 55 S	151 45 E	59
Newcastle upon Tyne, Eng.	55 00 N	01 35 W	42
New Delhi,* India	28 19 N	77 15 E	53
Newfoundland (isl.)	49 30 N	57 30 W	79
Newfoundland (prov.), Canada	51 30 N	55 45 W	79
New Guinea (isl.)	05 00 S	141 00 E	57
New Hampshire (state), U.S.	43 30 N	71 45 W	78
New Haven, Conn.	41 18 N	72 55 W	78
New Ireland (isl.)	04 00 S	152 00 E	62
New Jersey (state), U.S.	40 00 N	74 30 W	78
New Mexico (state), U.S.	34 30 N	106 00 W	76
New Orleans, La.	29 57 N	90 04 W	77
Newport News, Va.	36 58 N	76 25 W	78
New Siberian (isls.)	75 00 N	142 00 E	47
New South Wales, Austl.	32 00 S	147 00 E	59
New York, N.Y.	40 45 N	74 00 W	78
New York (state), U.S.	43 00 N	76 00 W	78
New Zealand	41 00 S	173 00 E	59
Niagara Falls, Ont.	43 06 N	79 03 W	79
Niamey,* Niger	13 31 N	02 07 E	68
Nicaragua	13 00 N	85 00 W	80
Nicaragua (lake)	11 30 N	85 30 W	80
Nice, France	43 42 N	07 16 E	42
Nicobar (isls.)	07 45 N	93 30 E	53
Nicosia,* Cyprus	35 12 N	33 22 E	52
Niger	17 00 N	08 00 E	68
Niger (river)	04 17 N	06 04 E	68
Nigeria	09 00 N	08 00 E	68
Niihau (isl.)	21 53 N	160 10 W	76
Nile (river)	31 50 N	32 00 E	69
Ningbo, China	29 54 N	121 32 E	55
Niue (isl.)	19 02 S	169 52 W	63
Nizhniy Novgorod, Russia	56 20 N	44 00 E	45
Norfolk (isl.)	29 02 S	167 57 W	62
Norfolk, Va.	36 51 N	76 17 W	78
Norman Wells, N.W. Terrs.	65 17 N	126 51 W	79
Normandy (region)	49 00 N	00 00 E	42
Norrköping, Sweden	58 30 N	16 10 E	43
Norrland (region)	66 00 N	20 00 E	43
North (cape)	71 11 N	25 40 E	39
North (isl.), N.Z.	39 00 S	176 00 E	59
North (sea)	55 20 N	03 00 E	42
North Battleford, Sask.	52 46 N	108 17 W	79
North Bay, Ont.	46 16 N	79 30 W	79
North Carolina (state), U.S.	35 30 N	79 00 W	78
North Dakota (state), U.S.	47 30 N	100 30 W	76
Northern Ireland, U.K.	54 30 N	06 30 W	42
Northern Marianas	18 00 N	145 45 E	62
Northern Territory, Austl.	20 00 S	134 00 E	59
North Magnetic Pole	75 00 N	100 00 W	71
Northwest Territories, Canada	64 00 N	120 00 W	79
Norton (sound)	64 00 N	164 00 W	42
Norway	65 00 N	11 00 E	43
Norwegian (sea)	70 00 N	00 00 E	39
Nottingham, Eng.	52 58 N	01 10 W	42
Nouakchott,* Mauritania	18 06 N	15 57 W	68
Nouméa,* New Cal.	22 17 S	166 26 E	62
Nova Scotia (prov.), Canada	45 00 N	63 00 W	79
Novaya Zemlya (isls.)	74 00 N	57 00 E	46
Novosibirsk, Russia	55 02 N	82 53 E	46
Nubian (desert)	21 00 N	33 00 E	69
Nürnberg, Germany	49 20 N	11 05 E	42
Nunavut (terr.), Canada	64 00 N	90 00 W	79
Nuuk (Godthab),* Greenland	64 11 N	51 45 W	73
Nyasa (lake)	12 00 S	34 30 E	70

O

NAME	LATITUDE	LONGITUDE	PAGE
Oahu (isl.)	21° 30´ N	158° 00´ W	76
Oakland, Calif.	37 48 N	122 16 W	76
Ob' (river)	66 45 N	69 07 E	46

NAME	LATITUDE	LONGITUDE	PAGE
Skeena (mts.)	56 30 N	129 00 W	79
Skopje,* Macedonia	42 00 N	21 26 E	44
Slovakia	48 30 N	19 00 E	44
Slovenia	46 00 N	15 00 E	44
Snake (river)	46 12 N	119 02 W	76
Society (isls.)	17 00 S	152 00 W	63
Socotra (isl.)	12 30 N	54 00 E	52
Sofia,* Bulgaria	42 42 N	23 20 E	44
Solomon (sea)	08 00 S	152 00 E	62
Solomon Islands	09 00 S	160 00 E	62
Somalia	05 00 N	47 00 E	69
Somerset (isl.)	73 30 N	93 30 W	79
South (isl.), N.Z.	44 00 S	171 00 E	59
South Africa	30 00 S	25 00 E	70
Southampton (isl.)	64 45 N	84 30 W	79
Southampton, Eng.	50 55 N	01 28 W	42
South Australia, Austl.	31 00 S	136 00 E	59
South Bend, Ind.	41 40 N	86 15 W	78
South Carolina (state), U.S.	34 00 N	81 00 W	78
South China (sea)	15 00 N	115 00 E	56
South Dakota (state), U.S.	44 30 N	100 30 W	76
South Georgia (isl.)	54 20 S	36 40 W	88
South Orkney (isls.)	60 38 S	45 35 W	71
South Sandwich (isls.)	56 00 S	26 30 W	12
South Shetland (isls.)	62 00 S	58 00 W	71
Spain	40 00 N	04 00 W	42
Spokane, Wash.	47 40 N	117 26 W	76
Spratly (isls.)	08 00 N	113 00 E	56
Springfield,* Ill.	39 48 N	89 39 W	78
Springfield, Mass.	42 06 N	72 35 W	78
Springfield, Mo.	37 13 N	93 18 W	78
Springfield, Ohio	39 55 N	83 48 W	78
Sri Lanka	07 00 N	81 00 E	53
Srinagar, India	34 07 N	74 45 E	53
Stanley,* Falk. Is.	51 42 S	57 51 W	88
Stanovoy (mts.)	55 40 N	126 00 E	47
Stavanger, Norway	58 58 N	05 45 E	43
Stikine (river)	56 37 N	132 21 W	79
Stockholm,* Sweden	59 16 N	18 00 E	43
Stockton, Calif.	37 57 N	121 17 W	76
Strasbourg, France	48 35 N	07 45 E	42
Stuttgart, Germany	48 40 N	09 10 E	42
Subotica, Yugo.	46 06 N	19 40 E	44
Sucre,* Bolivia	19 03 S	65 18 W	86
Sudan	13 00 N	30 00 E	69
Sudan (region)	12 00 N	10 00 E	68
Sudbury, Ont.	46 32 N	81 15 W	79
Sudd (swamp)	08 00 N	30 00 E	69
Sudeten (mts.)	51 00 N	17 00 E	44
Suez (canal)	30 45 N	32 20 E	69
Sulu (arch.)	09 00 N	120 30 E	57
Sulu (sea)	09 08 N	120 00 E	57
Sumatra (isl.)	00 00	102 00 E	56
Sumba (isl.)	10 00 S	120 00 E	57
Sumbawa (isl.)	08 30 S	117 26 E	56
Sunda (isls.)	09 00 S	105 00 E	57
Sunda (strait)	06 28 S	105 24 E	56
Sundsvall, Sweden	62 23 N	17 19 E	43
Superior (lake)	87 00 N	48 00 W	77
Surabaya, Indon.	07 16 S	112 44 E	56
Surat, India	21 10 N	72 50 E	53
Suriname	04 00 N	56 00 W	87
Sutlej (river)	30 00 N	73 00 E	53
Suva,* Fiji	18 08 S	178 24 E	62
Svalbard (arch.)	79 00 N	19 00 E	71
Swansea, Wales	51 58 N	03 55 W	42
Swaziland	26 30 S	31 30 E	70
Sweden	62 00 N	16 00 E	43
Swift Current, Sask.	50 17 N	107 46 W	79
Switzerland	46 48 N	08 00 E	42
Sydney, Austl.	33 52 S	151 10 E	59
Sydney, N.S.	46 09 N	60 10 W	79
Syracuse, N.Y.	43 03 N	76 09 W	78
Syrdariya (river)	46 03 N	61 06 E	45
Syria	35 00 N	38 00 E	52
Szczecin, Poland	53 50 N	14 30 E	44

T

NAME	LATITUDE	LONGITUDE	PAGE
Tacoma, Wash.	47° 15′ N	122° 26′ W	76
Tagus (river)	38 45 N	09 00 W	42
Tahiti (isl.)	17 38 S	149 25 W	63
Tai'an, China	36 12 N	117 07 E	55
T'aipei,* Taiwan, China	25 02 N	121 31 E	55
Taiwan	24 00 N	121 00 E	55
Taiyuan, China	37 52 N	112 35 E	55
Tajikistan	39 00 N	71 00 E	46
Takla Makan (desert)	39 20 N	83 00 E	54
Tallahassee,* Fla.	30 27 N	84 17 W	78
Tallinn,* Estonia	59 25 N	24 45 E	43
Tampa, Fla.	27 57 N	82 27 W	78
Tampere, Finland	61 30 N	23 45 E	43
Tampico, Mex.	22 13 N	97 51 W	80
Tana (lake)	12 00 N	37 20 E	69
Tanganyika (lake)	06 00 S	29 30 E	70
Tangier, Morocco	35 48 N	05 45 W	68
Tangshan, China	39 38 N	118 11 E	55
Tanzania	07 00 S	35 00 E	70
Tapajós (river)	02 24 S	54 47 W	87
Taranto (gulf)	40 15 N	17 15 E	44
Tarawa,* Kiribati	01 27 N	172 58 E	62
Tashkent,* Uzbekistan	41 20 N	69 18 E	46
Tasman (sea)	35 00 S	160 00 E	62
Tasmania, Austl.	42 00 S	147 00 E	59
Tatar (strait)	50 25 N	140 30 E	47
Taurus (mts.)	36 45 N	32 00 E	44
Taymyr (pen.)	76 00 N	104 00 E	46
T'bilisi,* Georgia	41 42 N	44 46 E	45
Tegucigalpa,* Honduras	14 06 N	87 13 W	80
Tehran,* Iran	35 41 N	51 26 E	52
Tehuantepec (isth.)	17 00 N	95 00 W	80
Tel Aviv-Jaffa, Israel	32 02 N	34 49 E	52
Tenerife (isl.)	28 15 N	16 35 W	68
Tennessee (river)	37 04 N	88 33 W	78
Tennessee (state), U.S.	36 00 N	86 00 W	78
Terre Haute, Ind.	39 28 N	87 24 W	78
Texas (state), U.S.	31 00 N	99 00 W	76
Thailand	14 00 N	101 00 E	56
Thailand (gulf)	10 00 N	102 30 E	56
The Hague,* Netherlands	52 05 N	04 20 E	42
The Pas, Man.	53 49 N	101 14 W	79
Thessaloníki, Greece	40 39 N	22 56 E	44
Thimphu,* Bhutan	27 29 N	89 37 E	53
Thompson, Man.	55 45 N	97 52 W	79
Thunder Bay, Ont.	48 24 N	89 19 W	79
Tianjin, China	38 59 N	117 24 E	55
Tian Shan (mts.)	42 12 N	78 13 E	54
Tiber (river)	41 44 N	12 14 E	42
Tibesti (mts.)	20 30 N	18 00 E	68
Tibet, China	30 00 N	90 00 E	54
Tierra del Fuego (isl.)	54 00 S	68 00 W	88
Tigris (river)	32 30 N	45 45 E	52
Tijuana, Mex.	32 32 N	117 01 W	81
Timişoara, Rom.	45 45 N	21 20 E	44
Timmins, Ont.	48 28 N	81 19 W	79
Timor (isl.)	09 30 S	125 00 E	57
Timor (sea)	11 00 S	125 00 E	59
Tinian (isl.)	15 01 N	145 38 E	62
Tiranë,* Albania	41 20 N	19 48 E	44
Tisza (river)	45 15 N	20 17 E	44
Titicaca (lake)	16 00 S	69 00 W	86
Tlalnepantla, Mex.	19 33 N	99 12 W	80
Tobago (isl.)	11 15 N	60 40 W	81
Tocantins (river)	01 50 S	49 10 W	87
Togo	08 00 N	01 00 E	68
Tokelau (isls.)	09 00 S	172 00 W	63
Tokyo,* Japan	35 42 N	139 46 E	55
Toledo, Ohio	41 39 N	83 33 W	78
Tol'yatti, Russia	53 31 N	49 26 E	45
Tomsk, Russia	56 30 N	84 58 E	46
Tonga	21 00 S	175 15 W	63
Tonkin (gulf)	19 40 N	107 30 E	56
Topeka,* Kans.	39 03 N	95 40 W	77
Toronto,* Ont.	43 38 N	79 27 W	79
Torrens (lake)	31 00 S	137 45 E	59
Torreón, Mex.	25 33 N	103 26 W	81
Torres (strait)	10 25 S	142 12 E	59
Toulon, France	43 08 N	05 56 E	42
Toulouse, France	43 36 N	01 27 E	42
Trail, Br. Col.	49 06 N	117 43 W	76
Transantarctic (mts.)	85 00 S	175 00 W	71
Transylvania (region)	47 00 N	23 30 E	44
Trenton,* N.J.	40 14 N	74 44 W	78
Trinidad and Tobago	10 30 N	61 15 W	81
Tripoli,* Libya	32 54 N	13 11 E	68
Tristan da Cunha (isl.)	37 00 S	12 30 W	12
Trivandrum, India	08 29 N	76 55 E	53
Trois-Rivières, Qué.	46 27 N	72 30 W	79
Tromsø, Norway	69 40 N	18 58 E	43
Trondheim, Norway	63 25 N	10 26 E	43
Troy, N.Y.	42 44 N	73 41 W	78
Truk (isls.)	07 25 N	151 45 E	62
Tuamotu (arch.)	17 00 S	142 00 W	63
Tucson, Ariz.	32 13 N	110 58 W	76
Tuktoyaktuk, N.W. Terrs.	69 27 N	133 03 W	79
Tula, Russia	54 12 N	37 36 E	43
Tulsa, Okla.	36 09 N	96 00 W	77
Tunis,* Tunisia	36 48 N	10 10 E	68
Tunisia	35 00 N	10 00 E	68
Turin, Italy	45 04 N	07 40 E	42
Turkana (lake)	03 30 N	36 00 E	69
Turkey	39 00 N	35 00 E	44
Turkmenistan	39 00 N	60 00 E	46
Turks and Caicos (isls.)	22 00 N	71 30 W	81
Tuscaloosa, Ala.	33 12 N	87 34 W	78
Tutuila (isl.)	14 17 S	170 40 W	63
Tuvalu	08 00 S	178 00 E	62
Tuz (lake)	38 00 N	33 30 E	44
Tuzla, Bosnia	44 32 N	18 41 E	44
T'ver, Russia	56 50 N	35 55 E	43
Tyrrhenian (sea)	39 00 N	13 00 E	42

U

NAME	LATITUDE	LONGITUDE	PAGE
Ucayali (river)	04° 30′ S	73° 26′ W	86
Ufa, Russia	54 43 N	55 55 E	45
Uganda	01 00 N	32 00 E	69
Ukraine	49 00 N	32 00 E	44
Ulaanbaatar,* Mongolia	45 55 N	106 53 E	54
Ul'yanovsk, Russia	54 20 N	48 24 E	43
United Arab Emirates	24 00 N	55 00 E	52
United Kingdom	55 00 N	02 00 W	42
United States	44 58 N	103 46 W	76-77
Ural (mts.)	56 00 N	60 00 E	46
Ural (river)	47 00 N	51 48 E	45
Urfa, Turkey	37 10 N	38 50 E	44
Urmia (lake)	37 35 N	45 05 E	52
Uruguay	33 00 S	56 00 W	88
Uruguay (river)	34 05 S	58 20 W	88
Ustyurt (plat.)	43 00 N	56 00 E	45
Utah (state), U.S.	39 30 N	111 30 W	76
Utica, N.Y.	43 06 N	75 13 W	78
Utrecht, Netherlands	52 05 N	05 08 E	42
Uzbekistan	41 00 N	62 00 E	46

V

NAME	LATITUDE	LONGITUDE	PAGE
Vaal (river)	29° 04′ S	23° 38′ E	70
Vaduz,* Liechtenstein	47 08 N	9 31 E	42
Val-d'Or, Qué.	48 07 N	77 46 W	79
Valencia, Spain	39 29 N	00 23 W	42
Valencia, Ven.	10 11 N	68 00 W	86
Valladolid, Spain	41 39 N	04 43 W	42
Valletta,* Malta	35 53 N	14 30 E	44
Valparaíso, Chile	33 01 S	71 38 W	88
Van (lake)	38 36 N	42 49 E	45
Vancouver (isl.)	49 40 N	125 50 W	79
Vancouver, Br. Col.	49 15 N	123 08 W	79
Vänern (lake)	59 00 N	13 30 E	43
Vanua Levu (isl.)	16 30 S	179 15 E	62
Vanuatu	17 00 S	168 30 E	62
Vārānāsi, India	25 17 N	83 08 E	53
Varna, Bulgaria	43 13 N	27 55 E	44
Vatican City	41 54 N	12 30 E	42
Vättern (lake)	58 20 N	14 30 E	43
Venezuela	08 00 N	66 00 W	86
Venice, Italy	45 26 N	12 20 E	42
Veracruz, Mex.	32 25 N	115 05 W	80
Verde (cape)	14 43 N	17 30 W	68
Verkhoyansk (mts.)	65 00 N	130 00 E	47
Vermont (state), U.S.	44 00 N	72 45 W	78
Vernon, Br. Col.	50 16 N	119 16 W	76
Verona, Italy	45 29 N	11 00 E	42
Victoria (falls)	17 57 S	25 52 E	70
Victoria (isl.)	71 00 N	110 00 W	79
Victoria (lake)	01 00 S	33 00 E	69
Victoria, Austl.	37 00 S	145 00 E	59
Victoria,* Br. Col.	48 27 N	123 25 W	79
Vienna,* Austria	48 20 N	16 30 E	44
Vientiane,* Laos	17 58 N	102 37 E	56
Vietnam	16 00 N	108 00 E	49
Vilnius,* Lithuania	54 41 N	25 19 E	43
Virgin (isls.)	18 20 N	64 40 W	81
Virginia (state), U.S.	37 30 N	76 30 W	78
Visalia, Calif.	36 20 N	119 18 W	76
Vistula (river)	54 20 N	18 50 E	44
Viti Levu (isl.)	17 50 S	178 00 E	62
Vladivostok, Russia	43 06 N	131 50 E	55
Volcano (isls.)	24 43 N	141 20 E	62
Volga (river)	46 15 N	48 24 E	45
Volgograd, Russia	48 42 N	44 30 E	45
Volta (lake)	07 00 N	00 00	68
Volta (river)	05 45 N	00 41 E	68
Voronezh, Russia	51 40 N	39 00 E	45
Vyatka, Russia	58 33 N	49 42 E	45

W

NAME	LATITUDE	LONGITUDE	PAGE
Wabash (river)	37° 48′ N	88° 01′ W	78
Waco, Tex.	31 33 N	97 08 W	77
Wake (isl.)	19 18 N	166 38 E	62
Wales, U.K.	52 30 N	04 00 W	42
Wallis and Futuna (isls.)	13 18 S	176 10 W	62
Walvis Bay, S. Afr.	22 57 S	14 30 E	70
Warsaw,* Poland	52 10 N	21 00 E	44
Wasatch Range (mts.)	41 00 N	111 35 W	76
Washington, D.C.,* U.S.	38 54 N	77 01 W	78
Washington (state), U.S.	47 15 N	121 00 W	76
Waterloo, Iowa	42 30 N	92 20 W	78
Weddell (sea)	70 00 S	40 00 W	71
Wellington,* N.Z.	41 19 S	174 47 E	59
Weser (river)	53 30 N	08 34 E	42
Western Australia, Austl.	25 00 S	122 00 E	59
Western Ghats (mts.)	15 00 N	74 30 E	53
Western Sahara	25 00 N	14 00 W	68
West Palm Beach, Fla.	26 43 N	80 03 W	78
West Virginia (state), U.S.	38 30 N	81 00 W	78
Wheeling, W. Va.	40 04 N	80 43 W	78
White (sea)	65 30 N	38 00 E	43
Whitehorse,* Yukon Terr.	60 45 N	135 04 W	79
White Nile (river)	15 37 N	32 31 E	69
Whitney (mt.)	36 35 N	118 18 W	76
Wichita, Kans.	37 42 N	97 20 W	77
Wiesbaden, Germany	50 05 N	08 15 E	42
Wilkes-Barre, Pa.	41 15 N	75 53 W	78
Willemstad,* Neth. Ant.	12 07 N	68 57 W	81
Wilmington, Del.	39 45 N	75 33 W	78
Windhoek,* Namibia	22 34 S	17 06 E	70
Windsor, Ont.	42 19 N	83 02 W	79
Windward (isls.)	13 00 N	62 00 W	81
Windward (passage)	20 00 N	73 50 W	81
Winnipegosis (lake)	52 30 N	100 00 W	79
Winnipeg (lake)	49 50 N	97 10 W	79
Winnipeg,* Man.	49 53 N	97 10 W	79
Wisconsin (state), U.S.	44 30 N	90 00 W	78
Woods, Lake of the (lake)	49 30 N	94 30 W	79
Worcester, Mass.	42 16 N	71 48 W	78
Wrangel (isl.)	71 00 N	180 00	47
Wroclaw, Poland	51 10 N	17 02 E	44
Wuhan, China	30 35 N	114 16 E	55
Würzburg, Germany	49 48 N	09 58 E	42
Wyoming (state), U.S.	43 00 N	107 30 W	76

X

NAME	LATITUDE	LONGITUDE	PAGE
Xi'an, China	34° 16′ N	108° 54′ E	54
Xiantao, China	30 25 N	113 25 E	55
Xingu (river)	01 44 S	51 56 W	87

Y

NAME	LATITUDE	LONGITUDE	PAGE
Yablonovyy (mts.)	52° 30′ N	113° 00′ E	47
Yakima, Wash.	46 36 N	120 31 W	76
Yamoussoukro,* Côte d'Ivoire	06 49 N	05 17 W	68
Yamal (pen.)	70 00 N	70 00 E	46
Yangon (Rangoon)*, Myanmar	16 48 N	96 09 E	56
Yaoundé,* Cameroon	03 53 N	11 32 E	68
Yap (isl.)	09 30 N	138 10 E	62
Yarmouth, N.S.	43 50 N	66 07 W	79
Yaroslavl', Russia	57 35 N	39 50 E	45
Yekaterinburg, Russia	56 50 N	60 38 E	45
Yellow (sea)	37 00 N	123 00 E	55
Yellowknife,* N.W. Terrs.	62 27 N	114 21 W	79
Yellowstone (river)	48 00 N	104 00 W	76
Yellowstone Nat'l Park, U.S.	44 30 N	110 30 W	76
Yemen	15 00 N	44 00 E	52
Yenisey (river)	69 35 N	84 25 E	46
Yerevan,* Armenia	40 11 N	44 30 E	45
Yogyakarta, Indon.	07 48 S	110 22 E	56
Yokohama, Japan	35 25 N	139 31 E	55
York, Pa.	39 57 N	76 44 W	78
Yorkton, Sask.	51 13 N	102 28 W	79
Youngstown, Ohio	41 06 N	80 39 W	78
Yucatán (pen.)	20 00 N	89 00 W	80
Yugoslavia	44 00 N	21 00 E	44
Yukon (river)	62 36 N	164 46 W	79
Yukon Territory, Canada	65 00 N	137 00 W	79
Yuzhno-Sakhalinsk, Russia	46 58 N	142 42 E	47

Z

NAME	LATITUDE	LONGITUDE	PAGE
Zagreb,* Croatia	45° 48′ N	16° 00′ E	44
Zagros (mts.)	34 00 N	47 30 E	52
Zambezi (river)	18 50 S	36 15 E	70
Zambia	14 00 S	27 00 E	70
Zanzibar (isl.)	06 00 S	39 30 E	70
Zaozhuang, China	34 53 N	117 34 E	55
Zaporizhzhya, Ukraine	47 50 N	35 10 E	44
Zaragoza (Saragossa), Spain	41 39 N	00 51 W	42
Zhengzhou, China	34 48 N	113 39 E	55
Zhytomyr, Ukraine	50 16 N	28 40 E	44
Zibo, China	36 47 N	118 01 E	55
Zimbabwe	19 00 S	30 00 E	70
Zürich, Switz.	47 22 N	08 22 E	42

World Statistics

THE CONTINENTS

	Area in: Sq. Miles	Sq. Kms.	Percent of World's Land		Area in: Sq. Miles	Sq. Kms.	Percent of World's Land
Asia	17,128,500	44,362,815	29.5	Antarctica	5,405,000	14,000,000	9.4
Africa	11,707,000	30,321,130	20.2	Europe	4,057,000	10,507,630	7.0
North America	9,363,000	24,250,170	16.2	Australia	2,967,893	7,686,850	5.1
South America	6,879,725	17,818,505	11.9				

DIMENSIONS OF THE EARTH

	Area in: Sq. Miles	Sq. Kilometers
Superficial area	196,939,000	510,072,000
Land surface	57,506,000	148,940,000
Water surface	139,433,000	361,132,000

	Distance in: Miles	Kilometers
Equatorial circumference	24,902	40,075
Polar circumference	24,860	40,007
Equatorial diameter	7,926.4	12,756.4
Polar diameter	7,899.8	12,713.6
Equatorial radius	3,963.2	6,378.2
Polar radius	3,949.9	6,356.8

Volume of the Earth	2.6×10^{11} cubic miles	10.84×10^{11} cubic kilometers
Mass or weight	6.6×10^{21} short tons	6.0×10^{21} metric tons
Maximum distance from Sun	94,600,000 miles	152,000,000 kilometers
Minimum distance from Sun	91,300,000 miles	147,000,000 kilometers

OCEANS AND MAJOR SEAS

	Area in: Sq. Miles	Sq. Kms.	Greatest Depth in: Feet	Meters
Pacific Ocean	63,855,000	165,384,000	36,198	11,033
Atlantic Ocean	31,744,000	82,217,000	28,374	8,648
Indian Ocean	28,417,000	73,600,000	25,344	7,725
Arctic Ocean	5,427,000	14,056,000	17,880	5,450
Caribbean Sea	970,000	2,512,300	24,720	7,535
Mediterranean Sea	969,000	2,509,700	16,896	5,150
South China Sea	895,000	2,318,000	15,000	4,600
Bering Sea	875,000	2,266,250	15,800	4,800
Gulf of Mexico	600,000	1,554,000	12,300	3,750
Sea of Okhotsk	590,000	1,528,100	11,070	3,370
East China Sea	482,000	1,248,400	9,500	2,900
Yellow Sea	480,000	1,243,200	350	107
Sea of Japan	389,000	1,007,500	12,280	3,740
Hudson Bay	317,500	822,300	846	258
North Sea	222,000	575,000	2,200	670
Black Sea	185,000	479,150	7,365	2,245
Red Sea	169,000	437,700	7,200	2,195
Baltic Sea	163,000	422,170	1,506	459

LARGEST ISLANDS

	Area in: Sq. Miles	Sq. Kms.		Area in: Sq. Miles	Sq. Kms.		Area in: Sq. Miles	Sq. Kms.
Greenland	840,000	2,175,600	Victoria, Canada	83,896	217,290	Luzon, Philippines	40,420	104,688
New Guinea	305,000	789,950	Ellesmere, Canada	75,767	196,236	Iceland	39,768	103,000
Borneo	286,000	740,740	Celebes, Indonesia	72,986	189,034	Mindanao, Philippines	36,537	94,631
Madagascar	226,656	587,040	South I., New Zealand	58,393	151,238	Ireland	32,589	84,406
Baffin, Canada	195,928	507,454	Java, Indonesia	48,842	126,501	Hokkaidō, Japan	30,436	78,829
Sumatra, Indonesia	164,000	424,760	North I., New Zealand	44,187	114,444	Sakhalin, Russia	29,500	76,405
Honshu, Japan	88,000	227,920	Cuba	42,803	110,860	Hispaniola, Dominican Republic-Haiti	29,399	76,143
Great Britain	84,400	218,896	Newfoundland, Canada	42,031	108,860	Banks, Canada	27,038	70,028

PRINCIPAL MOUNTAINS

	Height in: Feet	Meters		Height in: Feet	Meters		Height in: Feet	Meters
Everest, Nepal-China	29,028	8,848	Huascarán, Peru	22,205	6,768	Kenya, Kenya	17,058	5,199
Godwin Austen (K2), Pakistan-China	28,250	8,611	Chimborazo, Ecuador	20,561	6,267	Ararat, Turkey	16,946	5,165
Kanchenjunga, Nepal-India	28,208	8,598	McKinley, Alaska, U.S.A.	20,320	6,194	Vinson Massif, Antarctica	16,864	5,140
Lhotse, Nepal-China	27,923	8,511	Logan, Yukon, Canada	19,524	5,951	Blanc, France	15,771	4,807
Nanga Parbat, Pakistan	26,660	8,126	Kilimanjaro, Tanzania	19,340	5,895	Matterhorn, Switzerland	14,691	4,478
Annapurna, Nepal	26,504	8,078	Citlaltépetl (Orizaba), Mexico	18,700	5,700	Whitney, California, U.S.A.	14,494	4,418
Nanda Devi, India	25,645	7,817	Damavand, Iran	18,605	5,671	Mauna Kea, Hawaii, U.S.A.	13,796	4,205
Ismail Samani Peak, Tajikistan	24,590	7,495	El'brus, Russia	18,510	5,642	Mauna Loa, Hawaii, U.S.A.	13,677	4,169
Cerro Aconcagua, Argentina	22,831	6,959	St. Elias, Alaska-Canada (Yukon)	18,008	5,489	Kosciusko, Australia	7,310	2,228

LONGEST RIVERS

	Length in: Miles	Kms.		Length in: Miles	Kms.		Length in: Miles	Kms.
Nile, Africa	4,145	6,671	Paraná-La Plata, S. America	2,630	4,232	Zambezi, Africa	1,950	3,138
Amazon, S. America	4,007	6,448	Mekong, Asia	2,610	4,200	São Francisco, Brazil	1,930	3,106
Mississippi-Missouri-Red Rock, U.S.A.	3,710	5,971	Niger, Africa	2,580	4,152	St. Lawrence, Canada-U.S.A.	1,900	3,058
Chang Jiang (Yangtze), China	3,500	5,633	Yenisey, Russia	2,500	4,028	Rio Grande, Mexico-U.S.A.	1,885	3,034
Ob'-Irtysh, Russia-Kazakhstan	3,362	5,411	Mississippi, U.S.A.	2,348	3,778	Indus, Asia	1,800	2,897
Huang He (Yellow), China	2,950	4,747	Murray-Darling, Australia	2,310	3,718	Danube, Europe	1,775	2,857
Congo, Africa	2,780	4,474	Volga, Russia	2,290	3,685	Brahmaputra, Asia	1,760	2,832
Amur-Shilka-Onon, Asia	2,744	4,416	Madeira, S. America	2,013	3,240	Salween, Asia	1,675	2,696
Lena, Russia	2,734	4,400	Purus, S. America	1,995	3,211	Euphrates, Asia	1,650	2,655
Mackenzie-Peace-Finlay, Canada	2,635	4,241	Yukon, Alaska-Canada	1,979	3,185	Orinoco, S. America	1,600	2,575

PRINCIPAL NATURAL LAKES

	Area in: Sq. Miles	Sq. Kms.	Max. Depth in: Feet	Meters		Area in: Sq. Miles	Sq. Kms.	Max. Depth in: Feet	Meters
Caspian Sea, Asia	143,243	370,999	3,264	995	Great Slave Lake, Canada	11,031	28,570	2,015	614
Lake Superior, U.S.A.-Canada	31,820	82,414	1,329	405	Lake Erie, U.S.A.-Canada	9,940	25,745	210	64
Lake Victoria, Africa	26,828	69,485	270	82	Lake Winnipeg, Canada	9,417	24,390	60	18
Lake Huron, U.S.A.-Canada	23,010	59,596	748	228	Lake Ontario, U.S.A.-Canada	7,540	19,529	775	244
Lake Michigan, U.S.A.	22,400	58,016	923	281	Lake Balkhash, Kazakhstan	7,081	18,340	87	27
Aral Sea, Kazakhstan-Uzbekistan	15,830	41,000	213	65	Lake Chad, Africa *	7,000	18,130	25	8
Lake Tanganyika, Africa	12,650	32,764	4,700	1,433	Lake Ladoga, Russia	6,900	17,871	738	225
Lake Baykal, Russia	12,162	31,500	5,316	1,620	Lake Onega, Russia	3,761	9,741	377	115
Great Bear Lake, Canada	12,096	31,328	1,356	413	Lake Eyre, Australia *	3,500	9,066	—	—
Lake Nyasa (Malawi), Africa	11,555	29,928	2,320	707					

* Figures subject to great seasonal variations.